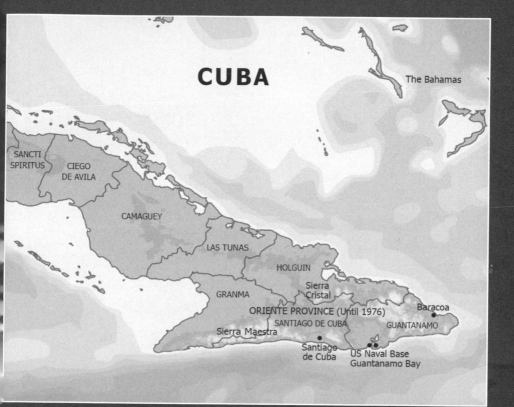

CUBA

The Bahamas

SANCTI
SPIRITUS
CIEGO
DE AVILA

CAMAGUEY

LAS TUNAS

HOLGUIN

Sierra
Cristal

GRANMA

Baracoa

ORIENTE PROVINCE (Until 1976)

SANTIAGO DE CUBA

GUANTANAMO

Sierra Maestra

Santiago
de Cuba

US Naval Base
Guantanamo Bay

CUBA

LAS TUNAS

GRANMA

THE
★ CUBAN ★
CONNECTION

THE
★ CUBAN ★
CONNECTION

NIXON, CASTRO, AND THE MOB

WILLIAM WEYAND TURNER

Prometheus Books

59 John Glenn Drive
Amherst, New York 14228–2119

Published 2013 by Prometheus Books

Cover image © Bettmann/Corbis/AP Images
Cover design by Grace M. Conti-Zilsberger

Inquiries should be addressed to
Prometheus Books
59 John Glenn Drive
Amherst, New York 14228–2119
VOICE: 716–691–0133
FAX: 716–691–0137
WWW.PROMETHEUSBOOKS.COM

17 16 15 14 13   5 4 3 2 1

Library of Congress Cataloging-in-Publication Data

Turner, William W.
    The Cuban connection : Nixon, Castro, and the mob / by William Weyand Turner.
        p. cm.
    Includes bibliographical references and index.
    ISBN 978-1-61614-757-0 (cloth : alk. paper)
    ISBN 978-1-61614-758-7 (ebook)
    1. United States—Foreign relations—Cuba. 2. Cuba—Foreign relations—United States. 3. United States—Foreign relations—1953-1961. 4. Nixon, Richard M. (Richard Milhous), 1913-1994. 5. Castro, Fidel, 1926- 6. Cuba—History—Revolution, 1959. 7. Organized crime—United States—History—20th century. 8. Organized crime—Cuba—History—20th century. 9. Subversive activities—Cuba—History—20th century. 10. Espionage, American—Cuba—History—20th century. I. Title.

E183.8.C9T87 2013
327.7307291—dc23

                                                                    2013001488

Printed in the United States of America on acid-free paper

To
MARGE
the light of my life

CONTENTS

ACKNOWLEDGMENTS

So many contributed so much to the production of *The Cuban Connection* that I don't know where to start. So I'll begin at home with a salute to Marge Turner, who kept cool in the face of the editorial bedlam that surrounds the making of a nonfiction book. This cool led to her intuitive discovery of a lost manuscript from an earlier era that provided background for the current one. Where was it? On a ledge in the garage, of course. And thanks go to my daughter, Lori Turner, for her able assistance in my research. Still in the neighborhood, my fellow author and colleague Marilyn Dineen was kind enough to critique the early text to start it on its way. One more neighborhood support was Linda Hepworth, our local waitress and author of *Turning the Tables*, who emulates Dorothy Parker at the informal Chalet Basque "Round Table."

To make the transition from proposal to contract—the bridge of sighs, I call it—the author more often than not needs some outside help. I recall my first book, *The Police Establishment*, which was published by G. P. Putnam's Sons in 1968. I was standing around the punch bowl at a holiday party thrown by San Francisco literati when I met John Dodds, the editorial director of Putnam's, and an esteemed figure in the Eastern literary world. At this point I had yet to contemplate writing a book—it all seemed too exotic for Westerners. But John seemed intrigued by my FBI stories—I had spent ten years as one of Hoover's finest, working on everything from counterespionage to bank robbery as well as the Migratory Bird Act. John asked if I had any book proposals prepared, then told me to compose an outline.

A week after I sent him the outline, John sent me a contract and a $3,500 advance. I found out later that the FBI had a snitch inside Putnam's and I was on J. Edgar Hoover's most-wanted list for criticizing his false alarms on the Communist Party USA and his dereliction on organized crime.[1] The

Bureau wanted not only to silence me but also to make me an example to deter other agents from speaking out. The Bureau was leaning heavily on Putnam's executives to smother the book. Initially there was a tendency to cave in to Hoover, but in the end, the American tradition of a free press prevailed. *The Police Establishment* went on to literary and financial success. One national reviewer titled his piece, "Pull Over, Officer."

I owe a tip of the cap to Dr. Cyril Wecht, a foremost pathologist and friend for over thirty years. When I learned that Cyril's latest work bore the imprint of Prometheus Books, I contacted him, and Cyril was kind enough to put in a good word for me with the publisher.

I was very fortunate to be granted an interview with Carlos Prío Socarrás, president of Cuba until ousted by Batista. In the interview, Prío provided the information about Castro's plan to offer a strategic alliance with the United States and his rebuff at Nixon's hands, which is the tipping point of this book. Prío played a significant role in Cuban politics in the 1950s; his graft-fed fortune was thought to be the largest in Cuban history. His showplace estate, La Chata, was the guesthouse for many international celebrities.

When I interviewed Mike McLaney, proprietor of the Casino Internacional in Havana, he was reluctant to talk because he said the federal government has a long memory. But he poured me a drink and settled down to talk. His language was colorful, as when he called one of the pilots he had retained for his own operations "all flaps and no throttle." I later found out that one of the hangers-on with McLaney was a tall, thin man with horn-rimmed glasses named Sam Benton, who was actually an assassination broker. (Yes, he took a percentage of the price of the hit contracts he "sold.") So I am grateful to McLaney, not for what he didn't say, but for what he put me onto: the involvement of Sam Giancana, the Chicago Mafia boss, and his underlings in the "snuff Castro" crowd.

I was also the beneficiary of the great paramilitary journalist Andrew St. George's ceaseless digging for the core of the story. Andrew was the golden boy of Time-Life's Henry Luce (the Founder, as Luce was sarcastically referred to inside the organization). Warren Hinckle, the bad-boy journalist who founded *Ramparts*, kept a parakeet christened Henry Luce in his San Francisco office. Hinckle had apprenticed at the *San Francisco Chronicle*, and his incomparable nose for news endowed me with my cub credentials by some strange osmosis.

Enrique "Harry" Ruiz-Williams was a commanding presence when I interviewed him in 1974 at his office papered with maps and geological charts. I published some of his story in *Deadly Secrets* but recently discovered pertinent information that Harry was forced to withhold from me. As it turns out, Harry was playing lifeguard to Commander Juan Almeida Bosque, a hero of the Cuban Revolution. Along with Che Guevara, Almeida had grown disillusioned with Fidel Castro. They took action. Almeida with the aid of the Americans would arrange a coup. Che would leave Cuba and build his own forces as he traveled through the hinterlands of South America. The Almeida story was a time bomb, and I'm deeply in debt to Harry Williams for briefing me on the existence of the defection without betraying the commander.

I know I haven't mentioned my editor yet, which may be a case of saving the best for last. Well, sort of. Carol Callahan is without a doubt one of the premier freelance editors listed in the white pages today. She came to my rescue when I was having difficulty getting this volume properly structured. She is a pro in every way, and a pleasure to work with. To put up with my quips is a talent in itself.

PREFACE

It was the first blush of dawn in Havana as Fidel Castro Ruz paid a surprise visit to the sprawling estate called La Chata, the home of the former Cuban president, Carlos Prío Socarrás. Castro felt a sudden need to talk to Prío on the intricacies of the American government as he prepared for a trip to Washington that would begin that afternoon.

One of the security guards Prío had on staff roused him from his slumber at La Chata, his expansive estate, saying, "Fidel wants to see you."[1] The guard was fairly bursting with excitement. It was a short four months since Fidel Castro had descended from his redoubt in the Sierra Maestra range of eastern Cuba to claim victory. Castro had kicked off his revolution there, taking on the despot Fulgencio Batista, who had begun his term of president as populist as an ex–army sergeant could be, even flirting with the Communist Party of Cuba. But Batista began to drift to the right and was brought full circle by his formation of the Bureau for the Repression of Atheism and Communism (BRAC). This outfit became so brutal in its methods that Nixon felt compelled to dispatch CIA inspector Lyman Kirkpatrick to Havana to tell Batista to cool it.[2] American prestige was at stake because Nixon had vigorously supported the regime since Batista had pulled off the coup in 1952 that ended constitutional government in the island state.

When Castro forsook a career in America's favorite pastime, baseball, for the political hustings, he squeezed his initial financing out of Carlos Prío, who as the elected president of Cuba had refined the fine art of grafting to a Rembrandt level.

At that time, Prío was convicted in Florida of gunrunning in support of his own paramilitary force based in the Escambray range. A sign on the trail to Prío's bivouac taunted, "No Communists Allowed." But the combatants in this fluid revolution changed sides with remarkable alacrity. To wit,

Major William Alexander Morgan, in charge of the Second National Front of the Escambray irregulars, a pudgy Ohioan sporting tattoos and speaking broken Spanish.[3] He was awarded a Hero of the Revolution medal after he flipped at the last moment. And Frank Sturgis, the future Watergate burglar ("I don't know what I was doing there, I'm a Democrat!" he told me[4]) had first flown supplies for Prío, then switched to Castro, who was more of a fighter. The macho Sturgis was a dedicated anti-communist from the start, the coda E. Howard Hunt exploited to recruit him for the Watergate team. Hunt was considered by many to be the mastermind of the Watergate conspiracy. His political bent was hard right.

All the elements of this book non-harmonically converged on the open city of Havana in early January 1959. Fidel Castro, now standing in a Jeep and waving as it crawled through a rapturous throng cheering thunderously. Fidel was a Robin Hood type of hero, his only stamp a Cuban nationalist. Ahead of him, William Morgan was trying to capitalize on the new leader's tardiness in reaching the capital by rallying his troops at the Presidential Palace, the symbol of power in Cuba. But Che Guevara stood in his way, so Morgan loudly proclaimed his allegiance to Fidel.

Ex-president Prío had returned from exile when Batista fled and was waiting at La Chata for Fidel to name him to a "top post" in the new government. The pledge was made in 1956 when Prío donated $100,000 to Castro to buy the decrepit yacht *Granma* to ferry his landing party to Oriente Province in eastern Cuba where Santiago de Cuba was considered the Cradle of the Liberty in the battle against Spain.[5] The sanctuary of the Sierra Maestra range was nearby, and that was the location from which Fidel directed the guerilla war that bellowed to the world, as the *Chicago Tribune* and *New York Times* reported the heroics of the revolutionaries.

Not once during the period between the purchase of the *Granma* and his triumphal entry into Havana did Castro notify Prío of events as promised.[6] So Prío apprehensively awaited his appointment to office. He would attend administration meetings of the new government in the hope that Fidel would spot him from the podium and announce what ministry he would head. Then there was Castro's outdoor speech at Camp Columbia before a huge crowd as the Student Revolutionary Directorate (DRE) and

Second Front forces turned in their arms. "The worst part of the revolution against [the 1930s despot] Machado," he lectured, "was that afterwards gangs of revolutionaries roamed around fighting each other."[7] As he spoke a white dove released from the audience landed on his shoulder. It was hailed as an omen for peace—but not for a "top post."

Now it has been four months since the victory and still no word, but here is Fidel showing up at La Chata at the crack of dawn without his administrative aide, Juan Orta. The president stood well over six feet with deep-set dark brown eyes, an aquiline nose, dark chestnut hair, and a short beard and mustache. As usual, he was dressed in olive-drab fatigues, combat boots, and a legionnaires cap. As usual, his clothes did not seem to have had a recent pressing. He did not have a Cohiba jutting from his mouth. But it was Castro all right. Was he going to offer a "top post" to Prío, or did this clandestine visit have something to do with an invitation from the American Society of Newspaper Editors (who knew a good story when they saw one) to go on a lecture tour?

Prío, a dapper, genial man with a wife who resembled Dorothy Lamour, was disappointed again. It turned out that the seemingly independent leader had sustained a case of the jitters, fearing he would seem lost in dealing with the American press and White House team. He had been in the hills too long to be comfortable with the inside of an executive suite. Not that Fidel was a rube; he had retained a standout public-relations firm in the American seat of government to keep his iconic image intact. Fidel needed Prío's advice on how to deal with the Americans. He said that he had been brushing up on his English since receiving the invitation for a tour lasting eleven days. He was told that protocol called for him, as Cuba's head of state, to be invited to the White House for a session with President Eisenhower.[8] Did Prío have such a session?

Castro seemed to be concerned that he might not be received with equal honors by Eisenhower, but Prío assured him that he himself had been received by the American president with full honors and Castro would be as well. Fidel seemed relieved. He remarked that it was fortunate that both he and Eisenhower were military men; they should understand each other well.

I talked with Carlos Prío on November 24, 1974, at the Miami home of his brother Paco, a former mayor of Havana. The interview was made possible by the good offices of Louis Wolfson, owner of the champion racehorse Affirmed. Prío told me his advice to Castro was "No matter what you discuss with officials, don't tell the press . . . and don't sell American [*sic*] all of our sugar and tie Cuba too closely economically." The rookie president nodded in agreement, saying he didn't want to ask the United States for anything. But then Castro tapped his breast pocket and enunciated a proposal so stunning in its conception and so simple in its complexity that Prío could only sit in silence. Not that he intended to say much in any event. Against the backdrop of the Cold War, Castro was going to propose to the Eisenhower White House that the Republic of Cuba and the United States form an alliance, a strategic alliance in which Cuba would side with the United States against the Soviet Union in the event of hostilities.[9] Noticing Prío's lack of reaction, Castro elaborated that the time had come when every third world country should align with one superpower or the other. Prío was surprised by Castro's prescient understanding of world affairs. Cuban presidents were not usually well-versed in foreign affairs.

Prío did not comment to Castro on his alliance proposal simply because he still longed to serve out his term as elected president and didn't want to inadvertently annoy the new head of government.

After dropping his bombshell, Castro began to fidget and appeared ready to leave. Prío offered him a ride to the airport, thinking he could brace him on the promised "top post." It would be his calling in a chip. But Fidel had brought his town car and driver with him, and left for his flight to Washington, DC. Little did he know that he would soon be meeting Richard "Dick" Nixon; Prío hadn't prepared him for that.

★ ★ ★

But Castro was not going to meet Eisenhower. When the cranky old man received word that the young Cuban head of state was coming, Ike pouted, writing later in his memoirs, "I was more than irritated by news of the invitation."[10] For Ike to express himself this forcefully was unusual, but

Fidel's 1957 polemic pitch for agrarian reform had alarmed conservatives. So he booked a golf game at Pinehurst, a course in North Carolina, though he was a member of a local club, Burning Tree in Washington, DC. In Eisenhower's estimation, Castro must buy his clothes at a war surplus store. This was just the type of put-down that churns class warfare. But Ike's avoidance of Castro might have been a strategic move to substitute Vice President Nixon, who was regarded as a tougher interrogator. In the four months since taking over, Castro's regime had not very well defined itself and its stance on communism was unknown to the White House.

From his point of view, Castro must have reasoned, the vice president of the United States had more important things to do than beat a dead horse. The Cuban leader said in the course of his lecture tour that in the event of hostilities between the Soviet Union and the United States, he would side with the United States. Nixon didn't seem to care about the strategic position of Cuba if, in fact, he understood it. The chimera of communism possessed him.

★　★　★

All of the players in Cuban politics felt that Castro's government would be a pushover, including the Mob. Every Cuban politician of the previous twenty years had been bought off by the National Crime Syndicate (NCS) so that the Syndicate actually functioned as the "invisible government." Led by Meyer Lansky, the Mob didn't feel threatened by Castro because they couldn't believe that he would close the casinos, which were stacking up some $200 million in profits a year, paying nominal taxes but lining the pockets of officials with graft. If the Havana casinos did close, the Mob would continue to buy up properties in Las Vegas, now that gambling had been legalized there.

The "invisible government" did decide to cover its bets when Castro flew to the United States for his lecture tour. He was accompanied by an entourage that included Frank Sturgis as his "director of security." When they arrived in Washington and checked in to the Statler Hilton, Sturgis was surprised by a visit from "Sally" Burns and Joe Rivers, two of Lansky's lieutenants, who claimed the visit was for social reasons.[11] Sturgis realized that the Mob was keeping tabs on Fidel, so he called some of the 26th of July irregulars who were part of the entourage and had the two goons thrown out. Burns and Rivers would later play a role in the Bay of Pigs fiasco. During the invasion, they were waiting on a boat three miles offshore for word to come that the invasion had succeeded. Once they received word, they were supposed to go ashore, retrieve a buried cache of $750,000, and turn the lights on in all the casinos.

Due to the fiasco of the Bay of Pigs invasion, the CIA decided to deploy armed cells throughout Cuba to wage a guerilla war of attrition against Castro.[12] They set up an anti-Castro action group called the Second Naval Guerrilla based in Nicaragua, led by Manuel Artime, who had been a member of the provisional government of Cuba in the Bay of Pigs invasion. In November 1961, Robert Kennedy set out to avenge a family humiliation by launching a low-profile, "plausibly deniable" operation, dubbed Operation Mongoose, that conducted sabotage raids, infiltration, black propaganda to stir internal dissent, and economic destabilization, all aimed at softening up Cuba for an eventual second invasion. Unfortunately, it relied on personnel like Artime, a proven incompetent.

As for Fidel, his intelligence services were more effective than the American agency. I met with Arturo Rodriguez, an electronic technician in Castro's security service, G-2, in Rio de Janeiro, Brazil, over the 1991 Labor Day weekend. He said G-2 had infiltrated Manuel Artime's camp in Nicaragua, recorded his radio transmissions, and tapped the phones.

The CIA had failed so miserably in its attempts to eliminate Castro that when he became president, Lyndon Johnson told E. Howard Hunt, "he didn't want to hear another thing about those goddamn Cubans."[13] So the CIA switched its covert operations to a dirty war in Vietnam where they were just as successful.

★ ★ ★

In this fashion was American policy toward Cuba turned inside out, resulting in a bitter enmity between the colossus of the north and the impoverished Caribbean island that has lasted through ten presidencies. Eisenhower initiated the economic blockade that endures to this day, and set in motion the disastrous Bay of Pigs invasion. John Kennedy came close to reversing the process when he secretly negotiated with Castro for rapprochement, an endeavor cut short by his assassination. Although Lyndon Johnson and Richard Nixon were preoccupied with the Vietnam War, they maintained the status quo by authorizing CIA operations against Cuba. Gerald Ford changed nothing. Jimmy Carter made conciliatory gestures until forced to suspend them by the Soviet invasion of Afghanistan. Ronald Reagan focused on the Soviet Union, that "evil empire," but he did contain Havana's expansionism by invading Grenada on the vaporous excuse that the Cubans were building an airfield there. Even though the Cold War was over, the Bushes *père* and *fils* were coldly antagonistic toward Cuba, a family trait stemming from their political exploitation of the powerful exile bloc in South Florida whose hatred of Castro knows no bounds. In 1990 Jeb Bush interceded with his father, then vice president, on behalf of serial terrorist Dr. Orlando Bosch, dubbed Dr. Death, when he re-entered the United States illegally.[14] In the late 1960s, Bosch was the evil genius behind Cuban Power, which claimed credit for bombing Cuban targets and entities they felt to be sympathetic to the Castro regime. In 1976, Bosch was imprisoned in Venezuela for engineering the midair bombing of a Cuban civilian airliner, which took seventy-three lives. The US Department of Justice maintained that Bosch "repeatedly expressed and demonstrated a willingness to cause indiscriminate injury and death" in ordering him deported, but the senior George Bush stepped in and the order was cancelled.[15] Just how cynical that is can be measured by current government policy under which families short of green cards are broken up in summary fashion.

For Bill Clinton, opposition to Castro was also a family affair. As *Time* put it in an article titled "Clinton's Cuban Road to Florida," by Douglas Waller, on October 28, 1996, a "core group" of Cuban-American Democrats convinced him "he could win Florida in '96 if he became even more anti-Castro than Ronald Reagan or George Bush had been." The group included Maria Victoria Arias, the wife of Hillary Clinton's brother Hugh Rodham, who had political ambitions of his own. Despite a Pentagon evaluation that Cuba posed no threat to the region, Bill Clinton pandered to the exile diehards and, as a result, carried Florida. It was one more example of how American foreign policy was held hostage to a special-interest lobby. When he ran for president in 2000, the younger George Bush benefited not only from the Cuban special-interest vote, but also from an exile goon squad that intimidated Miami-Dade County election workers into halting a recount bringing Al Gore closer to victory.[16]

Demonizing Fidel Castro as moral authority to do away with him actually began before his revolution succeeded, when Rafael Trujillo of the Dominican Republic (the Dom Rep) dispatched a mercenary sniper with US military links into the Sierra Maestra gunning for Fidel. For Trujillo, it was a personal grudge. Years earlier, during the Prío presidency, Castro had joined an expeditionary force bent on overthrowing the psychopathic Trujillo for humanitarian reasons. As soon as Castro rolled into Havana, Trujillo, with a nod from the CIA, formed his own expeditionary force composed of former Batista supporters. The fact that this tyrant enjoyed rosy relations with Washington while fitting Castro with a shroud spoke clearly of the double standards of American policy. Trujillo was in favor by virtue of his violent opposition to communism, which enabled him to count Richard Nixon, former ambassador William Pawley, and the Kennedy family—to whom he had been introduced by his son-in-law, international playboy Porfirio Rubirosa, a social contact of Jacqueline Kennedy—as friends. But in the family history was a time bomb that illustrated patriarch Joseph Kennedy's show-me-the-money standard: when son Jack was born, he named Trujillo his godfather.

The chronicle of US–Cuba relations has rarely been harmonious despite the geographic closeness. Some idea of the rancor that periodically stressed relations was the confiscatory occupation of Guantanamo and its conversion to a US Marine base. Each year a check arrives in the Cuban seat of government drawn on the United States Treasury for "rent," and each year Havana options not to cash it. The issue is deep in the hearts of Cuban nationalists who view it in terms of the island's sovereignty.

This book hopefully will be a shot over the bow of American foreign policy in the Caribbean region. The whole story of American involvement in the affairs of that region constitutes a plenary violation of the Neutrality Act and came close to igniting thermonuclear war. *The Cuban Connection* chronicles the disparate origins of the counterrevolution against Cuba, profiles the personalities who perpetrated it, and describes its plots and schemes ranging from the masterful to the ridiculous. It is the product of over a hundred interviews, conducted for the most part in the 1960s and 1970s. These are the core interviews:

- Dr. Carlos Prío Socarrás—President of Cuba until ousted by a Batista coup in 1952. Original funder of Fidel Castro. Snubbed by Castro after the victory, he relocated in Miami and became a major figure in the revanchism movement.
- Ambassador William D. Pawley—A wealthy anti-communist zealot, Pawley played Cardinal Richelieu to President Eisenhower to turn him against Castro. Secret emissary in trying to persuade Batista to step down in favor of a junta that would forestall Castro, and convincing Argentina and Peru to provide military backup to the Bay of Pigs invasion force.
- Rolando "El Tigre" Masferrer—Mortal enemy of Castro whose private army tried to hunt down the rebel leader while still in his mountain stronghold. Fled to Miami, from where he continued to go after Castro, sending in an assassination team. My interview with him took place in Miami at his home, where he weirdly appeared in an open garage door with his acolytes holding lit candles. Masferrer agreed to my interview through the auspices of Gordon Winslow, the county clerk of Dade County who was in touch with many in the Cuban exile community. The interview was taped not long before Masferrer turned the key to start his car and was blown away.
- Frank Sturgis, aka Fiorini—A soldier of fortune, he smuggled weapons to Castro in the mountains in 1958. Rewarded with a post in the new government, he switched sides when he perceived Castro to be a leftist. In Miami, Sturgis flew missions for the CIA while running his own action group funded by dispossessed casino

owners. Achieved notoriety in 1972 as one of the Watergate burglars. The initial interview with Frank in Miami in April 1974 was right after he was released after serving his time for the Watergate break-in. I made several more trips to Miami that year and touched base with Frank each time. By the end of that year, I was Frank's literary agent and was commissioned by the tabloid paper *Star* to solicit more information about the Watergate fiasco.

- Michael McLaney—Proprietor of the swanky Casino Internacional in Havana before being ejected by Castro, he formed his own air force to bomb strategic targets in Cuba. Partnered with the Chicago Mob to try to kill Castro. My interview with Mike at the Jockey Club in Miami resulted from a letter of introduction from my publisher, Houghton Mifflin; I explained that I was writing a book about the CIA's involvement with Castro (*Deadly Secrets*) and he told me to come on over.

- Gerry Patrick Hemming—A paramilitary specialist, he at first helped Castro, then turned against him, becoming a ubiquitous figure in South Florida anti-Castro circles. First to reveal the twin schemes to assassinate Castro when he visited Chilean president Salvador Allende in 1972. I was referred to Hemming by E. Carl McNabb in 1973 while I was conducting research for *Deadly Secrets*. I flew to Miami and booked into the Arrowhead Motel, a rather rundown facility that functioned as a home-away-from-home and safe house for many paramilitaries and soldiers of fortune. I invited Gerry to come to the Arrowhead for the interview. At the appointed time, I was shocked to find two huge men standing outside my door. Fortunately, they turned out to be 6'5" Gerry Hemming and his 6'5" brother Bob. I interviewed Gerry many times over the next few years because he was very plugged into the paramilitary community.

- Enrique "Harry" Ruiz-Williams—Wounded at the Bay of Pigs, he became Robert F. Kennedy's golden boy, spearheading a second invasion to be launched from the Dominican Republic. A penultimate meeting with the CIA was held on the very day that John F. Kennedy was assassinated. While researching for *Deadly Secrets*, I talked to Haynes Johnson at the *Washington Post*, who wrote a book on the Bay of Pigs, and he recommended I contact Harry, whom I subsequently interviewed in Fort Lauderdale at his office on the Coast Highway.

- General Fabian Escalante—Former director of Cuban Security G-2, his outfit discovered a CIA/Mafia plot to assassinate Castro coincident with the Bay of Pigs landing. It also penetrated the Harry Williams–led second-invasion preparations by bugging the Nicaragua base of Williams's ally, Manuel Artime. When I was an American delegate to the Rio Conference on the assassination of John F. Kennedy, I met the Cuban delegate Fabian Escalante and his aide-de-camp Rodriguez. Escalante introduced himself to me and subsequently sat down for an informal interview. Escalante had a commanding presence and was apparently a born leader.

A major source was President Fidel Castro, who in 1978 supplied information through an intermediary in Mexico City, and in 1981 authorized background interviews of Cuban officials in Havana.

CHRONOLOGY

June 1946: Lucky Luciano's prison sentence is commuted due to his support of the Office of Naval Intelligence in combating sabotage along the Atlantic Coast during World War II. He is deported to Sicily, but ends up in Cuba

December 1946: Luciano and Meyer Lansky invite Mob bosses to Havana Conference to establish a business plan for casino operations in Cuba

November 1948: Lansky and Cuban leader Fulgencio Batista establish pact to control the gaming industry in Cuba

March 1952: Batista engineers a bloodless coup, overthrows President Carlos Prío Socarrás, and takes over Cuba

Late October 1952: Richard Nixon visits Sans Souci casino in Havana with his slush-fund manager Dana Smith

Early 1953: Lansky begins buying controlling interests in casinos in Havana

July 1953: Castro takes up arms against the corrupt Batista regime. Moncada Barracks attack fails, Fidel and Raul Castro put in jail

December 1956: 26th of July Movement launches Cuban Revolution

April 1958: Rafael Trujillo of the Dominican Republic sends arms to support Batista's Cuban army and prevent the success of Castro's revolution

December 1958: At the behest of the State Department, William D. Pawley meets with Batista to suggest exile

December 1958: Ambassador Earl T. Smith warns Batista that the US government was in the process of withdrawing its support

January 1, 1959: Batista flees Cuba, as revolutionary troops enter Havana

January 1959: Fidel Castro takes control of Cuba, the Cuban Revolution is over

Late February 1959: Trujillo organizes the Cuban Liberation Army to invade Cuba

April 1959: Castro visits the United States on speaking tour, sponsored by American Society of Newspaper Editors

Late April 1959: Castro meets with Vice President Nixon, determined to establish rapport between the United States and Cuba

Late May 1959: On returning to Cuba after his disastrous meeting with Nixon, Castro has undergone an epiphany and now decides to move into the Soviet sphere

May 1959: CIA Director Allen Dulles sets up dummy corporation Double-Chek to handle covert operations against Cuba

June 1959: Castro sends Che Guevara to Cairo for the first official contact with the Soviet Union

August 1959: Trujillo's Cuban Liberation Army fails due to betrayal and bad timing

September 1959: Jack Ruby visits Havana

January 1960: Casinos close down in Havana

March 1960: Eisenhower authorizes the Cuba Project, a CIA operation led by Nixon for the purpose of overthrowing Castro

March 1960: French freighter *Le Coubre* blows up dockside in Havana, killing one hundred and injuring two hundred

November 1960: William Pawley travels to the Dominican Republic to try to persuade Trujillo to step down

April 1961: Assassination attempt of Castro by Mob hit man to coincide with Bay of Pigs invasion

April 17, 1961: Bay of Pigs invasion launched

April 19, 1961: Bay of Pigs invasion fails miserably

May 1961: Rafael Trujillo assassinated with support from CIA

November 1961: Operation Mongoose, an action plan designed to overthrow Castro's government, is launched by directive from John F. Kennedy

August 1963: Second Cuban invasion planned under Manuel Artime aborted by blunders

September 1963: Pawley's yacht, the *Flying Tiger*, drops band of mercenaries off Cuba for covert operation

November 1973: Interview with Enrique "Harry" Ruiz-Williams by author, in Fort Lauderdale

November 1973 and April 1974: Interview with Gerry Patrick Hemming by author, in Miami, Florida

April 1974: Interview with Frank Sturgis by author, in Miami, Florida

April 27, 1974: Interview with Rolando Masferrer by author, in Miami, Florida

November 1974: Interview with Carlos Prío Socarrás by author, in Miami, Florida

November 1974: Interview with William Pawley by author, in Coral Gables, Florida

December 1974: Interview with Mike McLaney by author, in Miami, Florida

August 1991: Interview with Fabian Escalante, head of Cuban counterintelligence, by author, in Rio de Janeiro

CHAPTER ONE
THE VIOLENT PAST IS PROLOGUE

"HISTORY WILL ABSOLVE ME."
—FIDEL CASTRO, 1953[1]

```
CUBAN PITCHER TURNS DOWN OFFER OF
    $5,000 BONUS TO SIGN WITH THE
NEW YORK GIANTS; WILL STUDY LAW AT
THE UNIVERSITY OF HAVANA INSTEAD.
```

This might have been the slug of the Manhattan press on that fine summer day when Fidel Castro Ruz opted for a legal career over a baseball one. The native of Cuba was scouted by Joe Cambria of the Washington Senators, who told him he didn't have a major league arm. But a Pittsburgh Pirates bird dog was more impressed, remembering, "He could set 'em up with the curve, blow 'em down with the heater." Castro tried out for several major league clubs, including the Philadelphia Athletics, but it was the New York Giants that showed a definite interest. The $5,000 figure was not random. Baseball rules at the time dictated that any amount over $5,000 tendered to a rookie required that he be kept on the roster of the big league club for a season. So the man with the golden arm would have been eligible for assignment to a minor league team, with the Havana Sugar Kings of the International League coming to mind. What may have offended Castro's sensibilities was that the Sugar Kings were owned by an official in the Batista regime. Fulgencio Batista was the Cuban Caligula, a dictator too long in power. But Castro never lost his love for the American national pastime, devotedly following Cuba's national squad and acquiring a batting cage of his own, though he was not destined to see his face on a bubble-gum card.

There are those, of course, who devoutly wish Castro had stuck with baseball. They don't include the Giants immortal Carl Hubbell, who undoubtedly would not have welcomed the stiff competition. But Castro himself found the stiffest competition imaginable when he later set aside his law books and took to the political hustings to deliver action-packed speeches that were distinguished by their length. But he spoke from the heart as he pleaded for an end to poverty in his homeland of eleven million people. The roads of Cuba never run straight, goes an old folk song.

At the University of Havana, Castro lost no time in becoming politicized in its hothouse environment. He was dominated by Cuban nationalism but affiliated with the Ortodoxo Party, which, like most Cuban political structures, was polemically flexible. Fidel's dominant theme in his speeches was the plight of the poor and what to do about it. He harped on agrarian reform that he saw as at least a partial solution in a country without rural electrification. Fidel had issued a manifesto on the subject in 1957 while still in the mountains. The move drew a furious response from the American legislator Harold Cooley, leader of the sugar lobby in Congress, and in the pockets of the corporate landholders such as United Fruit Company. But agrarian reform was a buzzword for American conservatives who viewed it as confiscatory socialism. It was not at all; usually the distributed acreage was unsuitable for agriculture. The Castro version was more like the *ejiido* model adopted in Mexico after the revolution.[2] It called for division of surplus land and land holdings within reasonable limits. Critics charged that United Fruit Company, a huge presence in tropical countries, was the prime target of Castro from day one because his father, an employee, had been mistreated.

Be that as it may, Fidel's matriculation at the Havana institution was marked by controversy that carried beyond the ivied walls. The Fidel who went to the University of Havana in October 1945 both attracted and repelled his fellow "students," some of whom even came to study, for this was a classic Latin American university system that was half devoted to learning and at least half devoted to fomenting political action.[3]

Castro's ability to deliver fiery speeches, albeit long-winded, gained him an approving audience in greater Havana that, when the time was right, coalesced into a solid political base. As a candidate he would have been a natural. Physically, Fidel stood out. He was markedly tall in a country of generally short men.[4]

He affected a somewhat rumpled look, perhaps the result of a conscious attempt to look unconventional. Yet he possessed the magnetic personality of a yacht salesman.

The conventional Cuban political scene was so turgid that it was perhaps preferable to be called a revolutionary. Consider the hapless Eduardo Chibás, a rotund little man who kept the political waters constantly roiled. "Every week on Sunday night, Chibás spoke," Hugh Thomas recorded in his landmark volume *Cuba or the Pursuit of Freedom*, and "crowds flocked to hotels or cafés to hear him." Like Castro, Chibás was an Ortodoxo. "He spoke with extraordinary passion and energy, denouncing the unbridled corruption of the regime and the gangsters associated with it." He believed that corruption was the most important problem Cuba faced. But Chibás had erred in identification. On August 5, 1951, he walked into radio station CMQ in Havana for his weekly radio broadcast. That day he had promised to furnish the evidence supporting his claim that education minister Aureliano Sanchez Arango was embezzling money. Instead, he talked about other topics, warned that Fulgencio Batista might attempt a military coup, and made a farewell statement. Chibás, who was also a senator, was supposed to present evidence from congressmen supporting his claim, who ultimately refused to do so. Chibás apparently believed that killing himself was the only way he could apologize for his inability to keep his promise, so he pulled out a pistol and shot himself in the head. Unfortunately, he had forgotten that his allotted radio time was only twenty-five minutes. The shot took place while the commercial ad with "Café Pilon" was running, thus eliminating the planned effect of "his grand finale." The corrupt regime, as Thomas put it, was the presidency of Carlos Prío Socarrás.

★ ★ ★

Cuba wasn't mighty militarily, but with the possessions of Guantanamo it was strategically on the map. It was rich in natural resources such as nickel and copper, and a major player in world sugar markets. Behold the Cuban cigars, their labels second to none. It was the pearl of the Antilles, playground to the sophisticated traveler who bends an elbow at the Floridita bar, or the Bodeguita del Medio, where mojitos are the politically correct drink. The packing-crate United States Interest Section building forlornly faces the Malecon waterfront. Outside Havana, the white-sand beaches defy surpassing beauty, and the highland lakes abound with bass.

In the 1950s it was golden to be president of Cuba. Batista presided over the growing number of gambling casinos and spent many an hour clinking glasses with visiting notables. One such was Richard Nixon, who showed up with his constant companion, Charles "Bebe" Rebozo, at his elbow. For Batista, the slots clanking in the background must have been music to his ears, as were the sounds of the roulette wheels spinning and the dice rolling.

One of Batista's most useful partisans was Rolando "El Tigre" Masferrer, who can best be described as a man for all political seasons. In his youth, the powerfully built Masferrer was a militant communist, fighting on the Loyalist side in the Spanish Civil War, losing a leg but gaining a reputation as an enforcer. It is safe to say that Masferrer was a Renaissance man, affecting silk scarves while scribing poetry, and painting landscapes while patronizing classical music. Speeding down the Malecon in a Cadillac convertible, he justified the acceptance of gangsterism to a German passenger, "Remember, *chico*, we're all gangsters. What did you expect? This isn't Europe."[5]

But Masferrer was also capable of fits of idealism, as was shown by his enlistment in the romantically named Caribbean Legion, which was formed for the express purpose of overthrowing the rogue dictator Generalissimo Rafael Trujillo of the Dom Rep. Trujillo was well known for his grievous trespasses against human rights. His only competitor for cruelty honors was François "Papa Doc" Duvalier of Haiti. The democratic rulers of other nations in the region had gotten together and decided that the only way to go was to muster a mobile strike force.[6] In recognition of his service in the Spanish Civil War, Masferrer was appointed an officer.

And who should come under his command but another volunteer, Fidel

Castro. It was the summer of 1947, and the tryouts with the Major League Baseball teams were two years away. Nevertheless, his athletic prowess was about to be tested. The Caribbean Legion trained on isolated Cayo Confites on the north coast of the Dominican Republic and, with the democratic rulers looking the other way, launched an invasion. It was a disaster. Trujillo's efficient spy network found out about the Legion's intent. The Dom Rep regulars trounced the eclectic Legionnaires. Fidel, who had been leading a platoon of Dom Rep citizen volunteers, dove into the choppy waters between the Dom Rep and the north shore of Cuba. It marked the beginning of the Castro legend. When he finished the marathon swim, he found himself within hitchhiking distance of his father's modest farm.

It was at this point that Masferrer became all tough-guy and formed his feared Los Tigres in Santiago de Cuba at the island's eastern tip, celebrated as the nation's Cradle of Liberty. From Santiago, Masferrer dispatched his Los Tigres into the hills to try and run his ex-comrade-in-arms to ground. But Fidel and his now-downsized band of insurgents had disappeared into the fastness of the Sierra Maestra range.

I interviewed Rolando Masferrer on April 27, 1974, at his home in urban Miami. He gave the impression of a street fighter, although his days as commander of his private army were long gone. Flanking him on both sides were khaki-clad individuals with stern faces who, if drugstore clerks, would only smile if someone forgot their change. I asked Masferrer if he had any criticism of Castro during the Caribbean Legion expedition, since the youngster was under his command. Masferrer replied, "I blame myself as the man who gave him rudimentary training in military affairs—he was in charge of a platoon and behaved very discreetly."

★　★　★

What Castro needed to start his revolution was money. He thought it would be a tough sell, but he knew his man, Carlos Prío Socarrás, had it. Prío had been regarded as the island's most corrupt president until he was unseated in Batista's bloodless coup in 1952. Ever since then, he had schemed to return to the baroque Presidential Palace. He had started his own paramilitary unit under the banner of the Autentico Party and merged with the Second National Front of Escambray that was physically much closer to Havana (the ultimate prize) than Fidel in the Sierra Maestra.

Prío provided funding for Castro to underwrite his revolution in the hopes that he would be allowed to finish out his term in office. But he worried that the Americans would somehow influence the outcome, and it wouldn't be in his favor. He made several trips to the State Department's Foggy Bottom headquarters in Washington to solidify his claim to be president-in-waiting as Batista's position deteriorated. "I told the head of the Cuban desk that we wanted a smooth transition—no massacres—and that it was the duty of the Americans to stabilize the situation," Prío told me.[7] State insisted that the situation would resolve itself.

As a source for financing, Castro also thought of the National Crime Syndicate (NCS) that was raking in millions of dollars a day through ownership of the casinos lining Havana's gamblers row, but the notion quickly passed. The Syndicate posed as legitimate businessmen but with few exceptions was under the rule of Meyer Lansky, the chief executive of the NCS. Just a percentage of the daily skim could finance Castro's revolution that had been staggering ever since the Moncada Barracks attack boomeranged in 1953.

That plan was to attack the barracks in Santiago de Cuba early in the morning when it could be anticipated that the soldiers would be dulled by hangovers, making the element of surprise the tipping point. The soldiers proved alert, however, and the Castro irregulars were routed, some escaping death only through the intervention of priests who happened upon the scene. The capture of the barracks was to be coupled with a general strike, but that never happened. Fidel, his brother Raul, and the surviving guerillas were hustled to the Isla de Pinos prison, where a panel of judges sat in Catalonian silence as Castro delivered his impassioned "history will absolve me" speech. He was sentenced to fifteen years in prison, and Raul to thirteen years, but both were released two years later, in 1955, in a Batista general amnesty.

In exile in Mexico, Castro formed the 26th of July Movement, named after the date of the Moncada assault. By this time, Castro was regarded by many Cubans as a reincarnation of Jose Marti, the hero of the fight for independence from Spain at the turn of the century. Soon the guerillas were pop heroes called *barbudos* ("bearded revolutionaries"), and their cause reverberated through the nation. Now out of prison and up in the hills, Castro's growing popularity attracted an eclectic group of people visiting his mountain redoubt: journalist Herbert Matthews of the *New York Times*; Jules Witcover of the *Chicago Tribune*; parajournalist Andrew St. George, a contributor to *Life*; and Frank Sturgis, who was ferrying guns and ammunition to Castro. It happened that Sturgis had formed a small import-export company grandly called Interamerica Business Corporation, and it came in handy as a cover for his smuggling. He bought quality weapons at a suburban Washington firm that dealt worldwide and was closely aligned with the CIA, then devised an ingenious system to supply the Havana underground. Using rented vans, Sturgis would drop off sixty-pound packages of guns and ammunitions to trusted Cuban families in Miami. They would buy old jalopies and conceal the contraband in false gas tanks and door panels, then drive to Key West and take the ferry to Havana. The jalopies were left in parking lots for pickup by underground contacts.[8]

But the only practical way to supply the rebel army in the Sierra Maestra was by air. One evening in early 1958, as shadows crept up the majestic turret of Pico Turquino, the loftiest peak in the Sierra Maestra, Castro lit a Cohiba and sipped Añejo rum as he conversed with Sturgis, a chain-smoking teetotaler. Castro disclosed that he was about to open new fronts and an urban underground in an expanding offensive. But the weapons coming through from Miami came at a snail's pace. Could Sturgis do better? He could and did. Sturgis assembled a small fleet of light planes that landed on remote stretches or made air drops. After watching Sturgis sideslip a Bellanca loaded with arms into a mountain clearing, Castro marveled, "My favorite *yanqui*."[9] Sturgis was also flying for Carlos Prío and his Second Front, but Sturgis ultimately dismissed Prío as just another politician and devoted full time to flying for the 26th of July Movement.[10]

Castro's popularity began to extend beyond the borders of Cuba due to the journalistic output generated from these meetings, and resulted in a multiplying effect for his cause, drawing in other rebels, like Che Guevara, and bringing in financial support from around the world. Teenagers put Castro and Che on their bedroom walls. His guerilla war of attrition became successful. Fidel was the Eisenhower of the hills.

In late 1958, Castro, fortified by additional troops and supplies, ordered an advance on Havana. The advance was turning into a rout, forcing some army soldiers to hide in caves. The precipitous departure of Batista left a vacuum that several of the action groups could try to fill. Only five days earlier, Castro had met secretly with General Eugenio Cantillo, commander of the Cuban Army forces on the eastern front in Oriente Province. Cantillo had helicoptered to the meeting site, a sugar mill, in an attempt to save the army from demobilization and Batista from criminal prosecution.[11] In addition to this, Cantillo harbored his own ambitions for the future of Cuba. The general promised that Batista would leave the country if the army was left intact. Castro was insistent, however, that the dictator be held for trial. Cantillo countered that the army would rise before 3:00 p.m. on New Year's Eve. Castro stood his ground that the army be dismantled. The talks broke off.

Now Castro's forces were advancing down the Central Highway toward Havana. It was a matter of hours, the glowing bulbs of the situation board showed, before the 26th of July banner hoisted on a Jeep would reach the Presidential Palace. Batista still had hopes of cutting a deal to participate in a rump government that would take over before Castro's lead columns reached the city center. But that didn't happen.

At the time the news hit, the CIA contingent attached to the United States Embassy in Havana was having cocktails on a glass-enclosed outer deck. The bearer of the tidings was E. Howard Hunt, the contemplative, pipe-smoking agent who would later be a major figure in the Watergate affair. Not to worry, Hunt said, Batista had given assurance that his air force had wiped out the invaders.[12] It was of course a canard.

CHAPTER TWO
THE EAGLE HAS LANDED

"CUBA HAS THE SAME EFFECT ON AMERICAN ADMINISTRATIONS THAT THE FULL MOON USED TO HAVE ON WEREWOLVES."[1]
—FORMER STATE DEPARTMENT OFFICER IN HAVANA

It was 2:00 a.m. on New Year's Day, 1959, and Cuban president Fulgencio Batista had a decision to make. As celebrants still roamed the cobblestone streets of Old Havana, the glowing bulbs of the situation board at army headquarters in Camp Columbia showed that hope was rapidly vanishing. Castro and his *barbudos* had spilled out of the Sierra Maestra range and consolidated their positions in Oriente Province to the east. Its principal city, Santiago de Cuba, was under siege. In central Cuba, Raul Castro and the Argentine revolutionary Che Guevara threatened to cut the central highway traversing the island. Rebel columns had captured Sancti Spiritus and Santa Clara, closer to Havana. Until now, Batista believed that his brutal, corrupt regime could somehow survive, or at least he could cut a deal to participate in a rump government that would take over before Castro's forces arrived. But it was too late. In a matter of hours, a rebel advance guard would enter the city.

Only five hours earlier, Batista had been driven in his limousine through the gates of Camp Columbia, the country's military headquarters in the outskirts of Havana, to the salutes of two sentries in natty khaki uniforms and white helmets. For the stubby dictator, who resembled a mestizo J. Edgar Hoover, it must have evoked memories of the day in 1933 when at this same army base he led a sergeants' revolt that propelled him into his first term as president. The limousine had proceeded to the airfield where it passed a row of biplanes—the Cuban Army's outdated air

37

force—and halted on the apron where two DC-4s of Aerovías Q, a civilian carrier, were parked with engines running. For two days they had stood by at a remote corner of the field with engines running and the pilots sleeping on board. Now Batista waited while forty-four relatives and aides boarded the lead plane. Into the president's plane soldiers loaded personal effects and satchels full of cash and jewelry, estimated to be worth more than $300 million.[2] Time had been too short to bring along the sixteen suitcases of silverware from the president's baronial mansion. Some critics charged that over the years Batista had looted as much as $700 million from Cuba's coffers.[3]

Since his arrival at Camp Columbia, Batista had attended a muted New Year's party in the officers' mess. But he must have been reminded of what might have been when he passed the obsolete biplanes. He had ordered fifteen Hawker Siddeley jets from Great Britain that might have made a difference if they had been delivered in time. The same might be said for the Staghound tanks that had been badly needed to blunt a major offensive by Fidel Castro's rebel guerillas, except that the tanks were unavailable because the United States and several Latin countries had slapped an arms embargo on Cuba due to egregious human-rights violations. The designation didn't make Cuba a leper colony, but it put on the brakes in more ways than one. Tourism slowed and exports were flat. Most important, international relations were affected.

An erstwhile army sergeant, Batista had been in control of the Cuban armed forces since the early 1930s. He became the strongman behind a succession of puppet presidents until he was himself elected to the presidency in 1940. At this stage in his career, he was the type of socially conscious ruler later exemplified by Gamal Abdel Nasser of Egypt. In fact, he had legitimately won the 1940 election by campaigning on a platform quaintly similar to Franklin Delano Roosevelt's New Deal, and he stitched together a coalition that mixed bankers and financiers with communists. But as his term progressed, Batista became more authoritarian, which eroded his popular support. As the State Department saw it, Batista's dalliance with communists might open the door to a communist takeover.

In 1944, after Batista ignored warnings through diplomatic channels,

State turned to Meyer Lansky to deliver the message in blunter fashion.[4] The collaboration of the Syndicate with the US government was already an established fact, due to the negotiations between the Office of Naval Intelligence (ONI) and Lucky Luciano during the war. Roosevelt knew that Lansky was on intimate terms with the Cuban leader, whom he viewed as a gangster anyway. So the president ordered naval intelligence to dispatch Lansky to meet eyeball to eyeball with Batista. The crime boss lectured the Cuban that the United States was engaged in a global conflict and would not hesitate to use military force to maintain stability in its own backyard.[5]

Batista got the message. He handpicked his successor for the 1944 elections, who unexpectedly lost to Ramon Grau. He went into "voluntary exile" in Florida, reportedly with millions of dollars in booty bulging out of his suitcases. Batista remained in the background of Cuban politics despite his election to the Cuban Senate *in absentia* in 1948. Returning to Cuba in 1952, Batista decided to run for president again. Three months before the elections, he staged a coup and began his reign as the country's iron man. Batista gradually shed his populist image and became a full-fledged dictator, establishing the Bureau for the Repression of Atheism and Communism (BRAC). By this time, he was on a glasses-clinking level with Dick Nixon, raising the question of what influence, if any, the Red-baiting member of Congress had on him.

Batista's reputation became so blighted by the BRAC excesses that it can be said his downfall started with "the BRAC thing" as a throttled press referred to it. Batista didn't think of himself as a dictator, especially when compared with Rafael Trujillo. In contrast, Batista only cracked down on those who threatened the state's security, while Trujillo was considered more promiscuous in his use of torture. In one instance in 1957, Batista was frustrated by his inability to defeat Castro's dug-in guerillas. His card-playing crony, US ambassador Arthur Gardner, proposed that he dispatch an FBI or CIA assassin to kill Castro. "No, no, we can't do that. We're Cubans," he said.[6] But the fact was that whether or not he realized it, he had grown tyrannical and more corrupt. Despite his chumminess with Nixon and other heavy hitters from north of the border, it was time for him to go.

Batista had considered the decision to go on December 9th when an American initiative to ease him into exile was handled by an old friend well connected in Cuba, in fact raised there.[7] He was William D. Pawley, a Truman ambassador to Peru. President Truman had been in awe of Pawley's leadership in forming the vaunted Flying Tigers to contest Japanese Zeros attacking supply routes. At war's end, Truman sent Pawley to Spain to negotiate the construction of Strategic Air Command sites with Francisco Franco. The soft-spoken Carolinian made his fortune during the Florida land boom of the 1920s. He founded Cubana (now the state carrier), the Havana transit system, and the bus line in Miami. In Florida, he owned Talisman Sugar Company, where he hired field laborers from Jamaica.

Pawley was key in the planning of the overthrow of the Arbenz government in Guatemala in 1956. I interviewed Bill Pawley on November 27, 1974, in his Coral Gables office. He was reluctant to see me, saying he was doing his own book. But when I pointed out his historical significance in Latin America and his footprints in the sands of the Caribbean, "Come on over," he said, "We can at least shake hands." Although he was a lanky, sandy-haired man, impeccably dressed with a Carolina accent, I felt as if I was engaged with a stern, didactic headmaster of a private school. At the end of the two-hour session, there was no doubt that he was a master of intrigue, operating behind the scenes to spur Ike to action against Cuba. At the same time, Pawley was a Daddy Warbucks using his yacht to carry out private missions. One was a bizarre plan in 1963 to kidnap two Russian missile technicians and spirit them off to Eisenhower's Gettysburg retirement farm to embarrass President Kennedy.[8]

In the course of his business and sub-rosa activities, Pawley came to know Batista well. It was because of this relationship that he was selected by the Eisenhower White House for a special mission to negotiate with Batista. Fidel Castro had become of concern even before he achieved a military victory. For one thing, Nixon was thick with Batista, as were other officials such as George Smathers, dubbed the Senator from Cuba because of his partiality for the Cuban dictator.

But there was a strong ideological pull as well. In 1957, when Castro issued an agrarian reform manifesto from his mountain base, it was a red alert. Bill Pawley had fits (colloquially), wrongly assuming Castro had in mind a Chinese version of reform. In the early spring of 1958, when everyone concerned agreed that the Batista presidency was doomed— it was only a matter of time—the question arose about the post-Batista future. In a lively caucus, Pawley voiced the notion that "everything we were doing was wrong. I told King that we should now, to try and save the peace, see if we can go down there to get Batista to capitulate to a care- taker government, unfriendly to him but satisfactory to us, which we could immediately recognize and give military assistance to in order that Fidel Castro not come to power."[9]

The reference to King was to a crusty ex–West Pointer, Colonel J. C. King, with whom Pawley walked in political lockstep. Like his compa- triot, King was quite a story. The colonel was a classic Cold War mixture of relentless anti-communist and buccaneer capitalist. As an entrepreneur, King built a condom factory in Brazil against the common wisdom that the predominantly Catholic country would obey the church's ban on birth control. The gamble paid off—King eventually sold out to the pharmaceu- tical giant Johnson & Johnson for millions of dollars. Now he was head of the CIA's Latin American Division.

In a series of conferences with CIA director Allen Dulles and State Department officials, Pawley and King presented this course of action in which Pawley would call on his friendship with Batista to persuade him to step down in favor of a five-man junta with one civilian, Jose "Pepin" Bosch of the Bacardi rum family.[10] The junta would immediately be rec- ognized as the legitimate government of Cuba by the United States and be supplied with $10 million in weapons with which to fend off Castro.

Standing fast against intervention that they saw as naked aggression, Roy Rubottom and William Wieland, both senior State officials, favored the option of a political settlement.[11] Pawley was adamant, "If you permit Castro to come to power, you are going to have more trouble than you have ever seen in your life."[12] It was an argument that Wieland had heard before. A few months earlier, the American ambassador to Cuba, Earl T. Smith, braced Wieland with the claim that Fidel's younger brother, Raul, was a communist and that his partner, Che Guevara, was a Marxist. In fact, Raul had belonged to the Young Communist League, but his membership had expired; and Che was a straight revolutionary. Wieland gave Smith, a Palm Beach socialite, a lesson in political reality based on his own experience as a reporter in Cuba. "We know all that, of course," he told Smith, "but that doesn't make it a communist-dominated movement. There are plenty of moderates in it as well. Far more moderates than radicals."[13] To State's careerists, the revolution was not beyond redemption.

Refusing to take no for an answer, Pawley sought a meeting with Undersecretary of State Douglas Dillon, an erudite Wall Streeter. President Eisenhower arranged it.[14] Pawley brought along the Senate's playboy, George Smathers. They complained bitterly about Wieland leaning to the left and urged Dillon to replace him with someone more amenable to blocking Castro. Wieland's superior, who was unexpectedly present, voiced resentment at the "outside pressure," and Dillon announced that he was unconcerned about Castro but greatly concerned about the right-wing dictator of the Dominican Republic.

Rafael Trujillo was regarded as a psychopath in some quarters and cut off by some Latin American states. Yet he was a friend of Pawley, Smathers, and Nixon. Pawley called for another caucus, this one with Assistant Secretary of State Henry Holland, whom he considered an ally, present with an aide. An agreement was reached in which Pawley would talk to Batista about stepping down. But at the insistence of Rubottom and Wieland, a stipulation was added. Pawley was to tell his old friend that the plan was his own idea and he was not speaking officially. He believed he could get Washington to agree.

"If he falls flat on his face," Rubottom told Wieland out of earshot of Pawley, "he won't embarrass anyone in government."[15]

Pawley did fall flat on his face. On the night of December 9, 1958, Pawley, after reviewing details with the Havana CIA station chief Jim Noel, met in the Presidential Palace with Batista for three hours. The American began by explaining the junta scenario and promising to "try to persuade the US government to back it to the fullest extent."[16] He guaranteed there would be no reprisals. Castro would have no place in the new government, elections would be held within eighteen months, and Batista could return to his Daytona Beach, Florida, ranch. By this time, however, the dictator had entered a depressive stage, turning moody and morose. He was given to such solitary pursuits as listening to recordings of telephone conversations made by his secret police. He angrily rejected his old friend's proposal, threatening to kick him out, so Pawley hurriedly departed.[17]

In Washington the right hand didn't know what the left was doing. Eight nights after Pawley's nocturnal visit, Ambassador Earl Smith appeared at Batista's door. He was unaware of Pawley's earlier visit, kept in the dark by Rubottom and Wieland due to his passionate partiality toward Batista. Smith had received a telegram from Rubottom that was not good news. It instructed him to tell Batista that, although the United States appreciated his past friendship, it was withdrawing its support for humanitarian reasons.[18] Batista spoke of setting up his own military junta, but Smith said it was too late. The dictator then asked if he could retire to his ranch in Florida. No, said Smith, he would have to go to another country first.

Here was Batista in effect saying he would leave Cuba if he could go to his own ranch in Florida. Smith didn't seize the opportunity; he stuck to the letter of his instructions. For his part, Batista still didn't know whether the offer bore the full marque of the US government. He realized that he was now a political leper, and he was bitter. "Your country has intervened in behalf of the Castros," he remonstrated.[19]

So instead of being blocked off by a powerful opposition junta, Castro took advantage of the lengthy stalemate and gained military strength. In the end, it was Castro who forced Batista to flee.

The bulbs of the situation board at Camp Columbia showed units of the rebel forces advancing through the Havana suburbs. Batista gave his last order, and the twin planes took off and banked to the northeast. There were murmurs of surprise among his entourage when Batista informed them they were bound for the Dominican Republic instead of the United States. The Dom Rep had been the only country to offer sanctuary to the fallen dictator.

Around 5:30 in the morning of New Year's Day, 1959, the phone rang in the Ciudad Trujillo (now Ciudad Domingo) home of Arturo Espaillat, aide to Rafael Trujillo. Groggy from a New Year's Eve celebration, he was jarred into sobriety by the raspy voice of his boss. According to Espaillat in his Trujillo memoir, Trujillo was confrontational, which was the case more often than not. "Remember that report you gave me yesterday regarding the Cuban situation?" he asked.[20] "You told me Batista was strong enough to remain in power another six weeks." The day before, Espaillat had returned from Cuba after evaluating Batista's position. He acknowledged his prediction. "Yes, I know you told me that," Trujillo said. "Now I want you to tell Batista that. He's at the airport now." When Batista's DC-4 had been only a few miles out, it had radioed for permission to land. Espaillat rushed to the San Ysidro Air Base to greet Batista and his entourage of uninvited guests, and put them up at the luxurious Hotel Jaragua. Trujillo was furious because Batista had allowed his regime to crater so precipitously that Castro, whom the dictator viewed as a communist, was practically invited into Havana. Trujillo received Batista icily, insisting that Dominican military aid to Cuba for fighting the rebels be recompensed. Batista dispatched his wife to the United States, where much of his fortune was deposited, to arrange the transfer of funds.

Batista simmered in Ciudad Trujillo for two weeks before calling Bill Pawley in Florida. He had to know the answer to a nagging question. When they met on December 9th in the Presidential Palace, it was clear to everyone concerned that the US government initiated the move for him to voluntarily go into exile in his Florida ranch. Pawley had claimed that it was not the government but he himself and several of his prominent business associates who were behind it as the most workable solution.

The deposed dictator had a pointed question for Pawley: did the initiative for him to go into exile have the full backing of the American government despite Pawley's story about himself and several other prominent businessmen?[21] Pawley admitted that the US government was fully behind the plan from the start. "In that case," Batista said, "I would have gone at once."

The upshot of this convoluted exercise in statecraft was that Pawley "fell flat on his face," as Rubottom and Wieland had set it up. But the consequence of their bureaucratic coup was down the line: the 1961 Bay of Pigs invasion, which ended in disaster, and the 1962 missile crisis, which came within a Cohiba cigar of nuclear warfare.

★ ★ ★

In Miami, early on New Year's Eve 1958, Carlos Prío's brother Francisco (Paco) Prío, a former Cuban senator, took a phone call from Havana. "Paco!" the caller was fairly bursting with news, "Batista's getting ready to leave right now!" Paco was dubious, but Carlos was inclined to believe it. In my 1974 interview with Carlos Prío in Miami, he was indeed dapper and cordial in dispensing information. "In early December Batista had put through an $80 million military appropriation," Carlos told me. "I suspected that it wasn't for the military at all, but that he was preparing to flee."

When the news was confirmed early the next morning, Carlos Prío chartered a plane and flew from Miami, with seven armed Autenticos, to Havana's Rancho-Boyeros Airport, but the runways were strewn with obstacles. The ex-president got on the radio and identified himself to the control tower, but the operator was under strict orders not to permit take-offs or landings. The situation was the same at the Camp Columbia airfield where Batista had departed only hours before. Prío reluctantly returned to Miami. But early that evening Rancho-Boyeros reopened and Prío was able to charter a Cubana plane capable of transporting his entire entourage. As he entered the terminal, soldiers with red-and-black 26th of July armbands accosted him, then broke into salutes as they recognized the "Cordiality President." Prío dragooned several to accompany him to his La Chata estate, for he knew Batista sentries would be posted. The sentries did not know that their commander-in-chief had flown the coop but, when told, meekly surrendered their arms. The opulent surroundings at La Chata contrasted with the scraggly appearance of the young 26th of July soldiers.

During Prío's presidency that began in 1948, the sprawling grounds were a kind of Camp David retreat where much of the business of Cuba was conducted. There was an Olympic-size swimming pool into which spilled an artificial waterfall. Around it, guests gathered to sip daiquiris. The stable of horses was blue-ribbon, as was the herd of cattle, and Prío often wore a Texas cowboy's hat.[22] There was a barber shop where the president and his cronies discussed politics and appointments while being shaved and manicured. Prío encouraged artists and writers, whom he invited to La Chata, and categorized his political philosophy as "democratic left."

Prío had taken full advantage of his tenure as president to become filthy rich. He helped finance the initial stage of the revolution and had kept watch for an opportunity to sneak back into the presidency. At least, Fidel had promised him a "top post" in his administration.

Ensconced at La Chata, Prío awaited the summons that he was sure would restore him to power. In fact, Prío was a prominent figure in the Autentico Party, which was one of two mainstream parties. I asked Prío what his arrangement was with Castro. "Simple," he said, "we agreed to stay in touch and notify one another of developments."[23] At this point he still hoped that Castro might allow him to finish out his presidency before taking over. Prío started doing his own thing, but he didn't rule out a higher post as promised. But after he sat in the parliament for weeks and nothing happened, he knew he was through. He had attracted notice during Castro's inaugural speech by being seated next to Hiocida March, a heroine of the revolution, and the second seat from Che Guevara. Prío looked out of place with a receding hairline and an off-the-rack suit, appearing dated among the casually dressed youth.

At the moment that Batista fled, Castro, stranded by cheering throngs in Oriente Province, ordered Che Guevara in Las Villas Province to race to the capital to secure it. They took over Camp Columbia, which had strategic importance, as well as the La Cabaña Fortress. But there was no governing Cuba without the Presidential Palace. When Che and his men of the 26th of July arrived at the ornate structure, they found it "occupied" by Major Rolando Cubela, who headed a group of hotspurs called the Student Revolutionary Directorate (DRE). Cubela belonged to the Senoritos of Cuban politics, dapperly dressed youth with white skin and slick black hair. But Cubela did not resist when Che showed up with his 26th of July Movement battalion. His patron was Carlos Prío, who expected a top job in the Castro administration. No slacker in the vanity department, Cubela saw himself as a rising star. But he didn't go anywhere, just as his patron Prío never got the call.

At this point in the Sugar Spring of the new regime, politics integral to the growing and marketing of the sweet commodity took over. The redistribution measure allowed over 200,000 Cuban families to buy land for the first time, but it was mostly the big American sugar companies that were forced to sell. On June 5, 1959, in the US Senate, George Smathers introduced legislation to reduce the Cuban sugar quota. Six days later, the Eisenhower administration complained that the compensation paid to the corporate landholders was based on tax-assessment rolls that were decades old, therefore not reflecting the current value (the complaint failed to mention that the landholders had enjoyed these artificially low tax rates for decades). The European landholders did not complain about Castro's compensation.

Prío admitted to a certain nostalgia for the presidency, but he felt the contingency in the position would bring about a feeling of stability in the country. He would've liked a longer talk with Castro, who was limited by the need to catch his flight to Washington. He left without ever hinting at a top post for Prío. After returning from the trip, Castro again stopped by La Chata, this time to brief Prío on his meeting with Nixon. According to Prío, the session ended with Nixon bracing Castro on the subject of elections. Castro retorted rather sarcastically that he got the "message" that he was imposing a contingency on him that he didn't on his friend Batista.

Prío got the "message" as well. Fidel's long silence meant he had no intention of promoting him to a top post in his government. Prío left La Chata for the last time. In Miami he assumed a prominent role in the counterrevolution, a "top post."

CHAPTER THREE

HAVANA SYNDICATED

"IT WAS A CRAZY MIXTURE OF SLOTS AND
GUYS WITH THE HOTS, FUELED BY HAVANA
CLUB [RUM]."[1]
—GERRY PATRICK HEMMING, 1959

It was New Year's Eve 1958. The casino proprietors who belonged to the National Crime Syndicate (NCS) were mad. They were facing a cool $200 million a year loss of income plus the skim, which they continued to pay to select public officials. Havana was the play yard of the Eastern part of the United States. And a wide-open play yard it was—sumptuary laws were rarely enforced. It was Sin City. "$39 round-trip and you were there," one Miamian who commuted weekends to Havana in its hedonistic heyday reminisced. "You got to know the Customs men, and you handed them a dollar like you were tipping a bellhop."

There was something for everyone. The rich and famous booked into the Hotel Nacional de Cuba, a grand hotel with stately twin bell towers, a magnificent tiled lobby, cascading chandeliers, bedecked women, and a spectacular view from every room. The elegant Monseigneur Restaurant featured strolling violinists, while the more budget-minded could be found at Sloppy Joe's with its long bar. In Old Havana there was the Floridita Bar, where Ernest Hemingway was often spotted, daiquiri in hand; and Bodeguita del Medio, whose stone walls bore the graffiti of countless guests, among them actor Errol Flynn, who wrote, "Great place to get drunk."

There were native gardens thick with bohemian ambiance, and the Shanghai Cinema screened the latest pornographic movies from around the world. Cabaret immortals were booked into the hotels: Eartha Kitt, Tony Martin, Lena Horne, Maurice Chevalier, Nat King Cole. The floor shows were Las Vegas in scale; the Tropicana had an outdoor rising stage with lithe dancers who lurked unseen in surrounding palm trees until a burst of spotlights heralded their act. There were cheap brothels in Old Havana, with their jukeboxes blaring Elvis Presley, but the Syndicate-run houses, which were luxurious, were in the suburbs near the international airport (the one above the Mercedes-Benz dealership was legendary). Tourists flocked to this playground of the Caribbean with its white beaches and historic sites. Was Papa Hemingway in residence at his villa in the hills, with the trophy swordfish dominating a wall?

It was about 6:00 on New Year's morning, 1959, when George Raft, the movie actor tough guy now the official greeter for the Riviera Casino, finally made it up to his room at the Capri. Quickly doffing his tropical silk tuxedo, he slipped between the bed sheets where there awaited a voluptuous Miss Cuba he had sent up a few hours earlier. "*Felix Ano Nuevo*," he whispered expectantly. Just then there was a loud burst of gunfire from outside, followed by the thud of heavier weapons. Raft rang the desk clerk. "Senor Raft, the revolution is here!" the clerk practically shouted, a note of fear in his voice, "Fidel Castro has taken over everything. He's here in Havana. Batista has left!"[2]

In fact Castro was still in Santiago, and in the vacuum of uncertainty, fighting would go on for days. Advance units of Castro's 26th of July irregulars, a blend of youth and peasants, were rolling into the center of the city to take over the functions of government while Fidel himself was standing in his Jeep on the central highway, waving to crowds, over one hundred miles away. The throng in central Havana grew thunderous, but the crowd din outside the Riviera was as loud. Some casinos, emblematic of Batista corruption, were trashed by roving gangs. A particular target was the parking meters, which were symbolic of the despised Batista administration by dint of its policies that produced higher incomes for the well-to-do who could hog the parking spaces.[3]

For George Raft, that New Year's Day was worse than a hangover. He feared for his safety. He put in a call to FBI chief J. Edgar Hoover, asking for protection from the rampaging mob.[4] It seems that the Bureau was linked through Frank Costello, the New York mobster, who shared a love of horse racing with the FBI chief. They would meet at a bench in Central Park to compare tout sheets. Costello, who was a tipster for Hoover, was in turn a "business" associate of Carlos Marcello, the New Orleans king of the slots; all of which accounted for Hoover's softness on organized crime. The top G-man's assistant director, Clyde Tolson, also a bachelor, spent considerable time alone in Havana. His visits aroused the curiosity of the FBI agents assigned to the American Embassy, who were at a loss to explain it. So a panicky George Raft had every reason to seek protection from the powerful FBI director.

Meyer Lansky and his wife, Teddy, had flown in to Havana the day before New Year's Eve with every intention of partying the old year out in a celebration of personal coups. Lansky certainly felt unwelcome with the advent of Castro, so unwelcome that he was about to make a hurried departure. He knew he was too close to Batista to be forgiven.

★ ★ ★

Lansky had begun his relationship with Batista in the 1930s, but it was consolidated during a stay at the Waldorf-Astoria in New York in the late 1940s when it was mutually agreed upon that, in exchange for kickbacks, Batista would offer Lansky and the Mafia control of Havana's racetracks and casinos. Batista would open Havana to large-scale gambling, and his government would match, dollar for dollar, any hotel investment over $1 million, which would include a casino license. To effectively bar outsiders, applicants for casino licenses would have to own at least a $1 million dollars' equity in a hotel. Import duties on construction materials would be lifted and corporate taxes waived, handing the gambling industry a privileged status. Lansky knew that successful casino operations would require skilled American or European managers, pit bosses, croupiers, and dealers, so the visa limit was stretched from six months to two years.

Lansky, of course, would place himself at the center of Cuba's gambling operations. With this pact in mind, Lansky was instrumental in bringing Batista back from exile in the United States in 1952. He began acquiring his inventory of casinos in 1953 after Batista usurped Prío and settled in for what was expected to be a long presidency because he was satisfied that Batista would be "his kind of guy." He took up permanent residence in the Nacional, retaining space for his business affairs. Lansky took over the fading Montmartre Club, using it for on-the-job training of Cuban help.[5] He approved of the ownership of the Deauville, Plaza, and Commodore by Santos Trafficante Jr., son of the Mafioso who had tended his properties during his absence; young Trafficante later acquired the glitzy Sans Souci from Gabriel "Kelly" and Sammy Mannarino of the Pittsburgh Mafia.[6] The Tropicana casino went to the brothers Martin and William Fox and a Cuban silent partner close to Batista.[7] The Casino International in the venerable Hotel Nacional was claimed by the Cleveland Syndicate headed by Moe Dalitz.[8]

★ ★ ★

Upon visiting Havana in the late 1930s, Lansky had gone straight to the sitting president (actually a puppet controlled by Batista) because he needed a steady supply of raw molasses to make rum from the sugar crop. Even with repeal pending, the Little Man (Lansky) envisioned a continuing demand for illicit booze, since the price was right. He had guided the NCS in forming the industry giant Molaska Corporation, which operated a dozen illegal distilleries in the eastern United States. By the time Batista came into power, Lansky had begun to expand into the Florida Gold Coast, a prime strip of seacoast stretching north from Miami. This is where Lansky located his inaugural venture, the Colonial Inn, which he styled a "carpet joint" because of its deluxe status. It became a public nuisance, however, after Senator Estes Kefauver came to town with his cameras and captured the faces of big-time crime for a national television audience. The Colonial Inn folded from the heat.

Havana's convenient location just ninety miles off Florida's shore and away from the glare of publicity enabled Lansky to expand his operations, signing up, for example, Moses Annenberg, who ran a national wire service for bookies, to a deal that plugged him into local gambling action. It is of more than parochial interest that Annenberg was eventually convicted of income tax evasion. He was also indicted with his son Walter Annenberg for sending obscene literature through the mail. After making a hefty contribution to Nixon's 1968 campaign for president, Walter was appointed ambassador to the Court of St. James. He and his wife became social intimates of Ronald and Nancy Reagan.[9]

With the Florida boom going bust, Lansky relocated his operations to Havana, leasing the Oriental Park racetrack from City National Bank of New York (now Citibank) and opening a gambling casino in the landmark Hotel Nacional. He might not make a killing, but in Cuba gambling was legal and there was less protection money to be paid out, so the profit margin was higher. The cruise ships and car ferries from Key West brought a steady stream of tourists with bulging wallets. With the outbreak of World War II, Lansky returned to New York. German submarines prowled the Caribbean sea lanes, and the cruise vessels were converted to wartime service. Before heading north, he designated Santos Trafficante Sr., an astute old Mafioso from Tampa, to manage his Havana and Florida enterprises.

Lansky inherited the mantle of crime boss from the boss of bosses, Charles "Lucky" Luciano, but his status in his subculture was recognized by Office of Naval Intelligence (ONI) during World War II when they alluded to it as "Operation Underworld." They co-opted Lansky to visit Luciano in prison and get him to convince the longshoremen to prevent sabotage on the docks and ensure that there would be no actions that would interfere with the war effort. Thus was consummated the deal that would form the New York–Havana crime axis. Luciano agreed to use his influence to deploy the longshoremen to check out any suspicious activity on the waterfront. In return, he hoped for an early release from his long prison sentence once the war was over.

Luciano was released from prison in 1946 and deported to Sicily but wound up in Cuba, the crossroads of the world heroin trade, where he took over a suite in the Hotel Nacional. As Luciano explained in *Havana Nocturne* by T. J. English, "When I got to the room the bellhop opened up the curtains on them big windows and I looked out. I could see almost the whole city. I think it was the palm trees and it made me feel like I was back in Miami. All of a sudden, I realized for the first time in over ten years that there was no handcuffs on me and nobody was breathin' over my shoulder, which was the way I used to feel even while I was wanderin' around Italy. When I looked down over the Caribbean from my window, I realized somethin' else; the water was just as pretty as the Bay of Naples, but it was only ninety miles from the United States. That meant I was practically back in America."[10]

At the Nacional he was visited by every NCS regional boss—and Frank Sinatra. The crooner flew down from Chicago with his pal, mobster Charles Fischetti. A nun saw a note in the local press that the teenagers' idol was staying at the Nacional. So she took a group of Girl Scouts to the hotel to present an award to their favorite singer, where the desk clerk innocently gave out Sinatra's hotel room number. When the nun and her group arrived at the door, it was ajar. She pushed the door open, revealing a fresco of men and women's clothing, whiskey bottles, and half-dressed men.[11]

Luciano and Lansky invited all the US Mafia bosses to Havana in December 1946 for the historic Havana Conference, to discuss mob rules, policies, and business interests. One important topic was establishing control over organized gambling in Cuba. Lansky shared his vision of a new Havana, profitable for those willing to invest the right sum of money. A city that could be their "Latin Las Vegas," where they would feel right at home, since it was a place where drugs, prostitution, labor racketeering, and extortion were already commonplace. To Lansky's dismay, Luciano proposed an ambitious, comprehensive plan that projected the Caribbean as his center of operations. The Isla de Pinos on the underbelly of Cuba was to become the Monte Carlo of the Western Hemisphere, with huge resort/casinos and its own private airport. Lansky felt that he himself deserved the grand-plan casino expansion, since he had pioneered the gaming industry in Cuba.

One night, Lansky dispatched a lieutenant for a quiet talk with an agent of the Federal Bureau of Narcotics (now the Drug Enforcement Agency) about Luciano. In his memoirs, *The Murderers*, chief narc Dr. Harry Anslinger, the last angry man in drug enforcement, reported that "Luciano had already become friendly with a number of high Cuban officials through lavish gifts."[12] It was determined that Luciano had invested in two smaller casinos but spent most of his time at the racetrack with Cuban beauties on his arm. Having found what Luciano was up to, Lansky wasted no time in prevailing on his friend Batista to work behind the scenes and pull the rug out from under him. But it was Harry Anslinger who was primarily responsible for Luciano's departure from Cuba in 1947. Anslinger persuaded President Truman to threaten an embargo on all shipments of medical drugs to Cuba unless Luciano left, and Batista had to comply. Grudgingly, Luciano returned to Italy, never knowing Lansky had double-crossed him.

In 1959, I was an FBI agent assigned to the inspection of the Los Angeles field office's performance against organized crime. Virtually all of the Bureau's information was lifted from the files of the LAPD Intelligence Division. The exception was the colorful mobster Mickey Cohen, on whom a wiretap had been placed. Cohen turned out to be Meyer Lansky's West Coast lieutenant, and as such he delivered cold cash to Richard Nixon during each of his political campaigns. In 1952, Nixon's foe, Adlai Stevenson, learned that Nixon was accepting the dirty funds but couldn't name the source. Nixon's place in Lansky's pocket was confirmed by the journalist Uri Dan when he interviewed the crime executive in retirement in Israel. Lansky gave a cryptic "yes" when asked if Nixon had been on his payroll, but would go no further.[13]

★ ★ ★

Taking a cut from each turn of a roulette wheel, each roll of the dice, each pull of a slot machine arm, Lansky ruled gaming supreme. How many millions were slipped to Batista as his share is a matter of conjecture because he stashed most of it in Swiss banks, but estimates ranged up to $200 million. A gauge of the take by Cuban officials was the reported $750,000 a month paid to the Havana police chief as "protection money."[14] Officials also exploited the government-run national lottery, the only organized game of chance the average Cuban could afford. The winning five-digit number was announced over the Havana radio station CMQ every Saturday at 2:00 p.m. But by that time the officials had obtained the numbers and shared them with their American mobster friends, piling up huge winnings at the expense of the Cuban citizens.

Havana exceeded Las Vegas in jackpots. Gaming expert John Scarnes disclosed that he spent five hours one night monitoring the action at a single dice table at the Statler Hilton casino. He counted that $3 million changed hands. Just how lucrative the Havana casino business was is indicated by the power grab of Albert Anastasia in 1959. Anastasia was the greediest of the New York Mafia bosses, and his threat to take over Cuba was considered so serious that the other bosses gathered at the famous Apalachin Meeting to find a solution.

In late 1957 in the southern tier of New York, over fifty men of various age groups converged on the timeless town of Apalachin, at the expansive home of Joseph Barbara, the local Canada Dry distributor. But they weren't there to discuss soft-drink sales. They were Mafia leaders from all over the United States. On the agenda was the matter of Albert Anastasia, a Mafioso from New York City who had turned greedy, too greedy. Anastasia was making a grab for control of the gambling scene in Havana. Kelly Marinaro of the Pittsburgh Syndicate was there. So was the ubiquitous Santos Trafficante Jr. of Tampa. Joe Sica from Southern California was present, as were the Magaddino brothers from Niagara Falls.[15] The Mafia heavyweights were not in a good mood. They had warned Anastasia off, but he was so infatuated with himself that he had not heeded.

Although the FBI had not shown up and the meeting was drawing to a close, a solitary visitor in the uniform of a New York State Trooper appeared. He had become suspicious of the influx of long, black cars with out-of-state license plates. When the trooper approached, half the men ran for the woods. "I saw nothing but assholes and elbows," the trooper was quoted.[16] The other half of the meeting meekly submitted to arrest.

The gathering went down in criminal history as perhaps the most significant conclave ever held. It also marked the end of the FBI's image of invincibility. Despite Hoover's attempt to sell it as an outing of petty hoods, the stigma endured. One FBI supervisor, Julius Mattson, complained, "Don't mention the Mafia. Hoover doesn't acknowledge that it exists."[17]

At the time of the Apalachin Meeting, the name Fidel Castro meant

nothing to the assembled Mafia. But he would be the one who would ultimately decide on the gambling in Cuba. Three weeks after the conference,
Albert Anastasia was shot to death as he was being shaved in a Manhattan
barber shop.

One of the few casino owners not mobbed up was the bulldog-tough
Mike McLaney, who bought controlling interest in the elegant Casino
Internacional, which had a Moroccan look about it. The New Orleans–
born McLaney had been a deputy sheriff in the 1930s, a low-handicap
golfer, and a nationally ranked tennis player. His exposure to the blazer
set of international sports provided the contacts he needed to become a
gaming entrepreneur. I interviewed him on December 12, 1974, in his suite
in the swank Jockey Club in Miami. He was skimpy on details because
"the government has a long memory." When I asked him about Meyer
Lansky, McLaney flushed. "Listen," he growled, "I met Meyer Lansky
once, and then only for thirty seconds." McLaney made his fortune developing the racetrack Totalisator with Carroll Rosenbloom, owner of the Los
Angeles Rams and Baltimore Colts. McLaney demonized Castro from
the beginning, figuring he was trouble. "But my brother Bill thought he
was Prince Charming," he said. According to Mike, Bill later changed his
mind, stating, "If it wasn't for that goddamn Castro, Caesar's Palace would
have been built in Havana."

One night in 1978 when I was conducting research for this volume,
I found myself in the heady situation of driving a rental car across the
Rickenbacker Causeway in Miami. As passengers I had Watergate burglar
Frank Sturgis; Eugenio Martinez, a boatmen in the CIA's bantam navy;
and Viriglio Gonzalez, a locksmith. What would the morning newspapers
say if we veered off into the turgid waters of Biscayne Bay?

Born Frank Fiorini in a grimy section of Philadelphia, Sturgis had a
silken voice and a Valentino body. He fought with Edson's Raiders (of the
1st Marine Raiders Battalion) in the Pacific. With the cessation of hostilities in World War II, he began a life of moving to where the action was. He
briefly married an Israeli intelligence agent and joined her in operations.
He gravitated to Miami when Fidel captured the imagination of idle paramilitaries everywhere. Sturgis first sought Carlos Prío, the ex-president of

Cuba who was overthrown by Batista in 1952. Like so many of his blue-collar compatriots, Sturgis was fiercely anti-communistic but not money hungry. He told me that he didn't know why he got involved in Watergate, because he was a Democrat. He then disclosed that E. Howard Hunt, the CIA officer who handled anti-Castro groups and individuals, told him that the motive behind Watergate was to prove Castro had donated $200,000 to the Democratic Party.[18] They found no evidence that he donated anything.

Castro had Sturgis to thank for the arming of his troops. First he flew weapons to Prío's action group in the Sierra Maestra range. He joined Prío's pickup squad of pilots, flying single-engine planes into remote mountain strips, attracting the notice of Castro, who talked him into switching to the 26th of July force. With the added weaponry, Castro was able to launch an offensive. He succeeded in taking Havana. "My favorite *Yanqui*," Castro would introduce him. "You see," Frank told me in explanation of the switch, "Prío was a politician. What he does is four-fifths talk, one-fifth action. Fidel and his guys were all action."

After Castro's victory, Frank was named security chief of the rebel air force. But he was transferred out after a friend, Air Force captain Pedro Diaz Lanz, bolted to Florida and testified before a Senate intelligence committee stacked against Castro. Despite the opinion of the American public, which largely still regarded Castro as a great liberator, the senators swallowed his line. Diaz Lanz labeled the Cuban leadership "a communist tool" and went on in perjurious prose to the press.[19]

At this point came one of the oddest pairings that can be imagined. When the revolution ended, Castro had shuttered the casinos only to reopen them when the unions loudly protested that thousands would be thrown out of work. The interregnum that ensued was rife with speculation over the ultimate fate of the industry. Frank Sturgis was rewarded with the position of commissioner of games of chance to make sure that the casinos, mostly owned by Mob syndicates, paid their taxes and to patrol the casinos for signs of trouble. It was a fitting role for this star-struck tough guy who rubbed elbows with the likes of George Raft, Errol Flynn, "Papa" Hemingway, and ordinary mobsters such as "Sally" Burns and George Levine,[20] who reported directly to Meyer Lansky. He became so friendly with Santos Trafficante, the former Tampa Mafia chief who owned the Sans Souci casino, that he was the only government official invited to his daughter's wedding at the Statler Hilton. Sturgis acted out his job with such gusto that he was asked not to wear combat fatigues in the casinos or dangle a registered .45 automatic from a webbed belt, in order not to scare off the tourists.[21]

Sturgis kept his eye on everyone. During the revolution, he would walk a long walk into Santiago de Cuba and report to the American consul on political developments in the Castro camp. This backfired when he wore religious robes as a disguise and Batista police detained him for days until back-door negotiations by the embassy freed him. After the revolution, he continued reporting to the American consul, and finally, fearing exposure, hightailed it to Miami.[22]

★　★　★

The casino crowd believed that gambling was forever—there was too much money at stake. After Castro's victory, the Mob was awakened to the question of whether Castro would leave the casinos open or shut them down. A CIA memo dated November 29, 1963, reported that Sturgis warned Trafficante that Castro would eventually shut down the casinos, but he waved off the idea. "Not in this world," Trafficante countered. "You think he's going to close up the hundred million dollars' worth that we get? He'll never do it."[23] So all was quiet on the green-felt front. But Sturgis saw a puritanical streak in Castro that he thought would be the tipping point for the casino question. A discordant note was a government contention that Cuban casino workers had been underpaid and a demand for "back wages." Mike McLaney was hit for $102,000,[24] and the others were dunned accordingly, but the hardnosed operators considered it no more than an expected shakedown. The amount was less than the cash tributes the Batista officials had exacted, and there was always the skim.

Within a week of Castro's victory, Cuban authorities put Trafficante and his mechanic, John Martino, in jail for thirty days because they attached "security devices to slot machines in the Deauville Casino owned by Trafficante."[25] Many of the Mob "players" were hustled out of town. George Raft recalls that pot shots were taken at the Capri Casino from Castro's headquarters in the Hilton. Then Raft was picked up by a squad of bearded rebels and taken to the airport, but he was kept off the plane and threatened with the firing squad for trying to smuggle dollars. The crisis passed when Raft suggested they search his luggage, and the leader asked the badly shaken film tough guy for his autograph. A supervisor at the Capri Casino, Nicholas "Fat Nick" Costanzo, was also scared out of his wits when a "goon squad" barged in and demanded money, forcing him to open the safe with the barrel of a cocked pistol between his teeth. He was so terrified he nearly forgot the combination, and without waiting to pack, he caught the next plane to Miami.[26]

The underworld heavies were not alone on the road to the airport. Honey Bruce, the widow of outrageous comedian Lenny Bruce, told me that at the time she and Lenny were staying at the Havana Hilton, where Castro occupied a suite. One afternoon, Lenny staged a broken-Spanish imitation of Fidel from their twelfth-floor balcony. "Lenny," Honey said, "those soldiers down below are looking at you awfully funny." The Bruces' room money was refunded, and they were given the well-known tumbrel ride to the airport.

The Mob had consistently underestimated Castro, regarding him as a "hillbilly soldier," though Lansky and the other Mob bosses had played both sides by investing in Fidelista bonds to support Castro during the revolution. The US Embassy had also underestimated Castro. "If you saved enough cereal box tops, you could send in for a toy soldier," joked one attaché at the embassy. "And if you sent in enough box tops, you got a Daddy Warbucks who would use his yacht for clandestine missions."[27]

Once in power, Castro eliminated the Batista peso and put in circulation the revolutionary peso, which left the casino owners stuck with hoards of the old money. Coupled with the tourist drought that reduced the flow of dollars to a trickle, they were in a squeeze so tight that underworld financiers tried to convert $22 million in old pesos for 13 cents on the dollar. At this bleak moment, Castro came up with an offer no casino owner could refuse: he would pay almost two revolutionary pesos for one dollar.

A minority partner in the Commodore casino was able to buy a quarter million dollars' worth of pesos for $150,000. Castro soon had dollars flowing into the country instead of out. But the new currency, pegged to the dollar, proved worthless. Banks in the United States refused to accept them even at slashed prices, and there was havoc in the secondary markets. Now the owners were losers. Meyer Lansky, whose holiday stay at the Nacional was disrupted by Castro's advance on Havana, lost no time in putting out a $1 million bounty on Castro's head.

I asked Fidel in writing whether he personally profited from the currency manipulations. He responded angrily, "Of course not," he said. "*No embargo. Sin embargo.*"[28]

The Cuban economy was in free-fall with the demise of the tourist trade, and labor unions counted job losses in the thousands. The casinos reopened, but by that time it was too late. Steamship companies such as Grace and Cunard were bypassing exotic Havana, and air traffic plummeted nearly 90 percent.[29] It was only a matter of months before the casinos were shuttered for good.

In January 1960, the Nacional and Riviera casinos were closed down. It had nothing to do with George Raft and Mike McLaney. It had everything to do with profits. E. Howard Hunt recalled that in the spring of 1960, when he visited Havana to size up the revolution, he went to "Sloppy Joe's bar where I lunched on draft beer and a poor-boy sandwich, alone at the great bar where once you had to fight for service."[30] At the Riviera, fifty guests were served by seven hundred employees, an imbalance the government was forced to subsidize because it had decreed no Cuban employee could be fired, and that was the trend everywhere. When Castro moved to shutter them as well, the unions protested that thousands of workers would lose their jobs. The premier left the casinos open, but there was a hitch: Cuban employees only. Journalist Murray Kempton remembered, after all American technicians were replaced by Cubans, "Some of us sat the next night in the empty bar of the Riviera. There were three customers and six waiters. The saloon of a luxury liner might feel like this when the passengers had taken to the lifeboats."[31]

Kempton remembered when Cuba's last American gambler came into the bar and told him, "Go to the casino. It's open night. I just played a hand of blackjack. I had a jack and a seven; the dealer had three sixes. I looked at him and said: 'Pay me, I got seventeen and you got fifteen.' The dealer looked at the cards and counted with his lips, then he paid me. Sure, it'll be lonely, but I'm living next to a casino where the dealer can't count. This is the place for me; the shills have taken over for the bosses."

★ ★ ★

A push was made to attract American tourists who had been put off by Fidel's cavorting with Russian premier Nikita Khrushchev at a United Nations session. Castro tried to reinvigorate the tourist trade with a campaign aimed at Americans with the slogan "See Cuba First." The National Institute of the Tourist Industry spent millions beautifying beaches and constructing new hotels.

With the demise of gambling, a number of casino proprietors whisked bundles of cash to safekeeping in south Florida, a speedboat ride away, and began financing paramilitary actions in the belief that Castro would be a soft target.[32] The NCS wanted its Sin City back.

The casinos might well have been taking bets on where the next B-26 would burst on the scene. On October 24, 1959, Frank Sturgis kicked off his personal counterrevolution in spectacular style when the American Society of Travel Agents was in convention at the Havana Hilton hotel. Castro had lured the convention to Cuba in a bid to revive the dying tourist trade, and he was waiting in the wings to give his pitch. It was the cocktail hour, and a grass-skirted Hawaiian troupe was dancing the hula.

Without warning, a B-26 swooped in from the north, passing over the Havana Hilton as its bomb bay doors opened and thousands of leaflets declaring Castro a communist tool created a blizzard over the hotel. In the pilots' seats were Sturgis and Pedro Diaz Lang. A frigate in the harbor opened fire, and rifle fire from the ground was visible. "I thought we were going to be hit," Sturgis told me when I interviewed him April 7, 1974. The B-26 completed its run, raised its flaps, swung back north, and disappeared. Fidel dashed across the street to CMQ television and went on

the air. He claimed that incendiary bombs had been mixed with the leaflets and there were civilian casualties. Calling the attack "Cuba's Pearl
Harbor," which was a slight exaggeration, since Cuba had no battleships,
Castro countered by addressing a next-day rally called by the labor unions
and attended by a half million people. "What reason have they to attack
Cuba?" Castro asked rhetorically, not knowing that his "favorite *yanqui*"
was the pilot of the renegade plane.[33] But Sturgis, the onetime commissioner of games of chance, had unwittingly put the brakes on tourism. The
tourist-agent group said that the frightening "attack" would make tourists
feel unwelcome coming to Cuba. They deemed it futile "to offer the tourist
splendid hotels, casinos, sumptuous nightclubs, and entertainment of all
sorts, unless the tourist feels he is welcome."[34]

★ ★ ★

In April 1960, Frank Sturgis began to direct the International anti-
Communist Brigade, a phantom organization running a network of safe
houses and naval installations, as well as a fleet of boats and planes. This
Brigade ran operations for the resettlement of Cuban exiles and innumerable
other activities, especially those related to paramilitary preparation in the
training camps and support missions for anti-Castro exile groups in Cuba.
Pedro Diaz Lang remained his faithful sidekick.[35]

The upshot of the revolution for the Mob was that virtually all Havana's
criminal class—Cuban gangsters, hit men, drug traffickers, Batista remit-
tance men, shakedown artists, and pimps—migrated to Miami. This was a
considerable number of crooks, as pre-revolution Havana was the Emerald
City of organized crime, free port for the Mob since the late 1940s when
Lucky Luciano established the Cuban connection in the world narcotics
trade. The Cuban connection was moved wholesale to Miami, which
became the drug-smuggling capital of the United States.[36]

CHAPTER FOUR
SIDEBAR: JACK RUBY

"IF YOU WANT TO HEAR ANY FURTHER TESTIMONY, YOU'LL HAVE TO GET ME TO WASHINGTON SOON!"[1]
— Jack Ruby to Chief Justice Earl Warren
of the Warren Commission

As part of Meyer Lansky's empire, the Tropicana was designated to play host to important guests and those doing business with Lansky Enterprises. One infamous guest was Jack Ruby, true name Jack Rubenstein, the Dallas nightclub owner who four years later silenced the accused killer of President Kennedy, Lee Harvey Oswald. Ruby walked through a police line—he seemed to know every cop in town—and pumped two bullets into Oswald's belly. Ruby claimed he did it to spare Jackie Kennedy the ordeal of having to testify in any trial, but the whole thing had the smell of contract murder. No one familiar with the nightclub owner's mistreatment of his female entertainers believed he was subject to sudden fits of charity.[2]

Ruby's choice of the Tropicana in Havana was not random. Although the Cuban owners of record were the Fox brothers, Martin and Pedro, who allegedly were implicated in gambling rackets and narcotics, the majority positions for the enterprise were held by Meyer and Jake Lansky, Norm Rothman, and Montreal Mafia overlord, Guiseppe "Pepe" Cotroni. Ruby was there for an eight-day stay as the guest of Lewis J. McWillie, a stylish, grey-haired man whose lowly title of craps-table supervisor belied the fact that he was a high-ranking casino executive.

Jack Ruby became a household name thousands of miles away, but he was a product of Chicago's South Side.[3] He was nicknamed "Sparky" because of his short-fuse temper that often flared into violence. Ruby was on the payroll of the corrupt Waste Material Handlers Union when he fatally shot an official, Leon Cooke, but claimed self-defense. The Syndicate outsourced him to Dallas with instructions to expand the territory. Soon a number of "bust-out goons" were in business, and Ruby bought the Carousel Club. When Ruby relocated to Dallas, he came under the jurisdiction of Don Joseph Civello of the Sunbelt Mafia, which stretched east to Carlos Marcello in New Orleans and Santos Trafficante in Florida. The relationship was confirmed in a report[4] to the FBI by Bobby Gene Moore, who supposedly had worked for Civello's Italian cheese–importing firm in the 1950s and afterwards filled in playing the piano at Ruby's Carousel Club. Moore fingered Ruby as "a frequent visitor and associate" of Civello, who was using the cheese business as a cover for smuggling narcotics, and as "connected with the underworld in Dallas."[5]

In the Tropicana casino over Labor Day weekend of 1959, Jack Ruby, a bulky, whey-faced man in conservative attire, mingled with the casually dressed, sun-tanned clientele. He struck up a conversation with several tourists from his hometown of Chicago. Ruby had come to Havana as a guest of McWillie, whom he had known from the bust-out days of Dallas in the 1940s. By his own account, McWillie had known Ruby since their boyhood days in Chicago, and they later linked up in Dallas.[6] A contemporary report of the Dallas Police Intelligence Bureau put them together in gambling activities. After eight days at the Tropicana, Ruby left. "I was bored because gambling isn't my profession," he later explained to the Warren Commission.[7]

The Commission accepted it as a pleasure jaunt and marked it down as Ruby's one and only trip to Cuba. Information that came to light during and after the Commission's probe, however, belies a label of innocence. It casts Ruby in a rather different light than the Runyonesque nightclub entrepreneur with a machismo hang-up depicted in the Warren Report. The real Ruby was tightly implicated with the Mob and gunrunning, connections that go a long way toward suggesting his true motivation in executing Lee Harvey Oswald.

In the first place, Ruby's portrayal of McWillie as a simple casino employee is highly misleading. The Senate Intelligence Committee dug up an FBI memorandum dated March 26, 1964, that places McWillie on intimate terms with Santos Trafficante and other Syndicate bigwigs. According to the memorandum,[8] "It would appear McWillie consolidated his syndicate connections through his association in Havana, Cuba, with Santos Trafficante, well-known syndicate member for Tampa, Florida; Meyer and Jake Lansky; Dino Cellini and others who were members of or associates of 'the syndicate.' . . . He left Dallas and went to Havana, Cuba, where he was known to associate with nationally known gambling characters such as Willie Bischoff, also known as Lefty Clark, Jake Lansky, Trafficante and others," a kind of *Who's Who* of the Mob.

During his Havana stay as McWillie's "guest," the voluble Ruby boasted that he was "in with both sides," according to correspondent Thayer Waldo, an old Havana hand for the *San Francisco Chronicle*.[9] The Dallas man claimed a close friendship with "El Tigre" Masferrer, the Batista ally who bought a surplus speedboat from the navy in Guantanamo and hightailed it to the sanctuary of Miami, and with Hamleto Batisti, like Masferrer, a former senator who ran the Seville Biltmore hotel/casino.

Although the Warren Report implies that Ruby returned directly to Dallas after the tropical interlude, he actually proceeded to Miami and then doubled back to Havana, the city he found so boring. A Miami Beach bartender said that in the summer of 1959 he received a phone call from Lewis McWillie in Havana advising that Ruby had visited him in Cuba and then in Miami Beach. Panitz looked up Ruby and met with him twice at Wolfie's Restaurant on Collins Avenue, which was a crossroads for all kinds of Caribbean intrigue.[10] An FBI report of Panitz's interview fails to mention what was discussed. It notes only that Ruby "said he had been in Cuba on a pleasure trip and was returning to Dallas."[11]

After being kicked out of Cuba, McWillie landed at the Cal-Neva Lodge, a gambling establishment on the north shore of Lake Tahoe. Frank Sinatra had bought the place the year before, with Chicago Mafia chieftain Sam Giancana as a silent partner. McWillie was to keep an eye on Giancana's investment and report back on Sinatra's activities. What he saw was gambling by Sinatra's high-profile friends, Marilyn Monroe and Peter

Lawford, the brother-in-law of John and Robert Kennedy, among them. But the Nevada gaming authorities were fixing an eye on the Cal-Neva as well, and espied Giancana as another Sinatra guest. Since the mobster topped the list in the state's Black Book of persons forbidden to enter casinos, Sinatra lost the Cal-Neva. Giancana was also Bobby Kennedy's most wanted crime bigwig in his war on the Syndicate.[12]

Ruby kept in touch with the singer/casino executive whom he idolized. When the Kennedy clan pulled clear of Sinatra because of his hoodlum coterie, he turned ardent Republican. So did Ruby.

Whether Ruby ever owned a piece of the Havana action is not confirmed, but within a few weeks after Castro's victory, he was in touch with Robert Ray McKeown, well known as an arms smuggler for the 26th of July Movement.[13] Ruby told McKeown that "he had an option on a great number of Jeeps which were in Shreveport, Louisiana, and he wanted to sell them to Castro at $5,000 a piece, a very profitable figure."[14] The Dallas man offered $25,000 for an introduction to Castro, but the deal fell through when McKeown insisted on a $5,000 down payment.

Obviously Ruby had not played a major role in running guns to Castro if he required an introduction to the Cuban *jefe*. Yet reports persisted that he had been involved. One came from three women who had vacationed on Islamerada in the Florida Keys in 1958.[15] They stayed with a relative, James Woodard, whom the FBI verified was implicated in weapons smuggling both for and against Castro.[16] Woodard had apparently met Ruby when he served briefly as a Dallas cop. The women were introduced to a man named "Jack," living in a nearby motel, whom Woodard described as originally from Chicago, a member of the "Syndicate" there, and a nightclub owner in Texas. "Jack" had some crates supposedly containing arms and ammunition to be smuggled into Cuba. After the JFK assassination, the women recognized Ruby as probably the man they had met.

Tying the knot on these disparate reports is the contention of an aging Caribbean cargo pilot named Blaney Mack Johnson that a pilot named Eddie Browder was "associated with Ruby in the arms smuggling operation."[17] This was Edward J. Browder Jr., a tousle-haired soldier of fortune who ran a firm called Aero Munitions that had a warehouse on the Miami

River. His gunrunning to Castro was in conjunction with the Mafia. Interviewed in prison by the FBI, Browder denied knowing Jack Ruby.[18] Oddly enough, however, he was tied in with the same Tropicana Casino crowd as Ruby.

According to Johnson, Ruby had been "active in arranging illegal flights of weapons from Miami to the Castro organization in Cuba" and was "part owner of two planes used for these purposes."[19] The pilot also stated that Ruby "purchased a substantial share in a Havana gaming house in which Collis Prio [phonetic] was principal owner." This was an obvious reference to Carlos Prío, who, Johnson went on, "was within favor of the former Cuban leader Batista, but was instrumental in financing and managing accumulation of arms by pro-Castro forces." Whether Ruby and Prío held secret shares in a Havana casino is open to question, and Prío was certainly not on equitable terms with Batista. But Johnson seemed to know quite a bit about Ruby, Lansky, Prío, and Browder, even though he had some of his facts garbled.

As time went on and Castro's agenda turned more and more socialist, the weapons merchants, with few exceptions, switched sides. There were others who didn't care who got the merchandise as long as it was COD. Nancy Perrin Rich, a barmaid in Ruby's Carousel Club until she quit after being slapped around, tells of a deal that went down in the summer of 1962.[20] Perrin's husband, Jack, a small-boat pilot, had been offered $15,000 to make a delivery to insurgents for Cuba.

★ ★ ★

Another topic at the Havana Conference of 1946 was what to do about Bugsy Siegel. The outcome was one of the most notorious gangland rubouts. It took place on the night of June 20, 1947, when Bugsy Siegel was cut down by a fusillade of shots in his Beverly Hills bungalow. The irony of Bugsy Siegel's demise is overpowering. The hit was probably ordered by Lansky, Siegel's old partner in the Bug & Meyer Mob, with the participation of Moe Dalitz, who was second only to the Little Man in the National Crime Syndicate (NCS) structure.

In late 1945, Bugsy Siegel and his "partners" came to Las Vegas, after the fledgling resort city piqued Siegel's interest due to its legalized gambling and its off-track betting. Hearing that William Wilkerson was seeking extra funding for his new resort project, Siegel and his partners, posing as businessmen, approached him and bought a two-thirds stake. Lansky pressured Siegel to represent the NCS in building the Flamingo project, reputedly named for the long, skinny legs of Siegel's girlfriend, Virginia Hill. Someone had to watchdog their interests. At Lansky's insistence, Siegel consented.[21]

The problem was twofold. First, Siegel wasn't much of a businessman; he often showed up at noon still wearing his tuxedo from the night before. Second, he had no experience in construction or design, causing costs to mount from constant changes and gouging from construction firms and suppliers—including, it was reputed, workers who delivered by day, stole by night, and resold the next day. Siegel may actually have bought some of the same materials twice thanks to this kind of scheming. Siegel lost patience with the rising costs, and his notorious outbursts unnerved his construction foreman. Reputedly, Siegel told him, "Don't worry—we only kill each other."[22]

In 1946, Siegel burned through $5 million of Syndicate money in construction of the Flamingo. Both Luciano and Lansky believed that Siegel was skimming money and depositing it in private bank accounts. Luciano demanded the return of the money, which was greeted by Bugsy with expletives. On June 20, 1947, it was curtains for the unruly impresario. At the time of the funeral for a man he once called "like a brother," Lansky sent his regrets, saying he was stuck in Havana.

The murder has never been solved officially, but in October 1947, Captain Connolly and Lieutenant Drury of the Chicago Police Department revealed that there was an accusation within the department that Lenny Patrick, Dave Yaras, and a William Block were given the contract on Bugsy Siegel.[23] The first two were old chums of Jack Ruby from his Windy City days. Ruby's sister, Eva Grant, confirmed to the Warren Commission that Ruby and Yaras were lifelong friends.

Lenny Patrick, a shirttail relative of Ruby, was an on-call contract killer[24] with twenty hits to his credit at last count. As for Dave Yaras, his curriculum vitae includes hit man for Sam Giancana, the Mafia boss of Chicago, and hired gun for Mafia interests in Havana. Yaras also ran a number of gambling operations on the island (Cuba).[25] After Batista fell, Yaras was the Chicago Mob's liaison to the Cuban exile community. In *Deadly Secrets*, Warren Hinckle and this author disclose that the McClellan Senate Rackets Committee "credited" Yaras with playing a significant Mob role in Havana.[26] His operations were carried out under the locus of a casino in which he had ownership points.

Back on the mean streets of Chicago in 1947, Yaras was booked for the murder of James Ragen, manager of the Continental Press Service, a racing sheet in dispute with the Mafia. Two witnesses identified Dave Yaras, Lenny Patrick, and William Block, according to the Chicago Police.[27] But after one witness was murdered, the charges were dropped. Years later, when interviewed by the FBI in the JFK case, Yaras admitted that he knew Jack Ruby for fifteen years in Chicago, but he furnished nothing more of substance. To be fair, the FBI did pick up some graphic conversation by wiretap in 1962 when Jackie Cerone commissioned Yaras to murder a local official. On the tape, Yaras gave the sales pitch, "Leave it to us. As soon as he walks in the door, boom! He won't get away from us."[28]

There is also confirmed evidence that Yaras and Ruby were in phone contact in the days preceding the JFK assassination.[29] Yet the FBI did not connect the dots in the killing of JFK, due to its reluctance to press an all-out probe. According to Peter Dale Scott, the Warren Commission covered up Ruby's connections with Yaras. In his book *Deep Politics and the Death of JFK*, he writes, "The Commission did not receive an important interview with Luis Kutner, a Chicago lawyer who had just told the press (correctly) about Ruby's connections to Chicago mobsters Lenny Patrick and Dave Yaras. All the FBI transmitted was a meaningless follow-up interview in which Kutner merely said he had no additional information. Apparently the FBI also failed to transmit a teletype revealing that Yaras, a national hit man for the Chicago syndicate who had grown up with Ruby, and who had been telephoned by one of Ruby's Teamster contacts on the eve of the assassination, was about to attend a 'hoodlum meeting' of top East and West Coast syndicate representatives,

including some from the 'family' of the former Havana crime lord Santos
Trafficante."[30]

★ ★ ★

Ruby's "friend in Havana" McWillie was really a trouble-shooter for
Lansky. He used Martin Fox's first name as his alias when he was at the
Tropicana. The Fox brothers, as Cuban nationals, were the front men for
Lansky's majority holding in the Tropicana. McWillie was a millionaire
in his own right because of his personal holdings in the casino. He was
supposed to be just a pit boss. The other pit employees called him "Slick"
McWillie because of his obvious connections, plus the fact that he had his
own limo and driver.

Five days before the assassination of JFK, McWillie called Ruby, who
then went to Las Vegas. There were two Lansky hotel/casinos in Las Vegas;
one was the namesake of the Tropicana in Havana and the other was the
Thunderbird Casino, which was the original home of the one-armed bandit
on the Las Vegas strip. Ruby visited the mobbed-up casino, where he used
McWillie's identity to cash a check. Then he met up with McWillie at the
Thunderbird. Two days later, Ruby is back in Dallas with sufficient cash to
pay off existing debts. He appeared to be in close contact with McWillie
during that time. One of the last voices he heard before he leaped onto
the national stage of history with his assassination of Oswald was that of
McWillie. When questioned by the FBI as to who would lead the list of
people who disliked him, Ruby named McWillie, because he felt that he
knew too much about who sponsored the JFK assassination. Ruby told the
FBI, as he would later tell the Warren Commission, "You've got to take me
to Washington where I can talk!"[31]

★ ★ ★

On the morning of November 22, 1963, Jack Ruby took a young lady by
the name of Connie Trammel to the office of H. L. Hunt in Dallas for a job
application. Hunt was the megabucks oil man who founded the John Birch

Society and similar extremist causes. In leaving Hunt's office, the nightclub impresario could have had a panoramic view of Dealey Plaza, which would later be the scene of JFK's assassination. That night, Ruby showed up at a press conference held by District Attorney Henry Wade. When Wade asserted that Oswald, who was being held as the prime and only suspect, belonged to the Free Cuba Party, Ruby interrupted to say, "No, he was a member of the Fair Play for Cuba Committee."[32] Although there had been a news dispatch out of New Orleans that afternoon outlining Oswald's political activities in the Crescent City the previous summer, it is doubtful that was the source of his information. There was considerable speculation that Oswald would confess, since it was a political crime and should invoke the death penalty. But all Oswald would say was, "I'm just a patsy."[33]

★ ★ ★

To follow up on the Ruby connection, in 1978, Seymour Ellison, a partner of Melvin Belli, called me to come to his house in San Anselmo, California. He related an interesting tale of a phone call he had received in 1963.[34] The theatrical Belli was away from the office at trial in Riverside County. Within hours of the Oswald shooting, Ellison received a phone call from a senior partner in a Las Vegas law firm where he had been employed, doing work for Moe Dalitz of the Desert Inn. The firm was connected with several organized-crime figures who had been stripped of their gambling casinos in Havana by the advent of Castro.[35] "Sy," the Las Vegas attorney said, "one of your guys just bumped off that son of a bitch that gunned down the president. We can't move in to handle it, but there's a million bucks net for Mel if he'll take it." The fee offered is very reminiscent of Lansky's bounty for Castro's assassination. The Las Vegas lawyer stressed that his clients wanted their relationship with Ruby kept strictly confidential. Before long, the lawyer called Ellison back and told him that the deal was off because they had just found out that Ruby had been in with another powerful element and his clients didn't want to get involved in any way.[36] The identity of this mysterious powerful element remains unknown. Could it have been the CIA?

CHAPTER FIVE
THE NIXON NOBODY KNEW

"IF YOU WERE MEYER [LANSKY], WHO WOULD YOU PUT YOUR MONEY ON? SOME POLITICIAN NAMED CLAMS LINGUINI? OR A NICE PROTESTANT BOY FROM WHITTIER, CALIFORNIA?"[1]

—WALTER SHERIDAN,
RENOWNED SENATE RACKETS INVESTIGATOR

It was not the event in his life that earned him the name "Tricky Dick," but it is relevant to his developing character as an adult. The Quaker kid obtained a job as a barker for a shady "Wheel of Chance" operation. According to biographer Earl Mazo in his book *Richard Nixon: A Political and Personal Portrait*, "Nixon barked for the legal front of the concession where the prizes were hams and sides of bacon, which was a 'come on' for a back room featuring poker and dice."[2]

A lapsed Quaker, Nixon was a product of his environment. Orange County in the 1950s was anchored by the newly created Disneyland of Walt Disney, who was impeccably conservative. It grew into a neon jungle of fast-food outlets, tanning salons, beer bars, bowling alleys, and fundamentalist churches—all flag-waving. As one orange grove after another was leveled by the bulldozer, car emissions replaced smudge pots as the smog source. Former California governor Goodwin Knight, a moderate Republican, quipped, "in Orange County, the orange trees all lean right."[3]

Nixon found his way into politics through the Orange County Republican mechanism. Within that rigid society, Red-baiting was Nixon's stock-in-trade. Despite the fact that he never came near a combat zone during the war in the Pacific, Lieutenant Nixon would suggest to constituents that he heard bombs exploding and guns firing.[4] On the campaign trail he would win no medals for chivalry, as was exemplified in his shameless—and groundless—attacks on pop diva Helen Gahagan Douglas in his 1954 Senate race, styling her a "pink lady."

It was natural for Nixon to become an anti-communist crusader, his most memorable case being that of Alger Hiss, a ranking State Department official charged with being a Russian spy. It had such props as a hollowed-out pumpkin and a typewriter the FBI couldn't identify.

His first scandal had come circa 1946 when it came to light that he was financed for Congress by an illegal slush fund.[5] The fund was the handiwork of Murray Chotiner, a loan arranger who was wired to the Mob[6] and was a fixture inside the Nixon staff. Nixon had known from the start what Chotiner was all about, but he was undeterred. So the "Mr. Smith Goes to Washington" demagogue caught his first whiff of the underworld that existed far beyond the precincts of tiny Whittier College. From Whittier College to responsibility for national security is a giant leap, but Nixon was a sunshine patriot, as the Watergate scandal would ultimately show.

Earl Mazo does not account for Nixon's fateful attraction to Cuba that he acquired as an adult, but it may have been a pending dream of his life. All that is known is that in 1940, shortly after he was married, he and his wife, Pat Ryan, traveled to Puerto Rico and Cuba on a United Fruit vessel. Captivated by the cobblestone charm of Old Havana, Nixon briefly thought of opening a law practice inside its portals.[7] But he would visit the wide-open city to test its gaming tables and drink heavily.

As Henry Kissinger saw it, Nixon was spellbound by the "Cuban mystique," which gave him neuralgic episodes resulting in severe headaches, he was so consumed by the spell. The lure was irresistible and, sans Pat, he made numerous trips there labeled as business or vacation or both, with Charles "Bebe" Rebozo at his elbow. He was seen clinking glasses with the Cuban dictator Fulgencio Batista, with whom he developed an investment as well as a social relationship.[8] The US naval attaché of the time stated that "Batista was a dictator. But he was our dictator."[9] Nixon may have paraphrased it as, "he's a bastard, but he's our bastard." The most absurd example of Batista's sympathetic view of major American corporations came in the case of a telephone company, a leading supplier of communications services to Latin America, to which Batista had granted outrageous rate hikes. The American company was so grateful for his bounty that it presented him with a solid gold statuette of a telephone.[10]

In 1952, when Batista pulled off his coup, Nixon, who was still a US senator, pulled off a stunt that could well have cost him the vice presidency. It was a mere ten days before the election in which he was Eisenhower's running mate, and it is fair to ask, what was the candidate doing in Cuba so close to the election? One answer to the riddle is that he was drinking and gambling with his slush-fund manager Dana Smith, a lawyer who was also a heavy drinker.[11]

It appears that Nixon, like the rest of his staff as well as the White House, was overconfident going into the stretch. He knew he had a godfather in Meyer Lansky. Dana Smith and Nixon were carousing in the Sans Souci Casino, owned by Santos Trafficante, a member of the National Crime Syndicate, which was situated in the upper-scale Country Club section on the outskirts of Havana.[12] The report of the incident has it that Smith gambled away $25,000 (factored for inflation). He had been extended credit by the casino's operating owner Norman "Roughhouse" Rothman, who was undoubtedly influenced by the presence of the vice-president-to-be. No sooner did Smith return home to Pasadena than he put a stop payment on the $25,000 check he wrote to cover the loss, and Rothman countered by filing a lawsuit in the Los Angeles civil courts. Nixon then stuck his neck out by writing a letter to the US State Department on official stationery seeking intervention with Rothman on Smith's behalf, and Rothman eventually dropped his action to collect.[13] This whole scenario doesn't compute. It was not like Nixon to be solely an observer; gaming action was part of him. When he was with his alter ego Bebe Rebozo—and this was most of the time—Rebozo would pick up the markers for him and pay them. Nixon never paid for anything, which makes it likely that it was he who rang up the $25,000 loss, leaving it to Smith to settle the account. When news of the curious letter broke, Nixon's office would only claim that he was "doing a routine service for a constituent."[14] It is more likely that the candidate was trying to separate himself from the fact that he was there with Smith, which could lead down a prickly path.

What role, if any, Meyer Lansky played in this elaborate act is anybody's guess. In either case, Rothman may have dropped the suit on instructions from Meyer Lansky, the chief executive of organized crime. Lansky told Israeli journalist Uri Dan that he and Dana Smith "knew each other well."[15] He would say that he "knew" Nixon. But those admissions were after he retired to Israel and was protected by Israeli law. A Lansky aide, Doc Stacher, was present at the interview and nodded in assent of the answers.

On October 30, shortly after Nixon wriggled out of the slush-fund scandal with his famous Checkers speech and five days before the election, veteran reporter Theodore Link, who specialized in organized crime, broke the story in the *St. Louis Post-Dispatch* that Nixon had been with Smith on the night he lost heavily at the Sans Souci.[16] And Nixon himself had been gambling heavily with political fund money. The pair had been on a combined holiday and political trip to Miami, staying at the exclusive Quarter Deck Yacht Club on Pirate's Key, when they decided to visit Havana, a puddle jump away. Link talked with the manager of the Quarter Deck, who confirmed that Nixon had accompanied Smith to Cuba. He also found five witnesses who had spotted Nixon's familiar face at the Sans Souci. At first Nixon hotly denied the story, which tided him over Election Day. Afterward, Link writes, "Nixon admitted that all the facts in the story were true," but then Link failed to ask if it was he himself who was the lone gambler.[17]

There is some authority for believing he did gamble heavily. It comes from Norman Casper, who occasionally did background checks for Bebe Rebozo, now in the real-estate and investments business.[18] Casper, whose source was locally well-known Arch Horner, said that Horner had observed Nixon and Rebozo at the Hotel Nacional's Casino Internacional when it was owned by the Cleveland Syndicate.[19] Nixon was gambling "pretty heavily," which prompted Horner to query a relative who was on duty in a money exchange cage.[20] Horner learned from the relative that Nixon "lost thousands of dollars—I think he said $50,000—and Bebe picked up the marker on it."[21]

Any doubt about Nixon's witting connection to Lansky and company is dispelled by an FBI document dated January 9, 1959, disclosing that Rebozo had business ventures in Cuba during the Batista era in which Nixon participated.[22] The information was attributed by the FBI to a "reliable informant," Bureau lingo for a tested source.

The Nacional was Meyer Lansky's flagship hotel, the venerable center of his operations. There is evidence that Nixon was comped—and compromised—at the Hotel Nacional, as Irish journalist Anthony Summers in his thoroughly researched *The Arrogance of Power* stated. Another former federal investigator, Jack Clarke, told him that later in the 1950s he was doing a black-bag job in the hotel's accounting office, looking for the goods on a man whose name began with "P" when he stumbled upon the name Nixon. "I took a quick look and snatched it," Clarke recounted. "It revealed that when Nixon stayed at the Hotel Nacional, which was owned by Lansky, they comped him a whole deal [paid his bill] and it was the presidential suite, before he was really something."[23] The hotel official who authorized the free stay was Vincent "Blue Eyes" Alo, a longtime Lansky lieutenant who in a 1997 interview with Summers cryptically confirmed that Lansky knew Nixon. "He met him in Havana in the old days," was all he would say.[24]

There is no evidence that Dana Smith ever darkened the doors of the Havana casinos again, which may have been prudent considering that Rothman was known as "Roughhouse" for a reason. From that point on, Bebe Rebozo was Nixon's lone companion haunting the casinos. Conceivably Lansky had gotten word to Nixon's erstwhile fund manager to stay away. But it is troubling news that Lansky flatly admitted that he "knew Smith well."[25] We are treading on dangerous ground here—a man who would be president was on open terms with the nation's top crime boss. The opportunity afforded Lansky by this relationship is boundless: graft, favoritism, and protection come to mind. Back home, Smith never left the Nixon coterie. "The Third Man Theme" would be an appropriate musical background.

As for Rothman, his fortune dimmed. He held an equity share in the glitzy Sans Souci. But in August 1956 he took a financial hit estimated between $200,000 and $400,000 when an illicit shipment of slot machines was intercepted by Customs agents in Miami. He had to give up his points in the Sans Souci, and he wound up managing a less-than-five-star-rated hotel in Miami. But Rothman missed his previous lifestyle. On June 5, 1969, he and three others were arrested in New York for the theft of $4 million in IBM and Burroughs Corporation stock from the vaults of Wall Street brokerage houses. He was tried and convicted and received a five-year sentence. From his jail cell in Atlanta Federal Penitentiary, he sent a note to another detainee, Frank Sturgis, who had been convicted for the Watergate burglary and was residing in a prison at Eckland Air Force Base. The note said, "Greetings, Frank, and welcome to the club."[26]

★ ★ ★

Bebe Rebozo was introduced to Nixon as early as 1951 by one of his Senate colleagues, George Smathers of Florida, "the senator from Cuba." Nixon was making regular junkets to Havana; two were vice presidential visits. In 1955, Nixon was photographed at a reception toasting the dictator and saying of him, "he admires the American way of life."[27] A year later, on a similar occasion, Nixon proclaimed that he was very impressed with the competency and stability of the Batista regime. Smathers selected Rebozo for introduction to Nixon because he felt he needed some sun and sea air, and Rebozo could supply that.[28] Smathers told Nixon to give Bebe a call when he checked in at the Key Biscayne Hotel. Nixon did, and soon he had a boon companion in constant contact. They would vote, swim, and golf together. On deep-sea-fishing excursions, they were the guests of Tatum "Chubby" Wofford, whose Wofford Hotel housed Meyer Lansky's "carpet joint" (a classy casino), the largest in Florida. According to former IRS agent Norman Casper, the really close relationship between Nixon and Rebozo began in Cuba.[29]

Rebozo indeed had a checkered career. During World War II, he was not subject to the military draft because he was a Cuban citizen. His father was an immigrant cigar maker in Miami, but Bebe aspired to greater things. During the war, he bought a tire-retreading business that he parlayed into a black market in tires. After the war, he became a flight attendant and gas-station-pump jockey. He went on to become an affluent real-estate investor and owned a small bank that handled his transactions and possibly provided a parking space for gaming profits.[30]

When the Florida White House was completed, Rebozo moved right in. Nixon and Rebozo prospered from crooked deals and their links to the Cuban exile community and the crime syndicate. Another strong contributor was Howard Hughes, for whom an ex-FBI agent named Richard Danner peeled off $100,000 in $100 bills to Rebozo as a campaign contribution to Nixon's 1968 run.[31] Danner again broke into the limelight in 1974 when, with Watergate closing in, he visited Nixon and Rebozo at the exclusive Camp David. Questions arose about the propriety of it all. A White House spokesperson explained that Rebozo's presence there was simply a discussion of old times.[32] That may have been the problem.

CHAPTER SIX
THE ALLIANCE NOBODY KNEW

**"THEY DON'T KNOW WHAT I WANT OR WHAT
I AM GOING TO DO."**
—Fidel Castro After Meeting
with Richard Nixon, May 1959

Accompanying Castro on his US lecture tour sponsored by the American Society of Newspaper Editors was Jose "Pepin" Bosch, head of the Bacardi rum distillery and a ubiquitous player in Cuban politics. Bosch had been minister of finance in the first Prío administration and was tapped during the dying days of the Batista regime to be the lone civilian member of the junta proposed by Pawley to dispose of Batista and block Castro. If there was any resentment on Castro's part, it didn't show. On the flight to Washington, DC, the conversation between the rebel army *comandante* and the well-tailored executive took a predictable bifurcation as Castro recited what the state could do for the people, and Bosch, what the people could do for the state.[1] Then they were drawn from their seats by the descent into Washington. In the distance, they could see the seat of American power; the Washington Monument, the United States Capitol, the Pentagon, and, with a closer look, the White House. Castro thought of the duplicate Capitol building the Cuban people had built decades ago out of admiration for the great democracy.[2]

Over the eleven days of his visit, Castro was the perfect guest, touring a zoo, eating hot dogs with relish, testifying before the Senate Foreign Relations Committee, signing autographs, and taking in the tourist spots—capped by a pilgrimage to the Lincoln Memorial, the assassinated president being a favorite of his. He was greeted with enthusiasm everywhere he went, but he was repeatedly braced as to whether he was a communist, a rumor planted by Cuban exiles who had fled to the United States before the takeover. Shortly after he arrived in the United States, Castro appeared on NBC's *Meet the Press*, fielding questions coolly. Representative Charles O. Porter of Oregon, who drove him to many of his engagements, recalled that in the presence of the editors, Castro insisted that he wasn't a communist, that he would hold elections in the near future, subject to the creation of a complete voters' process, that he would abide by the Organization of American States (OAS) charter and welcome private investment.[3] "I believe he meant what he said," Porter advised. The congressman assured Castro on behalf of the State Department that this country was willing to "triple existing aid programs" to keep "good will."

On the all-important question of war and peace, Castro stated at his appearances that in the event of hostilities with the Soviet Union, Cuba would side with the United States. The NBC panel, enchanted with Castro's pop-hero mystique in rumpled fatigues, didn't take him seriously and let the question go. The vision of Cuba becoming a base for nuclear missiles pointed at the United States was simply beyond their ken. A newsbreak on communist activities usually didn't exceed a single news cycle, the country having exhausted itself by the finger pointing of the McCarthy era.

★ ★ ★

It was nervous time again for Vice President Nixon, who would, after being forced out into retirement by his role in the Watergate scandal, title his autobiography *My Six Crises*. One of them was looming now. No, not the trans-Pacific dalliance with Marianna Liu,[4] a Hong Kong businesswoman, during the interregnum between narrowly losing a bid for governor of California against Edmund G. "Pat" Brown and his return to political life. In April 1959, Nixon was awaiting the decision of President Dwight David Eisenhower, the commander of allied forces for the invasion of Europe in World War II. He won the vice presidency in 1956 on Ike's coattails. Now in his second term as president, Eisenhower was slowed by two strokes, and the weight of government was slowly shifting to Nixon. The vice president was freighted with more and more duties.

What was keeping Nixon awake nights was whether Ike, as he was known, would recommend him for the presidential slot in the upcoming 1960 elections. Only weeks before, he had given his famous Checkers speech on television, using the emotional tug of the family pooch to offset the discovery that for the better part of his political career, he benefited from an illegal slush fund. But Ike hadn't given him his blessing yet, and Nixon was agonizing over the possibility that it might never come.[5]

Now there was a wild card to contend with: Fidel Castro, the new leader of Cuba, was in the United States on a speaking tour. Cuba might be a small country, but the image of Fidel Castro as Robin Hood was familiar to millions, giving it prestige beyond its size. For the embattled Nixon, Castro was bad news. The vice president had already participated in two attempts to block Castro from power. One was sending a friendly emissary to Cuba to talk about voluntary exile,[6] the other to cut off Castro by forming a military junta to block him from reaching the Presidential Palace.

The White House saw every move of Castro's as ideologically motivated. When he ordered the rates of the Cuban Electric Company, a monopoly owned by the American Foreign Power Company, slashed by 30 percent, Washington saw it as an intrusion on free markets. But Castro wanted to bring electricity to the multitudes in Cuba who hadn't owned a light bulb up to this point, a move more populist than socialist. For Castro in Washington, the prevailing atmosphere from the administration was pure disdain. One incident typifies the entire scene. Someone came into the room where the Cuban delegation was waiting and was announced as "Mister So-and-So, in charge of Cuban affairs." To which Fidel could only reply, "And I thought I was in charge of Cuban affairs."[7]

When it was time for the White House reception with the president, it didn't happen. Eisenhower, appalled that a head of state would be a rumpled revolutionary such as Fidel Castro, decided to violate protocol and absent himself over his visit. Ike got out of town, taking his golf clubs with him to North Carolina, and let his vice president handle the meeting. All the talk about agrarian reform was too much to stomach. Some believe the switch to Nixon was a setup to bring Nixon's stronger credentials as an interrogator into play. Others go with the theory that the spit-and-polish flag officer couldn't stand the idea of being of equal rank with a rumpled revolutionary.

Nixon did not stand in for his boss with great enthusiasm. When Castro arrived for the meeting, Nixon kept Castro out of the White House and instead led his guest into his old Russell Senate Office Building office. The site was an insult because visiting heads of state ordinarily are received in the White House as a matter of protocol. A minimal fifteen minutes was allotted (in reality, the meeting lasted three hours). When the two posed for photos before entering Nixon's office, Nixon put his right arm around Castro's shoulder and smiled for the cameras. It was his last friendly gesture. They retreated into Nixon's private office. The vice president's opening gambit was to brandish an FBI report alleging that the Cuban government was infiltrated by communists.[8] Castro didn't flinch. He knew his brother Raul had once been a member of the Young Communist League, but that ended when the Communist Party of Cuba disavowed Fidel's assault on the Moncada Barracks on July 26, 1956, to start the revolution.

Nixon asked Castro whether he intended to hold free elections, the holy water of democracy.[9] It was a question freighted with the North American experience. At the time of the Cuban Revolution, the *caudillo* tradition was widespread in Latin America, in which a benevolent strong man rules with the will of the people. It was particularly found in the poorer countries that couldn't afford democracy. Castro's reply to Nixon was that he would hold elections when political parties had been developed and an electoral process established.[10]

As the bare-knuckles session neared an end, Nixon volunteered that America wanted to help Cuba because of the condition in which the country had been left.[11] The younger man was not about to be gamed. "And when would you send all this aid?" he asked. He knew that Nixon would attach a contingency, and sure enough the vice president proposed that aid would come "as soon as you hold general elections."[12] Representative Porter, on behalf of the State Department, had offered aid with no strings. Castro was seething with Nixon's trickery and pushed back, "Democracy is more than just a word," pointing out that there can be no democracy where there is hunger, unemployment, and injustice.[13] The meeting ended with another exchange on the subject of elections, but Castro got the "message," the vice president was imposing a contingency on him that he had not on his friend Batista.

Castro knew from the moment he sat in Nixon's office, listening to his rants, that the White House hierarchy was scheming for his downfall. It was clear to the Cuban leader that the vice president was simply the point man.[14]

That night, when he returned to the Cuban Embassy, where he was staying, Castro was obviously not a happy camper as he was waved through the security post, swearing about Nixon to no one in particular, "That son-of-a-bitch Nixon, he treated me badly and he's going to pay for it."[15] After three hours at the hands of Dick Nixon, the Cuban saw clearly why the destroyer of character had been substituted. The vice president was a verbal axe man: not pretty with words but effective. Over the marathon exchange, he had embarrassed, humiliated, and slashed the composure of his visitor who was not exactly a slouch with words. The rank hostility radiated by Nixon from start to finish gave away the game. The Eisenhower administration had already made up its mind: the Castro regime was to be overthrown.

Ike's concern that Fidel was a communist dated back to May 1958, when he realized that his administration was paying too much attention to Europe and too little to that vast expanse of terrain known as Latin America.[16] So he linked with the OAS and reestablished the post of Assistant Secretary of State for Latin American Affairs. The ever-mobile William Pawley put in for the job, but Ike considered him too right-wing to fit. In line with his new attention to the region, the president dispatched Nixon to the troubled nations to soothe their leaders. It was a mistake in casting. Nixon's reception was hardly warm, and in Bogota, Columbia, riots broke out as the Nixon limousine was pelted with stones. Naturally, Pawley was on top of the story. He reported that at the height of the riots he heard a radio voice announce: "This is Fidel Castro. This is a communist revolution." Wanting to believe this convenient bit of artifice, Pawley briefed Ike that Castro was a self-professed communist.[17] The label stuck. There is no independent evidence of such a broadcast during Fidel's activist days, so the story was probably fictitious. Nevertheless, it kickstarted Pawley's pathological hatred of Castro.

At the embassy, in talking with Constantine Kanglas, a lawyer who represented the Cuban government, Castro told him that he had followed Prío's advice by not raising the matter of aid to Nixon but, as the lawyer quoted Castro, "I did say we needed help. He told me I had been a fine fellow, put in plenty of good reforms. Then he said in about six months we could meet and talk again. Six months!"[18] Castro believed that Nixon knew Cuba was broke, because his friend Batista had looted the treasury. "Castro didn't believe Nixon was interested in helping," Kanglas recalled. "He thought that Nixon wanted economic catastrophe to hit Cuba so that the people would overthrow Castro. He thought Nixon wanted to see him topple."

Castro may have had a few choice words for Nixon, but the indication was that he would yield to Nixon's fiats as far as possible in order to reach an accommodation. He told economic advisor Ernesto Betancourt, "What we have to do is stop the executions [of accused war criminals, which was Raul's doing] and the infiltration of communists into the government."[19] Probably Fidel was unaware of communist infiltration into his government until Nixon made the allegation. To one of his entourage, Rufo Lopez-Fresquet, Castro confided his plans, "Look, Rufo, I am letting all the communists stick their heads out so that I will know who they are. And when I know them, I will do away with them."[20] By this time, the smallish Communist Party of Cuba, which had strongly opposed Fidel, had thrown in with Raul's Young Communist League and with Che. This pair undoubtedly had something to do with packing the Cuban administration with conventional Communists.

The verbal duel between Nixon and Castro had been so heated, it left each man convinced he had won. Nixon let his staff know he had outargued the Cuban by proving that Castro was a communist. He was only slightly more temperate when he memoed Eisenhower that "he seems to be sincere; either he is incredibly naïve about communism or under communist discipline. We have no choice but to at least point him in the right direction."[21] What Nixon meant by this was not clear.

Castro had submitted to a CIA interrogation that found him "not only not a communist but a strong anti-communist fighter."[22] Deputy CIA director Richard Bissell explained that the session was set up because the

Agency was in doubt as to whether Castro was a committed communist or just leftward leaning. The report was the work product of Frank Bender, a slight, balding chain smoker who was the political action officer for Latin America and had a liberal slant. But it was drastically altered by staffers for presentation to Eisenhower. It deemed unconvincing Castro's promises that Cuba would be on the side of the West in the Cold War, and rated it a possibility that the land reform he was insisting upon might adversely affect certain American-owned properties in Cuba. The report concluded that Castro remained an enigma, but that there was still the possibility of developing a constructive relationship with him and his government. Eisenhower scribbled on the file margin, "We will check in a year."[23] In this passage, Ike revealed his lack of vision, which reduced Cuba to a backyard nuisance, not a potential player on the world stage. With its population of only eleven million, it was another Guatemala, easily hijacked if the need arose. By not ordering the pursuit of a constructive relationship, by not waging peace, Eisenhower let slip the opportunity to prevent Cuba from gravitating into the Soviet orbit. The void allowed the administration hardliners, headed by Nixon, to take over. Such was the poverty of American foreign policy at the time.

What was the cause of Nixon's knee-jerk repulsion of Castro—a feeling so strong that he intimidated Fidel from alluding to an alliance between the two nations? Surely it wasn't his anti-communism or his desire to trump the Soviets. Consider his subsequent efforts with the People's Republic of China. He would dispatch Henry Kissinger incognito in the 1970s to Beijing to open the golden door for trade with the United States and an exchange of diplomatic credentials. In 1974, Nixon would even reside in a compound in the land of the Great Wall for a short time. So Nixon was quite amenable to negotiating with a socialist nation if the time was ripe. No, ideology was not it. It might have been the loss of his gambling income from his gangbuster holdings in the Tropicana Hotel and casino. It may also have been the result of his debt to the Mob, which had been piling up since the 1950s for his gambling markers and being comped and compromised at every turn.

Upon taking over in January 1959, Castro shut down the casinos. But the unions so strenuously objected, saying it would throw out thousands of workers, that he backed down. But there was a bit of the puritan in him, and that April, before he met with Nixon, he began an orderly shutdown, starting with those that were in shaky financial shape. This meant the Casino Internacional, among others, and Mike McLaney now knew why Moe Dalitz, the Cleveland Syndicate's major domo, had been so casual in selling it to him after buying it only a few months before.

But Lansky and company might not have lost their glittering-gold chain of casinos in the first place if Nixon hadn't browbeaten Castro to the point of humiliation. For in his breast pocket the architect of the Cuban Revolution had carried a draft proposal for an alliance between the Republic of Cuba and the United States, in which the Latin neighbor would side with the United States in the event of hostilities with the Soviet Union.[24] It was a blockbuster of a deal. The rookie statesman had foreseen the necessity for third world countries to align with a superpower, and the United States was his first choice.

CHAPTER SEVEN

NIXON'S RED-BAITING BOOMERANGS INTO CASTRO EPIPHANY

"FOR THE THING WE SHOULD NEVER DO IN DEALING WITH REVOLUTIONARY COUNTRIES . . . IS TO PUSH THEM BEHIND AN IRON CURTAIN RAISED BY OURSELVES. ON THE CONTRARY, EVEN WHEN THEY HAVE BEEN SEDUCED AND SUBVERTED AND ARE DRAWN ACROSS THE LINE, THE RIGHT THING TO DO IS TO KEEP THE WAY OPEN FOR THEIR RETURN."[1]

—WALTER LIPPMANN, JULY 1959

There are opinions pro and con as to whether Castro was a communist before his revolutionary victory. Jim Noel, the CIA station chief in Havana, traveled to the Sierra Maestra range, where the revolutionary was based, to see for himself. His take was that Castro was not a communist.[2] Representative Charles Porter, who spent quality time with Castro in Washington, was convinced he wasn't in the shadow of Karl Marx.[3] The evidence stacks up that when Castro left Washington for home, he was not a believer in communism. This is convincingly illustrated by his vehement reaction to Nixon's charge that his administration was riddled with Communists.

Nixon could beat the air over the chimera of communism, but there was nothing to stick it to. The general public in Cuba regarded Castro as a heroic figure who was nothing more than a headstrong nationalist. CIA director Allen Dulles, who was already tuned in to a program to force him into the Soviet orbit to justify an intervention, previewed the potential for deploying punitive politics by drastically reducing Cuba's sugar allotment if he didn't toe the line. The one thing Castro was not was a communist. He told a Social Democrat in his delegation, Norberto Fuentes, that he was not a communist because "communism was the dictatorship of a single class and meant hatred and class struggle."[4] Castro still harbored resentment for the Communist Party of Cuba because it had falsely labeled his effort at the Moncada Barracks a "putsch." For his part, Castro maintained back at the embassy that he was nothing more than a staunch Cuban nationalist who belonged to the Ortodoxo Party, which was mainstream and majority. It had been his shibboleth on the Hill, as the University of Havana was called, and it was his position now. It was a saying on the Hill that a communist is someone who can't think for himself. At the University of Havana, Fidel's political gyro tilted slightly to the left.

It is worthy of note that Castro had invited two of Cuba's most powerful executives, Jose "Pepin" Bosch and Daniel Bacardi of the rum distilling empire, to join his entourage in Washington. On his blog, *Macrohistory and World Report*, Frank Smitha put it nicely, "He appeared to be a free enterprise nationalist but in search of remaking Cuban society."[5] In other words, Castro was a Social Democrat.

Castro left the United States telling the Cuban Embassy staff that he was going to continue to pursue a modus vivendi with the White House. Actually he felt embittered by the double standards Nixon had laid down. He arrived at the seat of American power full of promise to forge a Cold War alliance only to find it would have been futile as well as humiliating to even raise the point. In his biography *Castro: A Political Biography*, *New York Times* correspondent Herbert Matthews, who interviewed Castro extensively in the mountains in 1957, writes, "from his Havana University days Fidel would never take orders from anybody. In fact, he would rarely take advice."[6]

If this "lone wolf" characterization had been noted in the beginning by his Cuban middle-class enemies and by Americans in the State Department, there would have been less naïve zeal in picturing Fidel Castro as becoming a satellite of the Soviet Union.

Castro's dreadful experience with the vice president apparently caused a political vertigo that swept him to the left. On the return trip to Cuba, by way of Canada and Argentina, attending an economic conference in Buenos Aires, he was still fuming over his humiliation at Nixon's hands. He vented his feelings to Norberto Fuentes, "They [Ike and Nixon] don't know me. They don't know what I want or what I'm going to do. From now on it will always be that way."[7] By the time he landed at Camp Columbia, it was as if he had undergone an epiphany. Castro realized that he would not be able to work out an accommodation with the White House. The fact that he came away empty-handed from his brutalizing meeting with Nixon meant that he had lost his leverage with his brother Raul and with Che, who were advocating that the Ortodoxo Party convert to socialism. Fidel would not be able to stand alone against the party. As the wheels of his Bristol Britannia touched down at Camp Columbia, the smiling, hand-shaking celebrity was gone.

Eisenhower badly wanted Castro's demise before he left office at the end of 1960.[8] This contradicted his general foreign policy of containment. Nixon's contrite Checkers speech, in which he used his dog as emotional prop, hadn't as yet swayed the squeaky-clean general in Nixon's favor, and the suspense was killing Nixon. On the other hand, Eisenhower had to make a choice between turning thumbs down on Nixon's presidential bid or keeping him to direct the overthrow of the Castro regime. Ike finally chose the latter, endorsing his vice president for the Republican Party nomination. But he also appointed him White House Action Officer for the Cuba Project, as the effort to deconstruct the Castro regime was called. Ike had been impressed by Nixon's consuming anti-communism, his tendency to let expediency trump ethics, and, yes, his recklessness. A scary example of the latter had occurred in 1952 and could have cost both Nixon and Eisenhower their jobs. Nixon and his slush-fund manager, Dana Smith, were carousing in the Sans Souci Casino. The report of the incident has it that Smith gambled away a large amount of money, which could only have come from the political contribution funds he was managing.[9] Nixon was often seen drinking and gambling at the Havana casinos, but this was the first time such a huge sum was involved. And this was ten days before the presidential election. If the true story had hit the papers, the outcome of the election would have been different. And it would have been true that reporters wouldn't have Dick Nixon to kick around anymore.

So Eisenhower's conscious decision to in effect hand the 1960 election for president to the corruption-tainted Nixon was a roll of the dice based on practicality—his perceived potential to overthrow the Castro regime before Ike left office in January 1960—that trumped moral concerns. Eisenhower's old soldier pride had won the day for Nixon. But he lost the day when John F. Kennedy edged him out for president. The irony was that Nixon was muzzled on the Cuba Project for security reasons. On the other hand, Kennedy's camp was the beneficiary of several credible reports on an impending thrust against Cuba. It was an open invitation for Kennedy to spread his wings.

CHAPTER EIGHT
SETTING UP THE BAY OF PIGS AND OTHER DISASTERS

"[CUBA BECAME] A RED AIRCRAFT CARRIER ONLY NINETY MILES OFF THE COAST OF FLORIDA."
—NATHANIEL WEYL, *RED STAR OVER CUBA*, 1960

Early in 1960, after the United States cut off all imports of Cuban sugar, Cuba reacted by nationalizing all American businesses and commercial property. This provoked Eisenhower to announce that military action against Cuba was imminent. He would not "tolerate the establishment of a regime dominated by international communism in the Western Hemisphere," the president said.[1] The Soviets responded by announcing that they would buy all the sugar that had been allotted for the American market. Premier Nikita Khrushchev vowed that the Soviet Union would protect Cuba from any invasion, and Cuban foreign minister Raúl Roa declared before the United Nations assembly that his small country "could have no other course than to accept this assistance with gratitude."[2] The events that would lead to the Bay of Pigs invasion and the missile crisis were set in motion.

On a fine St. Patrick's Day in 1960, the red phone in the CIA director's office rang. It was President Eisenhower authorizing the Agency to engage in covert actions against the Castro regime, the so-called Cuba Project.[3] Allen Dulles was now set to implement his plan to terrorize the Cuban populace. Once again, the US State Department invoked the Monroe Doctrine of 1823 in order to intervene in Latin American affairs.

In 1954, famed aviator Jimmy Doolittle, who led a bombing raid on Tokyo during World War II (*Twenty Seconds over Tokyo* is the movie), was commissioned by Eisenhower to determine the CIA's capability in responding to the new threats created by the Cold War. On the Doolittle Commission sat the aviator himself and William Pawley.

Doolittle and Pawley, who had President Eisenhower's ear through his long public service, issued the report asserting that the United States had to abandon its concept of fair play "in the face of [an] implacable enemy and subvert, sabotage, and destroy enemies with more clever and sophisticated means."[4] If this sounds like automatic warfare, perhaps it was the intent.

Dulles was more than ready. On May 14, 1959, shortly after the Castro-Nixon verbal slugfest, an attorney named Alex E. Carlson filed corporate papers with the Dade County Clerk for a Double-Chek Corporation, whose business was stated as "brokerage." The company address was close to the Miami International Airport, and most of its clients were tramp airlines.

Dulles could now tap into the director's contingency fund to finance the operation—not that the tweedy, pipe-smoking Boston Brahmin's family didn't own large blocks of United Fruit stock.[5] The operation was nameless, but insiders called it the Dulles Bomber Wing. Double-Chek was a CIA front that would be subject to the Neutrality Act when it was enacted in late October 1962. It recruited ex-military pilots for missions over Cuba, strafing trains, firebombing cane fields, and hitting oil tanks, commercial buildings, and other targets designed to demoralize the population, commonly known as terrorism, to soften up the home front in preparation for a takeover by US Marines stationed at Guantanamo and the Panama Canal Zone.[6] Anyone curious enough to inquire about the strange company was given a flippant answer like, "We fly chickens to the Dominican Republic" or "We broker for Czech clients."[7] As it turned out, the CIA estimate of Castro's domestic support was significantly short.

So the Cuba Project was finally underway, with Nixon as its action officer, even though it was unauthorized until April 17, 1960, when Ike approved the covert operation. It is probable that Dulles ratcheted up a schedule of operations to please Eisenhower's wish that Fidel be overthrown before the end of his term.

Castro's air force consisted of leftovers from the Batista force, which would pose no threat to the CIA's fleet of B-26 light bombers refitted from

World War II, which were so common on the surplus market that they were difficult to trace. The registration numbers were painted out, and their bases were remote strips in Florida and Guatemala. The CIA fleet also had a few sleek P-51 Mustangs. All pilots were screened by Double-Chek.

To defend the homeland against these attacks, which showed no sign of abating, Cuba needed its own warplanes. Dulles learned that Castro had turned to Great Britain, which had sold seventeen Sea Furys to Batista that would even the score when delivered to Cuba. Castro changed the order to Hawker Siddeley jets that would give him the advantage. Britain apparently looked dimly on the aggressive feelings that the United States exhibited toward Cuba, and there was every indication that the deal would go through.

On December 2, 1959, the House of Lords debated the matter, then turned down the sale on the grounds that the military aircraft would introduce a new factor into a very delicate situation. Although the Americans cherished the thought that Dulles had put pressure on through his Old Boy network, Foreign Office records[8] declassified on March 22, 2001, reveal that a week before the House of Lords debate, Allen Dulles, who had connections deep inside the British intelligence services, let it be known to the British Embassy in Washington that his country looked with disfavor on the sale of aircraft to Cuba. The island was now unable to guard its airspace.

Allen Dulles's plan was to have the Soviets supply planes to Cuba by default. This would provide justification on the world stage for the US invocation of the Monroe Doctrine. Paradoxically, Dulles was in no small measure responsible for Cuba becoming, in the metaphor of its shriller detractors, "a Red aircraft carrier only ninety miles off the coast of Florida."[9]

★ ★ ★

On October 24, 1959, the B-26 sent to shower the American Society of Travel Agents in the Havana Hilton hotel with leaflets branding Castro a "communist tool," banked north and disappeared. Since the B-26 headed north, there was suspicion that it came from Florida. The United States Department of State declared it knew nothing about the mystery craft, and a check of registrations did not show a Frank Fiorini. State apparently was aware that Fiorini was Frank Sturgis, the man of many faces, including that of CIA operative. At the time he was flying "study flights" under the direction of Juaquin San Jenis, a ranking Agency officer who functioned under the cover of a Miami car dealership, upon being called and given the coordinates to slip through a gap in the picket line of US surveillance aircraft and penetrate Cuban airspace.[10] This would activate Cuban electronic defenses that would be picked up and analyzed by the spy ship *Pocono* in the Straits of Florida. In our 1974 interview, Frank said that he was paid by checks drawn on a food-products company and a department store. He had no contact with either.

Since it was a rump operation outside the Cuba Project, Dulles's Bomber Wing was able to hire pilots flying for anti-Castro action groups that proliferated in Florida. One particularly notorious example was the Insurrectional Movement for the Recovery of the Revolution (MIRR), which received CIA subsidies[11] but never yielded any degree of control over its activities. The maniacal head of MIRR was a pediatrician named Orlando Bosch, who once ran a coast-to-coast bombing conspiracy known as Cuban Power. The good doctor almost succeeded in knocking off Henry Kissinger in Costa Rica. But it was his role in the 1976 midair bombing of a Cuban airliner over the Caribbean that cost seventy-nine lives that brought him lasting notoriety. Despite this violent record, Bosch was lionized by the Bush family. Jeb Bush went so far as to use his influence to allow Bosch back into the United States.[12]

One of CIA-supported pilots was E. Carl McNabb, a United States Air Force (USAF) veteran who was a ringer for Paul Newman. I interviewed McNabb numerous times over a period of years. He told me that one night in Little Havana he was escorted to the headquarters of the Movimiento de Recuperación Revolucionaria (MRR)—in English, Movement to Recover the Revolution—an action group formed originally in Cuba by Manuel Artime. It was an unpretentious shingled house where an Anglo man was in a huddle with several Cubans. McNabb's escort turned him over to the

Anglo man, who got right to the point. His name was Alex Carlson, and he represented Double-Chek Corporation at the Miami International Airport. They were becoming operational due to the serious threat Cuba posed to American soil. They were countering this threat. Did Carl ever fly B-26s? Was he checked out on them? No, Carl replied, but he was checked out on P-51s and could maybe borrow one. McNabb asked if Carlson was looking for unpaid volunteers as well. No, Alex replied, the pay for pilots was $10,000 per month, and the company prefers orphans. It was a low blow, but McNabb was aware of the CIA's propensity for hiring those without family. The CIA knew that if someone was killed or missing in action, it was much easier when he or she didn't have relatives who might become a nuisance.

It is worth noting that this convenient practice would come home to haunt Carlson. He procured five Alabama Air National Guard pilots because of their experience in B-26s, which were favored by the Alabama National Guard. When the current operation was halted because it was being merged into the Bay of Pigs invasion, Carlson recruited the same five pilots. They cartwheeled into the sea after being shot down by Castro's defenders. It was left to the unfortunate Alex Carlson to inform the widows that their husbands had disappeared on a C-54 cargo flight to Central America. It was of course a lie.[13]

For the MRR, McNabb was based on a coffee plantation in Guatemala, flying a P-51 Mustang whose cannon was mounted in the spinner. The craft was supposed to be "borrowed" from Carlos Prío's fleet of seven. The most intriguing mission he flew was flying cover for a B-26 on a fire-bombing raid on a cane field in western Cuba. While en route, his radio cut in that they were to switch to a high-value target who was scheduled to attend a baseball game that night. Who could it be besides Fidel himself? Assassination was not in McNabb's contract. Feigning engine trouble, he returned to base. From that day on, he was under suspicion.

Frank Sturgis almost blew McNabb's clandestine work for the MRR when he heard of planes making bombing and strafing runs at targets in Cuba from bases in Central America. The man of many trades couldn't resist getting back into action. He told Michael Canfield and A. J. Weberman in *Coup d'Etat in America* that he made an appointment to see President

Miguel Ydigoras Fuentes of Guatemala with his sidekick, Diaz Lanz, "to arrange for bases there."[14] Ydigoras had restored authoritarian rule to the country after William Pawley engineered a 1956 overthrow. "So there were big headlines in the newspapers," Sturgis said, "all over Latin America, and on television and radio, that I was there trying to set up bases to invade Cuba, which really came about a year later."[15] So naturally the president was embarrassed, and Sturgis was hassled by State when he got back to Florida. The bases remained secret, but it had been a close shave. McNabb was subsequently transferred to an African "liberation" movement but "got sick of shooting up boats carrying nuns on Lake Tanganyika and quit."[16]

With the terror raids of the Dulles Bomber Wing—one explosive even hit a department store—the stage was set for the grand finale, the landing of the Marines in Cuba "from the Halls of Montezuma to the Shores of Tripoli."[17] Pawley had been there, done that, before. Cofounding the Flying Tigers was a stroke of genius. His success in business made him a powerful negotiator. It also enabled business connections with the Caribbean region's dictators, among them Batista, Trujillo of the Dominican Republic, and Samoza of Nicaragua. He socialized with them all, ordering the nation's favorite drink, Havana Club Rum. He became a diplomat sans portfolio, interacting with the dictators on the political level, and with Richard Nixon on the social level.

Pawley's diplomatic credentials were impressive. In 1950, President Harry S. Truman sent him on a mission to Madrid to negotiate with the Spanish dictator Francisco Franco on the construction of strategic air bases. Truman named him ambassador to Brazil and Peru. He became a confidant of Ike, who viewed him as a master of intrigue. It was with this set of credentials that Pawley became the point man in the campaign to bring about regime change in Cuba. Of course he had a financial stake in the outcome, but, absent that, he would still have pulled out all the stops. After all, he ranked second on Henry Kissinger's list of Fidel haters.[18] As with most White House officials, the ambassador thought Castro would be an easy mark.

Bill Pawley was a top planner of the Guatemala-invasion comic opera, with the plot centering upon the National Palace. It was hardly an invasion model, yet Pawley put great stock in it. Perhaps this is because all involved treated it with gravitas rather than as the farce that it was. Pawley commented that on the eve of the invasion, Ike summoned Allen Dulles and his brother, Secretary of State John Foster Dulles, and, clearly uneasy, told them that they had to succeed or else.[19] Years later, when the Bay of Pigs invasion of Cuba was being organized, there was an air of surety about the whole thing. Ike's only concern about Cuba, as expressed to Pawley, was to get it over and done with before he left office the following January.

In Guatemala, Jacobo Árbenz Guzmán had triggered a violent reaction by committing a personal agrarian reform and giving away some of his large land holdings. It was meant to be a humanitarian gesture, but to Pawley and Allen Dulles, who was on the board of United Fruit, it was ominous.[20] As Allen Dulles and Bill Pawley saw it, Guatemala had gone one more rung up the socialist ladder.[21]

The trouble was that the Army of Liberation assembled by the CIA, which was supposed to march into Guatemala City and take over, fled in dismay. It was left to the CIA's mercenary pilots to regain the initiative. Flying in relays, they bombed and strafed the city. At the same time, black-propaganda specialist David Atlee Phillips filled the airwaves with messages that rebels were closing in. After nine days, Árbenz lost his grip and capitulated. John Foster Dulles hailed the outcome as "a new and glorious chapter in the already great tradition of the American states."[22] But for the Guatemalan people, years of social progress went down the drain. American gamblers moved in, bribed the president's men, and opened casinos. United Fruit resumed business as usual. And Guatemala was lost for decades to right-wing militarists who failed to lift the country out of abject poverty but held power through death-squad atrocities against the opposition.

The Doolittle Report[23] left little to the imagination and provided a wide-open "pretext noir" for intervention in Cuba. When Castro dared to expropriate a large amount of United Fruit acreage in Cuba, retaliation was swift. Napalm bombs were dropped on cane fields and oil refineries.[24]

★ ★ ★

In late 1959, the CIA, still not sure, decided to try to resolve whether Castro was at heart a Caribbean capitalist or a socialist drifter. To carry out the venture, it chose Jacob M. "Jack" Kaplan, proprietor of the Southwestern Sugar & Molasses Company, which had operations in the Caribbean, including Cuba. Kaplan's public image was that of a generous philanthropist in support of Brandeis University and the New School for Social Research, and prominent liberal politicians such as Hubert Humphrey and Chester Bowles. Behind the scenes, Kaplan was allowing his tax-free Kaplan Fund to be used by the CIA as a conduit for subsidizing left-of-center but anti-communist regimes and organizations[25] in the Caribbean region as a firewall against communism, the prevailing policy at the time. By the time Castro came to power, however, Kaplan was in deep trouble. The IRS and the Patman Committee in Congress were probing his use of the Kaplan Fund as his "alter ego," pocketing the profit when stocks in the fund went up, and letting the fund take the loss when they went down (the CIA eventually lowered the "national security" curtain on Wright Patman, thereby saving Jacob Kaplan from criminal prosecution in shutting down the probe). Earlier, the CIA used Kaplan to travel to Havana and try to make a deal so favorable to Cuba only a socialist would turn it down.[26] A sweetheart deal, so to speak. But Castro, perhaps mindful of Prío's counsel, turned it down. For the CIA, this was "proof" of Castro's leftist leanings.

★ ★ ★

There is an incredible sidebar to the Kaplan collaboration story. It involves Jack Kaplan's nephew, Joel David Kaplan, a traveling executive of Jack Kaplan's Southwestern Sugar & Molasses Company, which had widespread operations in the Caribbean region.[27] Joel was privy to the arrangement in which the Kaplan Fund would be used as a conduit for funds to be distributed to left-of-center labor unions in the region to forestall any power grab by leftist elements, as had happened in Cuba.

But Joel was sympathetic to Castro's revolution, largely because of the abject poverty he had seen in his travels. The CIA was using Southwestern facilities to forward military supplies to bases in Guatemala intended as springboards for the Bay of Pigs invasion. In his position as a company executive, Joel Kaplan was able to divert the supplies to Castro-oriented units.[28] The CIA did not discover the treachery until after the invasion had failed. But Joel was an ongoing threat. Since he was Uncle Jack's close relative, murdering him was not an option.

Instead, Joel was framed in Mexico for a murder of a business partner, despite the fact that the body was patently not his. The putative murder victim was Luis Vidal Jr., son of a Dom Rep lobbyist. Joel's sister, Judy Dowis, got Warren Hinckle and this author interested in Joel's story, and in July 1967, I interviewed him in Lecumberri Prison in Mexico City. Joel recalled that Luis had boasted that "the old man had clean access to the White House—all the way up to Ike himself." Luis also showcased the claim that he was somehow related to Jacqueline Bouvier Kennedy. It may have been possible, since JFK himself was Trujillo's godson, thanks to the elder Joe Kennedy's idea of class. It was an anthropologist's nightmare.

The darkly handsome Vidal disappeared, coincident with the discovery of a body on a Mexican highway. It in no way resembled the playboy, but Joel was promptly arrested, tried, and jailed, and Vidal was heard from no more.

The CIA had Joel where it wanted him, but help was on the way. After Joel lost all appeals, his sister, who had been underwriting escape plots, insisted that I interview him in prison. He was obviously depressed underneath his prison pallor. As I scribed in my diary, "He just looked blank when I asked him if he was a CIA agent. He claimed his partner wasn't really dead. He kept mentioning Havana, saying I'd find some answers there. He told me that he had been framed but seemed reluctant to say who had framed him." Joel kept repeating, "Someone else's money was involved." I asked whose money, but the guard halted the interview and Joel was led away.

It was clear from the powerful forces arrayed against Joel that escape was his only way out. Several escape plans were tried, mostly involving bribery of Mexican officials, then a daring aerial one, proposed by Joel and developed by Vic Stadter, was selected.[29] Vic was a Californian with the style of a Texan, and he was a smuggler known by practically every Customs inspector on the US–Mexican border. Vic was the last of the rugged individualists who believed in the right of man to operate free of the restrictions of bureaucracy. He had been working on escape plans with Joel's sister, Judy, for several years when Joel was moved from Lecumberri to Santa Marta Acatitla Prison, high in the mountains outside Mexico City. On the evening of August 18, 1971, a helicopter descended into the prison courtyard in sight of the prison tower guards, who were frozen in place, not sure if it was the attorney general's helicopter, since Vic had painted it the same color as the attorney general's fleet. The helicopter pilot had been instructed to land in the courtyard, then count to ten and take off. Joel and his cellmate raced across the courtyard and scrambled onboard the helicopter, which took off immediately and disappeared into the night sky.[30] Joel linked up with a small plane in the outskirts of Mexico City and was flown to Stadter's house near Glendora, California. Vic knew all the smugglers' routes to avoid detection.

Warren Hinckle and I used Vic's home as a safe house to debrief Joel. From that debriefing, Hinckle and I produced a book, *The Ten Second Jailbreak*, which was later turned into a movie by Columbia Pictures, called *Breakout*, starring Charles Bronson and John Huston. Our book was a tough indictment of the CIA's role in Joel Kaplan's predicament, but in the process of making the movie, the CIA apparently got into the act and forced a rewrite that resulted in a Grade B potboiler. But the casting was superb.

Vic and Joel, the cowboy and boarding-school grad, later teamed up in business, speculating in gold. When last heard from, they were riding into the sunset in New Mexico.

CHAPTER NINE
MAJOR MORGAN'S TRIPLE PLAY

"REMEMBER THAT MORGAN, IN REALITY, WAS ALWAYS AN OFFICIAL OF THE NORTH AMERICAN SECRET SERVICES."
—FIDEL CASTRO TO AUTHOR, 1978

William Alexander Morgan, wearing a gold-plated .45 pistol at his belt, was a soldier of fortune straight out of central casting. He was one of those footloose adventurers who latch onto each revolution as it comes along and emerge as freedom fighters. Morgan was one of those smooth operators who could sell a rowboat to Cunard Lines. He left his mark in Cuban history books as a freedom fighter in Castro's Cuban Revolution, for which he was awarded a Hero of the Cuban Revolution medal. It was typical of Morgan that before he received the honor he had already changed sides. As a hero of the revolution, Morgan lived it up. People swarmed around him on the streets, and he cadged free food and drinks. He had a suite at the Capri Hotel in Havana and was permitted to "liberate" a luxurious mansion on Sexta Avenue in the Miramar district that was owned by a fugitive Batistite.[1]

In 1959, Morgan was thirty-one years old, a physically powerful man with blond hair and hard blue eyes. He laughed heartily, loved a practical joke, and had a penchant for women and liquor. A dead-end kid from Toledo, Ohio, Morgan enlisted in the army, his stint distinguished by brawling, robbing, going AWOL, and overpowering a guard to escape from the stockade. After being discharged, he held a string of inconsequential jobs. It seems highly incongruous that with this checkered career behind him, he would play a pivotal role in an abortive invasion of Cuba that preceded the one at the Bay of Pigs by close to two years.

In the spring of 1958, Morgan found his way to Miami and joined the Student Revolutionary Directorate (DRE), composed mostly of former University of Havana students, backed by Carlos Prío, who were waging a guerilla war against Batista in the Escambray range. It was in the Escambray that the Morgan mystique was born. Morgan conned his way into the counterrevolutionary forces by fabricating a military background, which is how he got his rank of major in the Second National Front of the Escambray. He was assigned some military responsibilities, but he was so undisciplined that he was soon relieved of them and placed in the reserves.[2] As David Grann so clearly explained in his article "The Yankee Comandante" in the *New Yorker* on May 28, 2012:

> Morgan had composed a more philosophical statement about why he had joined the rebels. The essay, titled "Why Am I Here," said:
>
>> Why do I fight here in this land so foreign to my own? Why did I come here far from my home and family? Why do I worry about these men here in the mountains with me? Is it because they were all close friends of mine? No! When I came here they were strangers to me I could not speak their language or understand their problems. Is it because I seek adventure? No here there is no adventure only the ever existent problems of survive [*sic*]. So why am I here? I am here because I believe that the most important thing for free men to do is to protect the freedom of others. I am here so that my son when he is grown will not have to fight or die in a land not his own, because one man or group of men try to take his liberty from him I am here because I believe that free men should take up arms and stand together and fight and destroy the groups and forces that want to take the rights of people away.

In his rush to overturn Cuba's past as well as his own, Morgan often forgot to pause for periods or paragraph breaks. He acknowledged, "I can not say I have always been a good citizen." But he explained that "being here I can appreciate the way of life that is ours from birth," and he recounted the seemingly impossible things that he had seen: "Where a boy of nineteen can march 12 hours with a broken foot over country comparable to the american Rockies without complaint. Where a cigarette is smoked by ten men. Where men do without water so that others may drink." Noting that U.S. policies had propped up Batista, he concluded, "I ask myself why do we support those who would destroy in other lands the ideals which we hold so dear?"

Morgan sent the statement to someone he was sure would sympathize with it: Herbert Matthews. The *Times* reporter considered Morgan to be "the most interesting figure in the Sierra de Escambray." Soon after receiving the statement, Matthews published an article about the Second Front and its "tough, uneducated young American" leader, citing a cleaned-up passage from Morgan's letter.

Other U.S. newspapers began chronicling the exploits of the "adventurous American," the "swashbuckling Morgan." The Washington *Post* reported that he had become a "daring fellow" by the age of three. The accounts were enough to "make schoolboys drool," as one newspaper put it. A retired businessman from Ohio later told the Toledo *Blade*, "He was like a cowboy in an Ernest Hemingway adventure." Morgan had finally willed his interior fictions into reality.[3]

Morgan traveled to Havana in 1959 as a principal in the proposed sale of Globemaster cargo planes to the Cuban government.[4] He thought they might be in the market for the planes for defense purposes. On March 21, one of the Globemasters was flown in from a surplus storage yard in Arizona for inspection. Privately Morgan promised the Cubans he would personally train the paratroopers. On April 1, the Cuban government announced that it intended to purchase between four and ten of the planes from Morgan's company Akro Dynamics. The selling price was $375,000 each, a markup of $200,000. The Cubans came to realize that the pricing was outrageous, and negotiations were stopped short of a test ride. It is quite likely that it was Frank Sturgis who nixed the Globemaster sale. At the time, he was minister of the Air Force and was fully informed on current pricing on the surplus planes market.

All the while, Morgan was double-dealing with Trujillo.[5] On February 24, 1959, he composed a long letter to the generalissimo detailing the training of Dominican exiles in Pinar del Rio Province in Cuba. The Cuban Revolution was contagious, he reported, and volunteers were streaming in. He was willing to betray Castro, he said, because the revolution was being betrayed. Not that Fidel was a communist, he explained, but Raul Castro and Che Guevara were, and the strategy and tactics of communism were taking over. On a personal sour note, Morgan disclosed that he and his men had been passed over for key positions in Castro's government, and now they weren't even being paid. He claimed that his Second Front force was virtually intact, and, with sufficient funding, could reestablish itself in the Escambray and do to Castro what Castro had done to Batista.

Trujillo reacted by calling for a meeting of the Organization of American States (OAS), charging that Cuba was "exporting revolution" by its planned military aggression.[6] Having set the stage, Morgan followed up by meeting with an emissary from Cuidad Trujillo. He was Fred Nelson, a wealthy, silver-haired American with Mob ties who had had business holdings in Cuba for more than a decade. When Castro took over, Nelson left for Miami posthaste with the first wave of Batista sympathizers. He aligned with the White Rose, a secretive counterrevolutionary organization composed of former soldiers of Batista's army, old politicians, and new capitalists. Their plans aligned perfectly with Trujillo's need for a fifth column and external support for an invasion. Morgan was offered one million dollars to bounce Fidel Castro from power, and after discussions with his fellow commander of the Second Front, Eloy Menoyo, he agreed to join the conspiracy. Nelson advised him that he would have to travel to Miami to firm up the plans with the Dominican consul there.[7]

The impulsive Rafael Trujillo lost no time in organizing the Cuban Liberation Army, which was composed of the evicted Batistanos with the aim of invading the island. In fact, in the days leading up to Batista's flight on New Year's Day 1959, he discussed the inevitability of Castro's takeover with his generals, raising the specter of the people's revolution spreading throughout the region and threatening the Dom Rep. Within one day of Castro's triumph, Rafael Trujillo set his plan in motion. He put the tough, brainy General Jose Pedraza in charge.[8] It is notable that Pedraza was once cashiered by Batista for being too ambitious. During the hiatus in his military career, Pedraza ran his own private army using a cattle ranch as a front; his "cowboys" rivaled Masferrer's Tigres[9] in cruelty and avarice.

According to General Fabian Escalante, head of Cuban G-2 counter-intelligence, whom I interviewed on August 27, 1991, in Rio de Janeiro, Brazil, "The CIA knew about the plans and reported them to the highest levels of the US government. Richard Nixon, then vice president of the United States, was interested in the details and gave the Agency the green light to send a senior official to meet with Trujillo and evaluate the seriousness of the anti-Cuba project." In February, Frank Bender (a.k.a. Gerry Droller) met with Trujillo and chief intelligence officer Johnny Abbes Garcia to appraise the plan.[10] Bender didn't believe Castro was a communist, but he was on assignment. He said he felt that the Cuban Liberation Army could be deployed as a kind of police force whenever needed.[11] With Bender's nuanced endorsement, Trujillo was assured that the United States would look the other way. But according to Rufo Lopez-Fresquet, the Castro government's first treasurer, who later defected, the CIA also lent logistical support to Trujillo through the Double-Chek Corporation[12] in Miami.

Morgan's master plan[13] called for the counterrevolution to be touched off by an air attack on Havana in which dynamite bombs would be dropped and explode in the air, causing a deafening noise while not injuring anyone—a psychological shock. At the same time, Morgan and his men would head for the Escambray and reconstitute the Second Front as a military force. In Miami, the White Rose would announce the start of the counterrevolution. The strategy called for Morgan and Eloy Menoyo of the Second Front to lead their force in a strike to seize and hold the airport at Trinidad, on the south coast. Then General Pedraza's eight-hundred-strong Cuban Liberation Army would be airlifted in from the Dom Rep, and on its heels, the mercenaries of the Anti-Communist Foreign Legion, numbering about six hundred. Rafael Trujillo wanted to bring in the mercenary army to add hardened steel to the venture. The nucleus was composed of members of the Spanish Foreign Legion who were loaned to Trujillo by Francisco Franco; many had fought alongside the German Blue Legion on the fascist side during the Spanish Civil War. Arms were to be airdropped to hundreds of Batista soldiers still hiding out in caves.

On April 15, 1959, Morgan traveled to Miami and made contact with the Dominican consul in that city. He explained the plan and the players and discussed reimbursements. It was decided that both Morgan and Pedraza would receive half a million dollars at the time of the invasion, and the other half would be placed in bank accounts. Morgan returned to Miami a week later to report on the progress of the conspiracy. At that time, he explained that Menoyo would participate in the plot only on the condition that the US government supported it. The Dominican consul provided Menoyo with the necessary assurances.[14]

The trips by Morgan and Menoyo to Florida began to arouse the suspicion that the G-2 was aware of their planned treason.[15] So Menoyo suggested to Morgan that they inform Castro of the plot. They agreed not to mention the money received, much less the extent of the plans, so that they would have all the cards in their hands when the moment came. If the legion landed in Cuba and consolidated its positions, they could again switch sides.

The next day, Menoyo arranged for a secret meeting with Castro. At the meeting, Morgan and Menoyo reported on the conspiracy, justifying their initial silence on the pretext that they waited to see how serious the plans were.[16] They gave Fidel all the details of the landing in Trinidad and the establishment of a provisional government in the Escambray Mountains. Castro authorized them to continue in the plot while providing information on a regular basis to his security agencies.

Meanwhile, the Dominican intelligence services distributed radio transmitters, directional antennas, and other necessary equipment to Morgan and the conspirators for the purpose of coordinating the progress of the plan. An arms deal was underway in Miami, and more funding flowed in to Trujillo from former Venezuelan dictator Marcos Perez Jimenez, who wanted to win favor in the hope that it might help him return to power at a later date.[17]

Through Morgan and Menoyo, the Castro security agencies soon were familiar with all the main elements of the conspiracy and began to move against it. On August 5, in Miami, Morgan picked up $170,000 in cash and a boatload of weapons from the White Rose exiles that were intended for the Second Front. He tipped off Castro and sailed to Havana harbor. According to General Escalante, Fidel inspected the booty: an entire arsenal which included forty 30-caliber machine guns, dozens of rifles, and a large supply of ammunition.[18] On the same day, the G-2 detained a US embassy security officer named Sergeant Stanley F. Wesson as he directed a meeting of the underground planning to carry out sabotage and disruptions in support of the Cuban Liberation Army's arrival.[19]

Now Morgan began the penultimate confidence game.[20] From his Miramar mansion and Las Villas headquarters he established shortwave radio contact with Johnny Abbes in Cuidad Trujillo. At first, they communicated clumsily in a code based upon an English dictionary's pages, but soon the American was chattering like a jaybird in "pidgin" Spanish about the impending invasion. While keeping Abbes satisfied that all was well, Morgan sprung a trap on the conspiracy's leadership. He had Menoyo summon all members of his "provisional government," among them the would-be president Arturo Hernandez Tellaheche and underground commanders, to the Miramar mansion for a final meeting.[21]

The place was packed. Also present were two members of the press: Jean Secon, a tall brunette representing United Press International, and Alex Rorke, who wangled an assignment from NBC television. Rorke had been contacted by a friend of Morgan's in New York to go to Havana if he wanted to film a rebellion. Suddenly, soldiers with machine guns surrounded the house and arrested its occupants. Castro was said to have been on the scene watching the arrests, taunting the big shots as they were led off, "And what were you going to be minister of?"[22] The arrestees were hustled off to Camp Columbia, where they were held incommunicado in a theater until the invasion played out.

The following day, Morgan got on the radio to Johnny Abbes from Las Villas and told him that his Second Front troops were attacking Trinidad, and its fall was expected momentarily. He called for the invasion phase to begin. Then, with Jean Secon under detention, Morgan faked a United Press International wire story that reported a popular uprising in the Trinidad area.[23] But in Cuidad Trujillo confusion reigned. General Pedraza was overwhelmed by doubt, and Trujillo's advisors, particularly General Arturo Espaillat and intelligence analyst Robert Emmett Johnson, were firmer than ever in their conviction that the whole thing was a ruse.[24] Trujillo took a tentative step by dispatching a Dominican transport to drop more arms, but Morgan complained to Abbes that all the parachutes had been blown out to sea.

On August 12, Morgan went on the radio again with the electrifying news that the Second Front had taken Trinidad. "I hold the town and am fighting off government troops," he told Abbes. "Send me arms."[25] Menoyo grabbed the microphone and exuberantly asked for a uniform similar to Trujillo's, to which the generalissimo sent a response that he would be rewarded with the country villa of the editor of *Bohemia*, a venerable Cuban magazine. The Dominican brain trust huddled around the radio in the National Palace, listening raptly as Morgan, with muffled explosions sounding in the background, described how pockets of resistance were being mopped up and peasants were joining the counterrevolution. Orson Welles could not have been more convincing.

Rafael Trujillo agreed to send a plane with his personal emissary that very evening. When the C-47 came to a halt on the Trinidad airfield, its propellers still spinning, out stepped a stout Spanish priest, father Ricardo Velazco. The cleric was greeted by shouts from Morgan's men of "Viva Trujillo! Down with Castro! Death to agrarian reform!" while others disguised as peasants lent credibility to the report of an uprising.[26] As gunfire was heard in the distance, Morgan and Fidel watched with amusement from behind a mango tree. Visibly moved, Velazco saluted from the staircase of the plane to several officials who applauded him. After the C-47 took off for its return to Ciudad Trujillo, Morgan got on the radio again with a request for machine-gun and mortar specialists. Thoroughly taken in by Velazco's enthusiastic report, Rafael Trujillo instructed General Espaillat to leave on a plane first thing in the morning and take charge of the forward elements. The invasion was on. He tapped Robert Emmett Johnson as the requested machine-gun expert, and assigned him double-duty as leader of the Foreign Legion. Almost desperately, both Espaillat and Johnson begged off.[27]

The first plane that took off for Cuba on the morning of August 14 soon returned to base with engine trouble. Then General Pedraza balked at moving his Cuban Liberation Army until the Trinidad salient could be secured by airborne units. Finally, a C-47 with ten men aboard, including a Spanish Foreign Legionnaire as the mortar specialist and Cuban exile Captain Raul Betancourt as the machine-gun master, made the trip to

Trinidad. As the craft rolled to a stop, it was hailed in the same lusty manner as the plane of the previous day. As the soldiers disembarked at the airstrip, which had been marked with lights, they could hear Morgan and his men shouting denunciations of Castro, and, as they joined in, the cries grew louder and more intense, converging, like voices at a stadium, in a deafening incantation: "Death to Castro!" But on a signal, Morgan's Cubans leveled their guns at the plane.[28] Soldiers from the strike force drew their guns, and for a moment the plotters and the counter-plotters peered at one another, as if still puzzling over who had crossed whom. Then a few of Trujillo's men opened fire, and everyone began shooting. One of Morgan's friends ran toward the plane and was killed. By the time the fusillade ended, two members of the strike force had died, and the rest had been apprehended. The invasion was over before it began.[29]

Rafael Trujillo placed a half-million-dollar bounty on Morgan's head. When Clete Roberts, the American broadcaster, visited Morgan's house, in September 1959, he found it surrounded by bodyguards with Thompson submachine guns. "I ought to tell you back in the United States that Mr. Morgan and I are sitting in what you might call an armed camp," Roberts said.[30] He asked Morgan, "How does it feel to have a half-million-dollar price on your head?" Morgan replied coolly, "Well, it isn't too bad. They are going to have to collect it. And that's going to be hard."

Castro reaped a propaganda windfall by casting Rafael Trujillo in the role of aggressor and charging that he had the support of the Organization of American States (OAS). The Dominican *jefe* was humiliated and stripped of the aura of invincibility that had rendered him the Caesar of the Caribbean. Chuckling that it was the "*carcajada del ano*" (joke of the year), Castro paraded the eight captured survivors from the C-47 before television cameras while playing tapes of Morgan's radio dialogues with Abbes.[31]

The Castro government made Morgan a Cuban "citizen by birth" and promised to protect him.[32] The Associated Press wrote that he had obtained "almost legendary stature" on the island. Morgan further bolstered his reputation when he handed over to the Cuban government seventy-eight thousand dollars that he had received from the Dominican consul, asking that the money be invested in economic development in the Escambray region.

When Morgan walked along the streets of Havana, people reached out to touch him; there was even a popular song celebrating his exploits.

★ ★ ★

On the afternoon of March 4, 1960, longshoremen were hours into unloading 7.5 tons of arms and ammunition from the French freighter *Le Coubre* in Havana harbor, the bulk being Belgian-made Fusil Automatique Lèger (FAL) rifles consigned to Castro's armories. In sight of the ship was the United States Interests Section, a squat edifice of plywood facing and an about-to-be-torn-down look. The building was hastily constructed after the rupture of relations and was now covered with pro-revolutionary graffiti. This symbol of American presence in Cuba was apparently as shabby inside as it was outside, according to an FBI agent posted there as legal attaché.[33]

Suddenly the bell towers of the Hotel Nacional de Cuba shuddered in a blast as *Le Coubre* exploded outward, according to accounts of witnesses who felt waves of heat as far away as a mile from the ship.[34] A huge black nimbus arose from shattered holds. It is estimated that seventy-five were killed and over two hundred wounded. Fidel, driving his town car, heard the blast on the Malecon. He sped to the scene and angrily pointed a finger at the United States. The odds are long against the cause being sponta- neous or accidental. But if it was deliberate, who did it?

On April 23, 1974, I interviewed Gerry Patrick Hemming, one of a number of paramilitary volunteers in Castro's rebel army who deserted when the army shifted to the left. Hemming recalled that he was in the harbor area, and about three hours before the blast, he spotted William Morgan with a few of his men coming off the vessel, carrying as many rifles as they could. He told me that when he ran to the vessel after the explosion, he again encountered Morgan, perhaps the most recklessly ambitious of the genre, dockside wearing his gold-plated .45. At the time, Morgan was in Castro's favor after pulling off the elaborate political sting against Trujillo. Hemming and Morgan both drew their handguns as Fidel Castro screeched to a halt on the dock in his town sedan. "Your shot or mine?" Morgan asked Hemming. But the moment passed, and both holstered. Both Hemming and Morgan had participated in Castro's military missions, and Hemming was in the process of quitting because he saw Fidel's politics swinging to the left.

At the time of the *Le Coubre* incident, Morgan was still the leader of Prío's Second National Front of the Escambray and was secretly trying to organize the agricultural oligarchies of central Cuba's Las Villas Province region of ranchers, cattlemen, and sugar producers, known as the Texas of Cuba, into a fighting force to spring surprise on the rebel army. He even ran a frog farm as cover. Did *Le Coubre*'s cargo figure in another attempt to overthrow the Castro regime? Or did the CIA callously destroy it in line with Dulles's plan to deprive Cuba of weapons? In any case, William Morgan appears to be a chief suspect due to his own skill set and fitting the profile of method, motive, and opportunity.

From the dock, Castro hustled to the nearby studios of Cuba's flagship TV station CMQ. Preempting programming, he instinctively blamed the CIA, or a CIA affiliate. If Morgan's mission was to destroy weapons consigned to Castro, he was acting in a CIA capacity. If he was providing a large punctuation mark to the Agency's campaign of destruction and terror to drive Cuba into submission, he was with the CIA. Not even if it was an abortive attempt to rip off arms for Morgan's private army, which was partly subsidized by the Agency for the Bay of Pigs invasion tentatively set for one year, would the Agency be out of the picture.

The results of forensic testing on *Le Coubre* after the blast were inconclusive. In Washington, the CIA denied any knowledge of the ship's fate. The detonation of *Le Coubre* foreshadowed the start of the electoral season. Eisenhower finally gave his approval of Richard Nixon as the Republican nominee while John F. Kennedy won a cliffhanger for the Democratic nod. What emerged as a prime issue in the campaign was "the Cuba thing." It became a contest as to who was more militant on the subject.

★ ★ ★

Morgan's double-dealing and anti-communist stance began to tell against him.[35] On October 21, 1960, Morgan was charged with conspiring against the regime. As General Escalante put it, he was arrested as he tried to organize—for the CIA—a band of counterrevolutionaries in the Escambray Mountains for the purpose of providing support for an invasion that was planned for the following months.[36] The Bay of Pigs invasion, which went on the CIA's drawing board during the Eisenhower administration, originally called for guerilla actions, and this was apparently to be Morgan's role. The chief witness against him was a youth he had selected as his chauffeur who delivered weapons to the Second Front in the Escambray, the same units he had duped during the Trujillo affair. Morgan also used his frog-farm trucks as transport.

Morgan was imprisoned at La Cabaña while awaiting trial. He spent much of his time trying to break free. He studied the design of La Cabaña and the routine of the guards, looking for a flaw in the system. "Morgan had all kinds of escape plots," another prisoner later told the CIA.[37] Morgan worked to regain his strength. A press attaché at the US Embassy later wrote, "Up at dawn, he would put himself through calisthenics, then march around the compound, shouting commands at himself."[38] An inmate who had given Morgan painkillers recalled, "He exercised like an athlete and marched like a soldier." Morgan turned increasingly toward his Catholic faith. He wore a rosary and often prayed.

Hiram González, a twenty-four-year-old revolutionary who had been arrested for conspiring against the regime, had just arrived at La Cabaña, and watched in despair as prisoners were taken out and killed by firing squads, while birds swooped down to "peck at the bits of bone, blood, and flesh."[39] Morgan, he recalls, tried to cheer him up, offering his mattress. When Morgan found him crying in a corner, he went to him and said, "*Chico*, men don't cry." Gonzalez replied, "At times like this, I'm not a man." Morgan put his hand on his shoulder. "If it helps your suffering, then it's OK." Morgan walked him around the prison yard until he felt better. "He was the only one to help," González recalls.

Two days later, on March 9, 1961, guards seized Morgan and escorted him across the compound to a room where a military tribunal was being held. Along the way, Morgan, trying to summon courage, murmured song lyrics to himself: "Over hill, over dale, we have hit the dusty trail / And those caissons go rolling along."[40]

There were eleven other defendants at the tribunal, including some tried in absentia. A few weeks earlier, Che Guevara had published an essay denouncing members of the Second Front. "Revolutions, accelerated radical social changes, are made of circumstances," he wrote.[41] "They are made of passions, of man's fight for social vindication, and are never perfect." The mistake of the Cuban Revolution, Guevara argued, was its accommodation of men like the Second Front commanders. "By their presence, they showed us our sin—the sin of compromise . . . in the face of the actual or potential traitor, in the face of those weak in spirit, in the face of the coward." He went on, "Revolutionary conduct is the mirror of revolutionary faith, and when someone calls himself a revolutionary and does not act as one, he can be nothing more than heretical. Let them hang together."

At the trial, Morgan was charged with conspiracy and treason. Later, Fabian Escalante, who served for many years as the head of Cuban counterintelligence, detailed the case against Morgan, claiming that he had been a longtime American intelligence operative—a "chameleon"—who, in 1960, had attempted to "organize, for the CIA, a band of counterrevolutionaries in the Escambray."[42]

At the tribunal, Morgan complained that his lawyer had only just learned of the charges against him. A prisoner who shared his imprisonment with Morgan recalled, "The whole prison was agog with the news that Morgan was actually going to stand trial. Not even the most zealous of the young rebels believed that Fidel Castro would shoot this man, who had played such a big role in the Cuban Revolution."[43]

Morgan denied that he had ever been a foreign agent and said, "I have defended this revolution because I believed in it."[44] He explained, "If I am found guilty, I will walk to the execution wall with no escort, with moral strength, and with a clear conscience."

The trial lasted little more than a day. A defendant's fate was usually signaled by which room he was taken to before the verdict. "If you went to the right, you went into a *copiea*, a little chapel-like room, and you knew you were going to get shot," a prisoner recalled.[45] "For most prisoners, if you went to the left, you got thirty years." Most of the defendants were led to the left. Morgan was led to the right and condemned to die the next day.

An American radio broadcaster at the trial told his listeners that he had witnessed "a farce."[46]

On the night of March 13, 1961, as Fidel clinked glasses at a reception in the new Chinese Embassy, Morgan was marched to a wall in the Moat of Laurels in La Cabaña Fortress and shot.

★ ★ ★

As a footnote to history, Morgan's Cuban wife, Olga Maria Rodriguez Farinas, was also a revolutionary. She was tried with him in absentia, found guilty of co-conspiracy, and sentenced to thirty years in prison. Rodriguez was released after twelve years, and she left for the United States during the Mariel boatlift. In a series of interviews with the *Toledo Blade* in 2002, she admitted that she and her husband had begun running guns to anti-Castro guerrillas because he was disenchanted by Castro's pro-Soviet leanings. She also said she wanted Morgan's US citizenship restored and his remains returned to the United States for reburial. The newspaper stories prompted two Democratic members of the United States House of Representatives, Charlie Rangel and Marcy Kaptur, to travel to Cuba in April 2002 to meet Fidel Castro and ask him to return Morgan's body. Castro agreed.

In April 2007, the US State Department declared that Morgan's US citizenship was effectively restored, nearly fifty years after the government stripped him of his rights in 1959 for serving in a foreign country's military.

★ ★ ★

According to the extensive *New Yorker* profile from writer David Grann, Morgan was only the second non-Cuban to earn the title of Comandante—the other being Che Guevara. As reported by the *Hollywood Reporter*, George Clooney and his producing partner, Grant Heslov, have optioned the article, "The Yankee Comandante," to produce as a directorial project for Clooney.[47] It will make an interesting movie because Morgan was a complicated figure—one in the middle of three governments, trying to stay alive during brutal fighting, though fatally flawed by his ambitions.

CHAPTER TEN

THE BEAST OF THE CARIBBEAN

"THE DEPARTMENT OF STATE INCREAS-
INGLY VIEWED THE DOMINICAN TYRANT
AS AN EMBARRASSMENT, AN AWKWARD
INHERITANCE FROM AN EARLIER TIME, NOW
LINGERING TOO LONG, IMPERILING THE
FUTURE AND UNWITTINGLY PREPARING THE
WAY FOR CASTROISM."
—ROBERT D. CRASSWELLER, *TRUJILLO,
THE LIFE AND TIMES OF A CARIBBEAN DICTATOR*, 1966

Rafael Trujillo hated Castro with a Latin passion. Castro had joined the Caribbean Legion in 1947, formed by advocates of democratic countries who felt Trujillo should be ousted for his crimes and civil-rights violations. Trujillo's Dominican regulars routed the ill-trained Legionnaires, but Trujillo never forgot Castro's dramatic escape. He swam a marathon distance through pods of sharks to reach the safety of a Cuban frigate that, in the Latin context, humiliated Trujillo. The general had never thought highly of Batista, considering him weak-kneed, but he absolutely detested Castro as a cultivator of the rabble and a menace to the Caribbean status quo; in his lexicon, a communist. The Dominican *jefe* had watched Batista's deconstruction with alarm. In April 1958 he delivered five plane-loads of weapons to the Cuban army, and in December, as Batista's plight worsened precipitously, he offered to land two thousand Dominican troops in the Oriente Province and two thousand more in the Santa Clara area, where the Second Front was dug in. But Batista summarily rejected the offer, saying he didn't deal with dictators.

In 1959, "the Benefactor," as Trujillo called himself, was at the peak of his power, the Caribbean's most formidable rainmaker, the possessor of its most potent armed forces. At age sixty-eight, he had the look of a wary trout and the scruples of an alley fighter. His paternal grandfather had been an officer in the Spanish secret police, and he himself had once commanded the Dominican national police. He was a comic-opera dictator, doting on gaudy uniforms and medals, and it was said that he never broke a sweat as he stood in the blazing sun for the pomp and circumstance. But he was distinctly unfunny. For three decades, he ruthlessly crushed opposition, and his torture chambers were infamous. As former US ambassador John B. Martin wrote, "Tortures to obtain confessions or satisfy sadism became bestial—naked prisoners were shocked in an electric chair; a prodder, an electrified metal rod used on cattle in stockyards, was applied to their genitals."[1] Trujillo was aptly called "the Beast of the Caribbean."

Nevertheless, Trujillo devoutly wished to be accepted and supported by the United States, and his grip on the American mainland was tight. He contracted with the International News Service in New York to publish fiction about what a nice place the Dominican Republic was,[2] to counter unfavorable newsbreaks, and he employed a public-relations firm fronted by society columnist Igor Cassini. He was the poster boy of the Cholly Nickerbocker column that was syndicated across the country. He laid out untold millions trying to influence politicians and decision makers. According to Arturo Espaillat, he drew up "price lists for the purchase of US Congressmen," with key committee chairmen running from $50,000 to $75,000.[3] Conflicted senators like Strom Thurmond, James Eastland, and George Smathers rose like robots to his defense. Blackmail was one of Trujillo's lesser vices. "Sometimes, when dignitaries from the United States visited the Republic," Martin disclosed, "his agents provided them with women and then secretly photographed them."[4] Everything he touched, he corrupted, but his "virtues" of anti-communism, merciless law and order, and name-your-price dealing endeared him to many an American policy setter. One of Trujillo's biggest fans was Vice President Nixon, who in 1955 ignored the dictator's odious reputation by showing up as his guest at the grand opening of the showpiece International Center in Santo Domingo. Nixon was so in the thrall of Trujillo that he even brought his wife, Pat, whom he rarely took anywhere. The germ of this cynical love-fest was a commodity that was sweetening the kitty of members of the US Congress: sugar. In the Caribbean, sugar was king and the royalties were substantial.

At this point, Rafael Trujillo's days were numbered. The Eisenhower administration was worried by his increasingly bizarre behavior in the wake of the Cuban-invasion fiasco. In February 1960 Venezuela had asked the Organization of American States (OAS) to censure Trujillo for "flagrant violations of human rights," and he retaliated by dispatching Johnny Abbes, the head of his secret police, to Caracas to arrange a car bombing that narrowly missed killing President Rómulo Betancourt.[5] Fearing that Trujillo's excesses would open the door to a Dominican counterpart of Fidel Castro, the OAS voted sanctions against his regime in August of that year. Several Latin American countries broke diplomatic relations with Ciudad Trujillo, and the United States felt compelled to follow suit.

Running a diplomatic leper colony rankled Trujillo, so he perversely negotiated a nonaggression pact with Cuba and made overtures to the Soviet Union. The threat of a new power alignment in the Caribbean alarmed Washington. As Robert D. Crassweller wrote in his 1966 biography *Trujillo*, "The Department of State increasingly viewed the Dominican tyrant as an embarrassment, an awkward inheritance from an earlier time, now lingering too long, imperiling the future and unwittingly preparing the way for Castroism."[6] Bucking State, however, was the powerful sugar lobby in Congress. Since 1934, the United States had subsidized raw sugar on the premise that it was necessary to pay more to ensure a steady supply. Although proponents of this system argued that it aided underdeveloped countries, the subsidies—paid for by consumers in the form of higher prices—were distributed by the sugar corporations more in the interest of profit maximization than social needs. Under Batista, Cuba was allotted the highest quota, leaving the bulk of Dominican cane to be sold to British brokers at the lower world-market price. Nevertheless, Dominican producers turned handsome margins because Trujillo kept the cost of labor low.

During the summer of 1960, Trujillo partisans in Washington waged a vigorous campaign to assign the lion's share of the Cuban quota, which had been cancelled after Castro took over, to the Dom Rep. Harold Cooley, who as chairman of the House Agricultural Committee reigned as sugar czar, made several expenses-paid junkets to visit Trujillo and was favorably disposed toward the Dominican bid. It was accepted, and Dominican exports doubled.

But by early fall, the Eisenhower administration, which by that time had committed to overthrowing Castro, reluctantly concluded that Trujillo had to be replaced for the sake of political balance. "It's certain that the American public won't condemn Castro until we have moved against Trujillo,"[7] Ike is quoted as telling Secretary of State Christian Herter by Bernard Diederich in his 1978 *Trujillo: The Death of the Goat*. The White House approved covert aid to Dominican dissidents and a contingency plan to be implemented if the situation kept deteriorating. According to a 1974 Senate Intelligence Committee report, the plan provided that the United States take political action to remove Trujillo from the Dominican Republic as soon as a suitable successor regime can be induced to take over.

But first it would try to coax him out. In November 1960, Rafael Trujillo, wearing his green, bemedaled generalissimo's uniform, squatted silently on a couch in the National Palace, blinking froglike at his two guests.[8] Normally Trujillo exuded cordiality when his old friend William Pawley came to call. For some time the American had been a financial advisor, drafting Dominican legislation on foreign investments and arranging the awards of mineral concessions. The two would have an animated conversation over snifters of brandy. But this time Trujillo had been tipped off that Pawley was not coming to discuss business matters.

Pawley, attired in the white linen suit and planter's hat he reserved for meetings in the tropics, brought with him Charles "Bebe" Rebozo, the close-mouthed, wavy-haired Cuban American who was Richard Nixon's boon companion and business front, as a proxy for the vice president.[9] Finally, the general broke his silence by inviting Rebozo to sit next to him, a rare honor intended to symbolize his warm feelings toward Nixon.

As Trujillo was aware, Pawley, who had been Eisenhower's ambassador sans portfolio in trying to convince Batista to abdicate, was there representing the president and vice president to persuade him to step down. In my November 1973 interview, Pawley told me that Trujillo reacted badly.

"What's the matter with me?" he snapped when Pawley delicately broached the subject. The dictator protested that he was the best friend the United States had in the Caribbean, and a staunch anti-communist to boot. When Pawley soothingly proposed that he might retire to a farm in America, Trujillo snorted, "The only way I'll ever leave is when they carry me out of here dead." He had no way of knowing how prophetic his words could be.

The last thing Washington wanted was for leftist factions to fill any vacuum left by Trujillo's downfall, as happened in the Cuba experience. So Ambassador Joseph Farland established contact with a dissident group regarded as moderately conservative and pro-American. At a cocktail party when one member of the group asked Farland for rifles with telescopic sights, it was clear that assassination was on their minds.[10] Farland relayed the request to the CIA's Western Hemisphere Division chief, Colonel J. C. King. King responded to Farland's proposal by querying State whether it would okay "sniper rifles or other devices for the removal of key Trujillo people from the scene."[11] The answer was yes.

Fortunately, the Agency had an assassination plan for Trujillo, named EMOTH, already underway.[12] The dissident group had requested ex-FBI agents to carry out the assassination; first with cameras fitted with hidden guns, then a slow-acting lethal poison that could be transmitted to Trujillo in a handshake, then fragmentation grenades. But shortly after Pawley's futile November mission, the plot assumed its final form. The dictator would be killed by an action group led by Brigadier General Juan Tomas Diaz, whom Trujillo had forced into early retirement; General Antonio Imbert; and Antonio de la Maza, the revenge-minded brother of a pilot who was ordered killed by Trujillo because he knew too much about a kidnap-murder of an American civilian.[13] A provisional government recognized by the United States would take over until elections could be held.

The EMOTH conspirators planned to gun down Trujillo in the apartment of his mistress.[14] They asked for automatic weapons on the excuse that a firefight might erupt, but in fact they wanted tangible proof that the United States stood behind the coup. The CIA broke down the weapons and packed them in specially marked food cans consigned to a Cuidad Trujillo supermarket owned by Lorenzo "Wimpy" Perry, an American who had once trained Dominican pilots. Perry delivered the cans to the EMOTH group. But Washington still had not given final approval. Ironically, Trujillo had received a temporary reprieve by John Kennedy's election victory. Kennedy advisor Adolph Berle was chairman of the giant Sucrest Corporation and a Trujillo partisan. Vice President Lyndon Johnson's attorney crony, Abe Fortas, was a Sucrest director. Ellsworth Bunker, a roving diplomat, was a past president of National Sugar Refining Corporation. All represented substantial investments in the Dom Rep, and they began to form a consensus that Trujillo might be redeemable after all.

The CIA informed the new president that some weapons had already been turned over to the conspirators and that it was prepared, if authorized, to transfer machine guns and grenades to their station in Cuidad Trujillo. The Agency refrained from making any recommendations as to whether to proceed; the ball was tossed to the White House. On May 29, 1961, Kennedy ordered the CIA to pull out of the conspiracy, "We must not run the risk of US association with political assassination since the US as matter of general policy cannot condone assassinations."[15]

On May 30, 1961, Trujillo's thirty-one-year rule ended as he was being driven down the seaside highway en route to a rendezvous with his mistress. His car was overtaken and forced to stop. Trujillo died fighting back.

In the Dom Rep, army loyalists clamped a news blackout on the capital as they searched for the conspirators. The State Department got wind of the assassination and relayed the news to JFK, who was in Paris meeting with Charles de Gaulle. There, Pierre Salinger casually mentioned Trujillo's demise during a press conference. It was the world's first notice that the dictator was dead.

Salinger's gaffe caused severe headaches in Washington; the news from Paris implied that the United States had advance knowledge of the assassination. "If people think we did anything to Trujillo," fretted Dean Rusk, "they might look at this as a license to go after Kennedy."[16]

Ramfis Trujillo, son of Rafael Trujillo, also happened to be in Paris. He reacted to the news of his father's death by chartering a commercial jet on the family credit card to return home. Upon landing, he had all the known conspirators run down and executed. At the White House, an over-eager presidential assistant named Richard Goodwin, who had supported EMOTH, was twisted in knots by the fact that the old regime survived. "He danced around the White House, demanding that we get Allen Dulles on the line and call out the fleet," an aide to George McBundy recalled.[17] "He was ready to send in the Marines! Fortunately cooler heads prevailed."

The American entrepreneur Perry, whose market had been used as the weapons terminal, was safely secreted out of the Dom Rep. If the younger Trujillo knew of the CIA connection to his father's murder, he saw no need to make a public issue of it. His father was gone, and the country was his.[18]

CHAPTER ELEVEN

LA BATALLA DE GIRÓN

"DURING THE EARLY HOURS OF 15 APRIL [1961] . . . WE DID NOT SLEEP. ALL THE SIGNS FROM ONE MOMENT TO ANOTHER WERE THAT THE INVASION WAS GOING TO TAKE PLACE. WE WERE ON GUARD."
—FIDEL CASTRO, SPEECH, APRIL 23, 1961

William Pawley set out to duplicate his feat in the overthrow of the Árbenz government in Guatemala by engineering an invasion of Cuba. He told me that it was his idea, but it was shared by Allen Dulles: "It is difficult to say who originally conceived the idea. . . . It may have been an almost-spontaneous thought of a number of people, including myself."[1] But Pawley took credit for helping convince Ike that Castro was a communist and rousing him to action. "I had several conferences with the president," the old Flying Tiger told me, "and finally he was convinced that the anti-communist Cubans in Florida should be armed and given every assistance to overthrow the communist regime." It was not an easy sell, primarily because Ike, who had survived a heart attack and a stroke, was not easily energized. By this late stage in his presidency, Eisenhower "had lost his enthusiasm for political battles at home and [the] cold war clashed abroad,"[2] writes Leonard Mosley, the biographer of Allen Dulles, "and his aides at the White House who sometimes caught him with a faraway look in his eyes soon learned that what he was thinking about was golf." Eisenhower soon approved the CIA plan titled "A Program of Covert Action against the Castro Regime" without any oversight other than to rush it along as fast as possible so he would be credited with the overthrow of Castro before he left office. The Agency assigned Richard M. Bissell to lead the project and E. Howard Hunt to coordinate.

Hunt was the consummate spook, so into tradecraft that he wrote spy novels on the side. He was just in from Uruguay, where his mugwumpery had irritated Ike himself. Nor was he held in the highest esteem by Dick Bissell, who remembered that just before the Guatemalan overthrow, Hunt had taken exile leaders, whose presence in Miami was supposed to be a secret, on a nightclub binge that nearly blew their cover. But he was a member of that winning team in Guatemala that in CIA lore achieved Super Bowl status. This was enough for Bissell's deputy, Tracy Barnes, to bring him in. Barnes dispatched Hunt to Havana to size up the situation, where he reported back that a popular uprising coincident with the invasion was not in the cards. But Hunt had a recommendation: assassinate Fidel Castro so his armed forces "would collapse in leaderless confusion."[3]

Nixon's top advisors had also hoped that the invasion would take place during Eisenhower's term in office. One advisor afterwards said that Nixon thought "it would have been a cinch to win" if the Eisenhower administration could destroy Castro before the voters went to the polls. Herbert G. Klein, who was at the time Nixon's press secretary, provided a revealing glimpse inside the campaign in a *San Diego Union* story on March 25, 1962: "From the start of the 1960 campaign many of us were convinced that Cuba could be the deciding issue in a close election. Certainly, in retrospect, it was one of the decisive factors in what was the closest presidential election of modern history."

What effect the Cuba issue had on the election is impossible to say. Certainly the Nixon camp thought Kennedy had blundered when he publicly called for the arming of exiles in the United States and attempted to capitalize on it. By the same token, Kennedy's strident stand may have won him converts among Cold War intransigents and those with a special interest in Cuba. On the night of the election, the Miami Cuban section erupted in joy.

It remained to be seen whether the president-elect would deliver on his campaign promise regarding Cuba, and the CIA plan seemed paralyzed by suspense. Uneasy, E. Howard Hunt went to Washington to try to find out what direction the project was taking. "Don't worry, boychick," he says Frank Bender reassured him.[4] "Bissell's well plugged into the Kennedy team. In a few days, after Bissell and Dulles have briefed Kennedy, it'll be full speed ahead."

On November 18, Bissell and Dulles flew to Palm Beach for that briefing about the full-scale invasion on the drawing board. Kennedy gave them a qualified go-ahead.

★ ★ ★

It was decided that no Americans would be recruited for the invasion at the Bay of Pigs, known as La Batalla de Girón in Latin America. It would have a decidedly Latin theme. "There will not be a white face on the beach," Bill Pawley and others declared.[5] The entire effort was supposed to be financed and executed by a group of rich Cuban exiles trying to get back their expropriated properties, or so the CIA would have everyone believe. It occurred to Pawley that certain South American countries might furnish troops to back up the main invasion force.

With Ike's blessing, Pawley and his wife, posing as tourists, traveled first to Argentina. When he was the US ambassador to Peru shortly after World War II, Pawley came to know Argentine president Arturo Frondizi well. The secret mission got off to an inauspicious start at the Buenos Aires airport, when he bumped into Roy Rubottom, there to greet another passenger. "Why Ambassador," the surprised Rubottom fumbled, "what are you doing here?"[6]

Pawley let the question hang as he hustled off to see Frondizi. He told this author that he played on the Russian scare that was prevalent at the time, with arms shipments from the Soviet Union that were creating "a military capability far larger than any army in Latin America."[7] He proposed that Argentina commit a shipload of troops to reinforce the invasion brigade. Pawley told me that Frondizi was enthusiastically receptive, saying, "You tell me how much and where. This is the first time the United States has used excellent judgment in dealing with a secret problem. You speak Spanish and come here incognito."[8] Pawley explained that for security reasons, no advance details could be given: the Argentine ship would have to stand off the Cuban coast at a designated time and place to await instructions from the invasion command.

Then Pawley hopped over the Andes to Peru, where he anticipated no trouble in swaying President Mario Prado. On December 8, only a few days before his arrival, anti-Castro Cubans raided the Cuban Embassy in Lima and pilfered a letter supposedly "proving" that Cuba was forwarding Soviet funds to the Peruvian Communist Party to finance a revolt. Relations between Lima and Havana were ruptured. Prado readily agreed to send a shipload of marines under the same conditions as Argentina.

Recruitment never reached the 1,400 combat troops needed, as determined by Pawley, and the invasion force mustered in Guatemala could not be readied in time to meet Ike's deadline. Pawley blamed foot-dragging in the State Department, notably on the part of Rubottom and Wieland, who harbored reservations over the repercussions such aggression would cause. But bad weather and internal bickering by the two factions in the training camps in Guatemala, one belonging to E. Howard Hunt and the other to Manuel Antonio de Varona, prime minister of Cuba under Prío, contributed to the downfall. Varona and Hunt had been at odds from the very beginning. Hunt presented himself as representing an international business group eager to recoup its lost Cuban properties. Varona saw through that farrago immediately and told Hunt that the CIA was too parsimonious in dispensing money for his counterrevolutionary operations in Cuba. They remained at loggerheads throughout the entire fiasco.

★ ★ ★

The denouement of the Bay of Pigs invasion force could have come straight out of *Saturday Night Live*. A key consideration in the plan was the makeup of the provisional government that would succeed Castro. The CIA had pulled together several exile groups under an umbrella organization called the Democratic Revolutionary Front (FRD), set up as the government in exile. The project chief, Richard M. Bissell, wanted moderate exile leaders like Jose Miro Cardona, first prime minister in the Castro government, and Prío's minister of education, Aureliano Sanchez Arango, to head the plan. But Nixon, one of the hands-on planners in the Cuba Project, had a conservative authoritarian in mind. Mario Kohly, a designate of the right-wing senator from Maine, Owen Brewster, was Nixon's choice to free Cuba from Castro's iron grip. The CIA had written off Kohly as a pompous blowhard whose only allegiance was to himself. But with Nixon touting him as a red-hot prospect to lead the Cubans, the Agency was compelled to hold a round of talks with him. Kohly was finally nixed by Bissell, who saw him as an ultraright loose cannon working at cross-purposes with what the CIA had in mind. To assuage Nixon, Bissell offered to include Kohly in the FRD. Kohly bristled at the idea, labeling the FRD moderates as "left-of-center Castroites."[9] In the end, the CIA determined that the invasion would be led by Antonio Varona, former prime minister and a senator at the time Castro appeared on the horizon, and Manuel Artime, the wealthy owner of a meatpacking company in Nicaragua and leader of the Movement for the Recovery of the Revolution (MRR) in Cuba.

★ ★ ★

The plan included many components. One was the creation of a responsible and unified Cuban opposition to the Castro regime located outside of Cuba. After Fidel Castro assumed power in Cuba in 1959, many Cubans emigrated in protest of the communist regime. Many of these immigrants chose Miami as their new home. As a result, Miami gained a certain magnetism to future Cuban immigrants wishing to settle in a land other than Cuba.

The next in importance was the creation and development of a covert intelligence and action organization within Cuba that would respond to the orders and directions of the exile opposition. As the invasion plans evolved, it had been assumed that the underground in Cuba, loosely coalesced under the Unidad Revolucionaria (UR) would be activated. An outbreak of sabotage, some of it strategic and some psychological to lend the appearance of having the upper hand in the cities, would be a valuable supplement to the advance of the invasion brigade. But for security reasons only a few of the UR leaders were told about the invasion.[10] The rest were proceeding on the assumption that they were in for some kind of protracted war of attrition and guerilla warfare that Castro had employed so successfully against Batista.

The UR was a creature of the CIA, and the Agency called the shots.

In the fall of 1960, Rafael Diaz Hanscom, the intelligence officer inside Artime's MRR in Cuba, slipped over to Florida and began two months of intensive CIA training. According to journalist Jay Mallin, Hanscom "was entrusted with a highly important mission," after which he returned to Cuba.[11] Traveling around the island at a frantic pace, he succeeded in gathering more than two dozen groups of varying size under the UR umbrella, although he did not reveal that the CIA was controlling it. In this fashion, the Agency consolidated its hold on the Cuban underground. "Once Castro was overthrown and victory achieved," Mallin states, "the CIA could pick Cuba's new leaders and determine the political path they were to take." For its part, the CIA would provide weapons and equipment as well as financial backing.

The final part of the invasion plan was the development of a paramilitary force outside of Cuba for future guerrilla action.[12] This last task also came under the purview of the CIA. The Agency established Point Mary in the Florida Everglades as the training center for the anti-Castro coalition forces in early 1960. The CIA recruits were paid $400 a month to train, with an additional allotment of $175 to support their wives, and more for their children. The Point Mary facility was under the direction of Johnny Rosselli, a suave Los Angeles representative of the Chicago Syndicate and a lieutenant of Meyer Lansky. Rosselli and John V. Martino, a slots mechanic working for Santos Trafficante, ran training for the paramilitaries and orchestrated clandestine operations. They got their kicks out of driving speedboats procured by the CIA through the latticework of waterways at high speeds.

The curriculum at Point Mary included sharpshooting, sabotage, small-boat handling, interrogation techniques, and communications. It also served as a launching point for incursions. At an inlet to the Gulf Stream was a fleet of speedboats for raids and infiltrations. An army specialist, Bradley Ayers, disclosed to Frank Sturgis that Johnny Rosselli worked closely with the chief of operations at the Miami CIA station JM/WAVE, David Sanchez Morales.[13] According to Ayers, they took the edge off the evening by downing martinis and barbequing steaks. They were an odd couple: the congenial mobster and the brooding spook.

★ ★ ★

By the time Kennedy took office in January 1961, he had already made serious commitments to the Cuban exiles, promising to oppose communism at every opportunity and supporting the overthrow of Castro.[14]

Eisenhower, Kennedy, and other high-ranking US officials continually denied any plans to attack Cuba, but as early as October 31, 1960, Cuban foreign minister Raúl Roa, in a session at the UN General Assembly, was able to provide details on the recruitment and training of the Cuban exiles, whom he referred to as mercenaries and counterrevolutionaries.

The original plan called for a daytime landing at Trinidad, a city on the southern coast of Cuba near the Escambray Mountains. A paratroop battalion was in training at a sugar plantation at San Jose Buena Vista, between Retalhulea and Guatemala City. The paratroopers would touch off the invasion by seizing the airfield at Santa Clara, north of Trinidad, and fanning out to cut road and communication lines. Seaborne diversions would be staged at Havana and near Santiago, in the hope of freezing the Castro troops concentrated in those areas. An Anzio-type landing would then take place in Trinidad, with the beachhead perimeter gradually expanded. Reinforcements would then be brought in by airlift to Santa Clara and Trinidad. Theoretically, the invasion Brigade 2506, using the membership number of Carlos (Carlyle) Rafael Santana Estevez, who had died in a training accident in September 1960, would then be able to march west and east, picking up recruits as it went.

But Kennedy thought the plan exposed the role of the United States too openly, and he suggested a nighttime landing at the Bay of Pigs, which offered a suitable airstrip on the beach from which bombing raids could be operated. Once the bay was secured, the provisional Cuban government-in-arms set up by the CIA would be landed and immediately recognized by the US as the island's legitimate government. They would then hold the beachhead for at least seventy-two hours. This was a critical element of the plan because it would allow the government-in-exile to be converted to a government-in-arms. Under international law, this new government would formally request military support, and a new "intervention" would take place. And due to a secret arrangement with Bill Pawley, that provisional government would be furnished with millions of dollars in further pursuit of Castro's overthrow.[15]

In his book *Reflections of a Cold War Warrior: From Yalta to the Bay of Pigs*, Richard M. Bissell writes, "It is hard to believe in retrospect that the president and his advisers felt the plans for a large-scale, complicated military operation that had been ongoing for more than a year could be reworked in four days and still offer a high likelihood of success. It is equally amazing that we in the agency agreed so readily."[16]

A nighttime amphibious landing (which, according to Bissell had only been accomplished successfully once in World War II) diminished the possibility that a mass uprising would be able to join the invading forces. In addition, the new location made it practically impossible to retreat into the Escambray Mountains.

The plan, however, seemed to breed what Néstor T. Carbonell describes in the book *And the Russians Stayed: The Sovietization of Cuba* as infectious optimism. "Castro's fledgling air force was to be destroyed prior to the invasion," he writes. "Enemy troops, trucks, and tanks would not be able to reach the brigade; they would be blasted from the air. To allay any fears of a Castro counteroffensive, the CIA briefer asserted that 'an umbrella' above would at all times guard the entire operation against any Castro fighter planes that might remain operational."[17]

Once Kennedy came to accept the plan, opposition to the invasion was subtly discouraged. Various memos and notes kept from meetings prior to the invasion warned of potential problems and legal ramifications. At a meeting on January 28, the chairman of the Joint Chiefs of Staff spoke strongly against invasion on the grounds that Castro's forces were already too strong. At the same meeting, the secretary of defense estimated that all the covert measures planned against Castro, including propaganda, sabotage, political action, and the planned invasion, would not produce "the agreed national goal of overthrowing Castro."[18]

On March 29, Senator J. William Fulbright gave Kennedy a memo stating that "to give this activity even covert support is of a piece with the hypocrisy and cynicism for which the United States is constantly denouncing the Soviet Union in the United Nations and elsewhere. This point will not be lost on the rest of the world—nor on our own consciences."[19]

A three-page memo from Under Secretary of State Chester B. Bowles to Secretary of State Dean Rusk on March 31 argued strongly against the invasion, citing moral and legal grounds. By supporting this operation, he wrote, "we would be deliberately violating the fundamental obligations we assumed in the Act of Bogota establishing the Organization of American States."[20]

At a meeting on April 4 in a small conference room at the State Department, Senator Fulbright verbally opposed the plan, as described by Arthur Schlesinger in the Pulitzer Prize–winning book *A Thousand Days*: "Fulbright, speaking in an emphatic and incredulous way, denounced the whole idea. The operation, he said, was wildly out of proportion to the threat. It would compromise our moral position in the world and make it impossible for us to protest treaty violations by the Communists. He gave a brave, old-fashioned American speech, honorable, sensible and strong; and he left everyone in the room, except me and perhaps the President, wholly unmoved."[21] In June 1967, I interviewed the senator from Arkansas (at his request to deal with the problem of CIA interference with his Fulbright scholars), and he confirmed the gist of this meeting.

Some ten days before the invasion, Colonel Jack Hawkins, the CIA commander of the Brigade's training camp in Guatemala, took aside the leaders, "Pepe" Perez San Román, Erneido Oliva, and Manuel Artime. There were "forces in the administration," he confided, that were trying to block the invasion.[22] Should a red light come from Washington, the Brigade was to take its American advisors prisoner, station an armed guard at each of the doors, sever communication with the outside, and continue training. Hawkins said that he would give the word, even though a prisoner, on when and how to get to their launch point, and that the American advisors would give them "the whole plan." Although stunned, the Cubans agreed. They assumed Hawkins was speaking for his superiors, for there was no way they could get to the launch point in Nicaragua without CIA assistance.

This desperate measure proved unnecessary, however. It was indeed true that Kennedy was uneasy, and that several aides had counseled against going forward. But in the end, the president was swayed by the CIA's optimistic hucksterism and by the glowing report of a personal emissary in whom he had complete confidence. The emissary, a Marine colonel with combat experience detached to the CIA, had been sent to Guatemala to appraise the Brigade. In early April, he cabled Kennedy: "My observations have increased my confidence in the ability of this force to accomplish not only initial combat missions, but also the ultimate objective, the overthrow of Castro."[23] The colonel spoke of the "fanatical urge" of the Brigade to join battle, and of their "supreme confidence" of winning. The dispatch ended, "I share their confidence." Kennedy was convinced.

Five days before D-Day, on April 12, Kennedy held his weekly press conference. Adolph Eichmann had gone on trial in Jerusalem after being kidnapped from Argentina. Major Yuri Gagarin of the Soviet Union had rocketed into space in the Vostok and become the first human to orbit the earth. The Pathet Lao guerrillas were routing the CIA-backed royalists in Laos. But the first question from the press corps was about intervention in Cuba. The president answered in his best Boston patois, "I want to say that there will not be, under any conditions, an intervention in Cuba by the United States Armed Forces. This government will do everything it possibly can. . . . I think it can meet its responsibilities, to make sure that there are no Americans involved in any actions inside Cuba. . . . The basic issue in Cuba is not one between the United States and Cuba. It is between the Cubans themselves."[24]

★ ★ ★

Stockbrokers tend to be a clubby lot, and in Washington they have their own intelligence system, picking up advance notice of government decisions affecting the stock market. The loosening of credit, international pacts, and legislation favoring an industry group are the kinds of inside information that can be converted into an overnight profit.

After the Castro takeover, the stocks of sugar and molasses farms that depended on Cuban production became greatly depressed. A number of CIA personnel who knew about the impending invasion began buying up these cheap stocks in the expectation they would vault in price once

Castro was defeated.[25] Word spread to their friends that a flyer in sugar shares might prove a sweet gamble. As the buy orders proliferated, some brokers became curious and began probing sources in the Pentagon. But their curiosity remained unsatisfied, for military knowledge of the invasion was restricted to the highest levels. One astute broker hit on the idea of calling the manager of a mutual fund believed to service CIA investors. Sure enough, the fund had been bullish on sugar stocks. So the broker recommended sugar shares to his firm's clients, and a new wave of buying began. The stocks were inching upward with the pressure when the bubble burst on the beaches of the Bay of Pigs.

★ ★ ★

The counterrevolutionary Brigade 2506 was assembled at Retalhuleu, on the west coast of Guatemala, where US engineers refurbished the airport especially for the mission. From there they were transported to a CIA base in Puerto Cabezas, Nicaragua. Six ships sailed from Puerto Cabezas on April 14, cheered by Nicaraguan president and US-friendly dictator Luis Somoza, who jokingly urged the soldiers to bring him some hairs from Castro's beard.

The Cuban government knew an invasion was coming but could not guess exactly when or where the attack would take place. When teams of US B-26 bombers began attacking four Cuban airfields simultaneously on Saturday, April 15, rattling the populace but doing little military damage, the Cubans were prepared and the planes were driven off by antiaircraft fire. Castro later testified that the few planes belonging to the Cuban Air Force had been dispersed and camouflaged, with some obsolete, unusable planes left out to fool the attackers and draw the bombs.

When the Brigade planes bombed the airfields, UR leaders were caught by surprise. Arturo Villar, the intelligence chief of the organization, set up an emergency meeting with his MRR counterpart, one "Guillot." Villar recounted, "I asked him what was happening. He didn't know. He didn't know what we should do. In those days our groups were in touch with the CIA through telegraphy. The telegraph operator for the DRE group contacted the CIA and asked what was going on. The only reply he received was a stream of names of Cuban vegetables."[26] This was undoubtedly E. Howard Hunt at work creating disinformation messages that he hoped would throw off the G-2.

As part of the CIA cover story, the attacking B-26 planes were disguised to look as if they were Cuban planes flown by defecting Cubans. An exile Cuban pilot named Mario Zúñiga was presented to the media as a defector and photographed next to his plane. The photo was published in most of the major papers, but the surprising omission of several serious details, and the overwhelming amount of information already gathered by reporters, helped bring out the truth much sooner than anyone expected.

Shortly after the attack started, US ambassador to the United Nations Adlai Stevenson II flatly rejected Cuba's report of the attack, telling the General Assembly that the attacking planes were from the Cuban Air Force and presenting a copy of the photograph published in the newspapers. In the photo, the plane shown has an opaque nose, whereas the model of the B-26 planes used by the Cubans had a Plexiglas nose. Within a few hours, the truth was revealed, and Stevenson was extremely embarrassed to learn that Kennedy had referred to him as "my official liar."[27]

Before the operation began, CIA operatives were sent to Cuba to aid the invading forces. Their task was to blow up key bridges and perform other acts of terrorism that would make it appear as if the people of Cuba were joining the invasion. José Basulto was one of those operatives. He flew straight into Havana airport, posing as a student from Boston College coming home on vacation. Basulto was never told when the invasion would begin. He was surprised to hear the attack had started, and he didn't have time to get around to completing his assignment. Instead, he drove out to Guantanamo and jumped the fence into the US base.[28]

At this time, the invasion fleet had another forty hours to go before reaching Cuba. The CIA had planned two further air strikes to finish off the work done by the first one and to coincide with the landing of the invasion force.[29] But Kennedy cancelled any further air attacks because he was concerned about plausible deniability for his government in the court of world opinion.

The undermanned Brigade 2506 landed at the Bay of Pigs on April 17, 1961, after a team of frogmen went ashore and set up landing lights to guide the operation. The invading force consisted of 1,500 men divided into six battalions, with Manuel Artime as the political chief.

On the eve of their departure, the CIA instructors told the brigade, "It's going to be easy. All you have to do is turn left and go onto Havana."[30] But the Cuban security force knew that an invasion was imminent and was on high alert. Two battalions came ashore at Playa Girón, and one entered at Playa Larga. But the operation didn't go as smoothly as expected. Frogmen went ashore first to mark the landing areas. They mishandled the landing and began to exchange shots with a patrolling jeep, while intense firing began on both beaches long before any substantial forces were landed. The landing was also complicated by ignorance of razor-sharp coral reefs lying offshore, which delayed or destroyed several landing craft. Some of the landing-craft engines themselves failed, so that landing (Playa Girón) was spread over about six hours.[31]

This series of delays allowed the militia in the area to radio the news to Cuban armed forces soon after the first landing. Many Brigade paratroopers lost all their equipment in the drops because they were landing too close to swampy areas. The air support for the invasion was either turned back or shot down by antiaircraft fire and the Cuban Air Force. It is interesting to note that when the aerial combat at the beachhead began, the five Alabama National Guard B-26 flyers were hit by enemy fire and cartwheeled into the sea. These were the pilots recruited by Alex Carlson of Double-Chek Corporation, who gave their widows a phony story about crashing in a C-54 cargo plane over Venezuela.

The Cuban Air Force was also able to drive the invasion support ships far off shore so that they could not resupply the invasion force, leaving them stranded and fighting an overwhelming force.

★ ★ ★

On Monday, April 17, as the invasion was well underway, US Secretary of State Dean Rusk gave a press conference. "The American people are entitled to know whether we are intervening in Cuba or intend to do so in the future," he said.[32] "The answer to that question is no. What happens in Cuba is for the Cuban people to decide."

After Ambassador Stevenson became aware of the true facts, he was so outraged that he publicly urged Washington to stop the attack and avoid further embarrassment. Soviet ambassador Zorin said, "Cuba is not alone today. Among her most sincere friends the Soviet Union is to be found."[33]

At 12:15, on April 17, Kennedy received a letter from Khrushchev in which the Soviet leader stated: "It is a secret to no one that the armed bands invading this country were trained, equipped and armed in the United States of America. The planes which are bombing Cuban cities belong to the United States of America; the bombs they are dropping are being supplied by the American Government.

". . . It is still not late to avoid the irreparable. The government of the USA still has the possibility of not allowing the flame of war ignited by interventions in Cuba to grow into an incomparable conflagration.

"As far as the Soviet Union is concerned, there should be no mistake about our position: We will render the Cuban people and their government all necessary help to repel an armed attack on Cuba."[34]

The expected supporting air cover by the US Air Force never came. In a political environment full of posturing, threats, and confusion, Rusk advised Kennedy to back off, concluding that additional strikes would tilt international opinion too far against the United States.

"At about 9:30 PM on April 16," describes L. Fletcher Prouty in *The Secret Team: The CIA and Its Allies in Control of the United States and the World*, "Mr. McGeorge Bundy, Special Assistant to the President, telephoned the CIA's General C. P. Cabell to inform him that the air strikes the following dawn should not be launched until they could be conducted from a strip within the beachhead."[35]

Prouty, the first focal-point officer between the CIA and the Air Force for Clandestine Operations, quotes the report by General Maxwell Taylor, a member of the Kennedy-appointed Cuban Study Group: "From its inception the plan had been developed under the ground rule that it must retain a covert character, that is, it should include no action which, if revealed, could not be plausibly denied by the United States and should look to the world as an operation exclusively conducted by Cubans. This ground rule meant, among other things, that no U.S. military forces or individuals could take part in combat operations."[36]

★ ★ ★

In a desperate last-ditch effort to support the invasion, a limited air strike was approved on April 19, but it would not be enough, and four American pilots lost their lives that day. At 2:30 p.m., brigade commander "Pepe" Perez San Román ordered his radio operator to transmit a final message from Brigade 2506. "We have nothing left to fight with," San Román said, his voice breaking, "Am taking to the swamps. I cannot wait for you. Over and out."[37]

Without supplies or air cover, the invading forces fell. To them, the lack of air cover was a direct betrayal. In the end, 200 rebel soldiers were killed, and 1,197 others were captured.

"There's no question that the brigade members were competent, valiant, and committed in their efforts to salvage a rapidly deteriorating situation in a remote area," wrote Bissell.[38] "Most of them had no previous professional military training, yet they mounted an amphibious landing and conducted air operations in a manner that was a tribute to their bravery and dedication. They did not receive their due."

"The reality," wrote Arthur Schlesinger, "was that Fidel Castro turned out to be a far more formidable foe and in command of a far better organized regime than anyone had supposed. His patrols spotted the invasion at almost the first possible moment. His planes reacted with speed and vigor. His police eliminated any chance of sabotage or rebellion behind the lines. His soldiers stayed loyal and fought hard. He himself never panicked; and, if faults were chargeable to him, they were his overestimate of the strength of the invasion and undue caution in pressing the ground attack against the beachhead. His performance was impressive."[39]

On April 20, President Kennedy discussed Cuba before the American Society of Newspaper Editors and continued to deny US involvement.

"This was a struggle of Cuban patriots against a Cuban dictator. While we could not be expected to hide our sympathies, we made it repeatedly clear that the armed forces of this country would not intervene in any way.

"But let the record show that our restraint is not inexhaustible . . . if the nations of this hemisphere should fail to meet their commitments against outside communist penetration—then I want it clearly understood that this government will not hesitate in meeting its primary obligations which are to the security of our nation."[40]

★ ★ ★

One of the Brigade 2506 volunteers, Enrique "Harry" Ruiz-Williams, a graduate of the Colorado School of Mines, was geologist who at first aided and abetted Castro's units in the revolution, hauling equipment with his geology company as a front.[41] Harry turned against Castro when he perceived the revolution to be turning left. Ruiz-Williams was not one to cling to the middle, so he enlisted in Brigade 2506 and was assigned to the heavy-gun battalion in the invasion. When the outcome tipped in Castro's favor, he urged his comrades to keep fighting. "I want you to go to the front and make sure of your direction of fire," he told them, "because we are going to put in the history of Cuba how many men we killed today." Just then, a shell exploded at his side, riddling his body with shrapnel. His comrades left him in a cottage by the beach. On the second day after the fighting ended, Harry saw a familiar face in the doorframe. It was Fidel himself. Ruiz-Williams reached for a gun on the floor of the cottage, but Castro grabbed it first. "What did you intend to do with it?" he asked Harry. "Kill you," was the blunt reply. Ruiz-Williams was transported to a hospital, and two years later he was repatriated after Castro was promised medical aid for Cuba in exchange for his release.

★ ★ ★

An ancillary effort named Operation 40 was headed by Joaquin Sanjenis, a veteran CIA operative. This group had been established in March 1960 by President Eisenhower when he signed a National Security Council directive authorizing the anti-Cuban covert-action program whose premise was the creation of a responsible and unified opposition to the regime of Fidel Castro outside of Cuba.[42] Its mission was to go ashore in the wake of the invasion brigade strictly as a political force, then go to the population centers of Cuba and kill left-wing political leaders. This assassination effort was strongly supported in graphic terms by the political-action officer for the Cuba Project, which included Operation 40, none other than Dick Nixon.[43] The approximately ninety operatives for Operation 40 never made it to the beach because the brigade was beaten back.

CHAPTER TWELVE

KENNEDY GETS HIS IRISH UP

"THE AGENCY WAS NOT INVOLVED WITH [MAJOR ROLANDO] CUBELA IN A PLOT TO ASSASSINATE FIDEL CASTRO, NOR DID IT EVER ENCOURAGE HIM TO ATTEMPT SUCH AN ACT"

—CIA DIRECTOR RICHARD HELMS[1]

"**Y**ou blew it!" exclaimed the cantankerous Joseph Kennedy, patriarch of the Kennedy clan, greeting his son John after the Bay of Pigs debacle.[2] The scolding was administered at the Kennedy family compound in West Palm Beach, Florida, according to James Stevenson, the FBI agent in charge of the Cuba Desk at the time. As far as Joe was concerned, his son had placed his trust in the wrong hands. "I know that outfit," he ranted with reference to the CIA, "and I wouldn't pay them one hundred bucks a week."

For all practical purposes, the decision to make a second try at overthrowing Fidel Castro was made in that room that day. The Kennedys were too humiliated by the drubbing at what the Cubans now triumphantly alluded to in a single word: Girón. It was all too much for the brothers to take lying down, Bobby especially. They sought encouragement from the Nixon camp to try again. The day after the white flag went up, Tricia Nixon took a phone message for her father. "JFK called," she said. "I knew it wouldn't be long before he gets into trouble, and has to call on you for help." Nixon returned the call immediately.[3] "What would you do now to Cuba?" Kennedy got right to the point, and Nixon did likewise. "I'd find a proper legal cover and go in. There are several justifications that could be used like protection of American citizens living in Cuba and defending our base at Guantanamo." Kennedy was dubious. "If the United States grabbed Cuba, Khrushchev might grab Berlin."[4]

So the Kennedy brothers began a new phase of the Cuba Project called Operation Mongoose. As General Edward Lansdale, who was to lead this new beginning in cooperation with the CIA, described it, the Kennedys were obsessed with the idea of regime change. "Bobby felt even more strongly about it than Jack," Lansdale said.[5] "He was protective of his brother, and he felt his brother had been insulted at the Bay of Pigs. He felt the insult needed to be redressed rather quickly."

Operation Mongoose was a secret program of propaganda, psychological warfare, and sabotage against Cuba to remove the communists from power, which became a prime focus of the Kennedy administration, according to Harvard historian Jorge Domínguez.[6] A document from the US Department of State confirms that the project aimed to "help Cuba overthrow the Communist regime," including its leader Fidel Castro, and it aimed "for a revolt which can take place in Cuba by October 1962."[7]

Lansdale was chosen due to his experience with counterinsurgency in the Philippines during the Huk Rebellion,[8] and also due to his experience supporting the Diem regime in South Vietnam. Samuel Halpern, a CIA co-organizer, conveyed the breadth of involvement: "CIA and the US Army and military forces and Department of Commerce, and Immigration, Treasury, God knows who else—everybody was in Mongoose. It was a government-wide operation run out of Bobby Kennedy's office with Ed Lansdale as the mastermind."[9] Lansdale's idea was that the project "take a very different course" from the "harassment" operations of the past and try to crack the Castro regime from within.

With the support of Bobby Kennedy, Lansdale outlined the coordinated program of political, psychological, military, sabotage, and intelligence operations, as well as assassination attempts on key Cuban political leaders. Each month, a different method was in place to destabilize the communist regime, including the publishing of views against Fidel Castro, armaments for militant opposition groups, the establishment of guerilla bases throughout the country, and preparations for an October military intervention in Cuba. Plans to discredit Castro in the eyes of the Cuban public included contaminating his clothing with thallium salts that would make his trademark beard fall out, dosing his daily cigars with a depilatory for the same result, and spraying a broadcasting studio with hallucinogens before a televised speech.[10]

The first initiative came from the Commerce Department—the imposition of a commercial embargo.[11] Walter Rostow, an adviser on national security for the Kennedy team, was sent as an envoy to the North Atlantic Treaty Organization (NATO) to tell its allies that the United States would look favorably on the Western European governments if they stopped trading with Cuba. A number of Japanese and European companies, importers and exporters alike, were pressured to cut economic ties.

Historian Jorge Domínguez states that the scope of Mongoose included sabotage actions against a railway bridge, petroleum storage facilities, a molasses storage container, a petroleum refinery, a power plant, a sawmill, and a floating crane in a Cuban harbor. Domínguez states that "only once in [the] thousand pages of documentation did a US official raise something that resembled a faint moral objection to US government–sponsored terrorism."[12] Many assassination ideas were floated by the CIA during Operation Mongoose. The most infamous was the CIA's alleged plot to capitalize on Castro's well-known love of cigars by slipping into his supply a very real and lethal "exploding cigar."[13] While numerous sources state the exploding-cigar plot as fact, at least one source asserts it to be simply a myth, and another, mere supermarket-tabloid fodder. Another suggests that the story does have its origins in the CIA, but that it was never seriously proposed by them as a plot. Rather, the plot was made up by the CIA as an intentionally "silly" idea to feed to those questioning them about their plans for Castro, in order to deflect scrutiny from more serious areas of inquiry.[14]

Other plots to assassinate Castro that are ascribed to the CIA include poisoning his cigars (a box of the lethal smokes was actually prepared and delivered to Havana); planting exploding seashells at a scuba-diving site; giving the gift of a diving wetsuit impregnated with noxious bacteria and mold spores or with lethal chemical agents; infecting Castro's scuba regulator apparatus with tubercle bacillus (which causes tuberculosis); and dousing his handkerchiefs, his tea, and his coffee with other lethal bacteria. The US Senate's Church Committee of 1975 stated that it had confirmed at least eight separate CIA-run plots to assassinate Castro. Fabian Escalante, who was long tasked with protecting the life of Castro, contends that there have been 638 separate CIA assassination schemes or attempts on Castro's life.[15]

One plan involved the CIA's favorite inside man in Havana, Rolando Cubela. It was now two years after the revolution, and Rolando Cubela was still sulking.[16] It had been his unexpressed desire to snatch the presidency away from Castro as the Batista administration collapsed in January 1959. For his service to the revolution, the leader of the Student Revolutionary Directorate (DRE) had been promised a "high post" in the nascent government, as had Carlos Prío. Now he was certain that the top post promised by Castro wasn't that at all, but a deliberate slight. Actually, Cubela had been given a middling position in the diplomatic corps as the Cuban delegate to the International Federation of Students, which required his absence from Havana most of the time. But he made trips back to the capital, which gave him access to Castro. What Fidel didn't know was that Cubela's huge ego was gnawing away at his judgment. Given his temperamental makeup, it was perhaps inevitable that Cubela would seize the opportunity for payback. He had been cultivated by the CIA through a lifelong friend aligned with the American service. He was deemed a valuable resource by the Agency because of his access to Castro and freedom of movement. To make an appointment to see the president, all he had to do was pick up the phone and call Castro's aide, Juan Orta. And the more he sulked, the more he became determined to act. The Agency set up AMLASH, a plan to assassinate Fidel Castro using Cubela's close proximity to the Cuban leader.[17] The plan has been referred to as a "basically one-person Cubela operation." By March 1961, Cubela let it be known that he was ready to defect, but the operation was called off when it appeared that Cuban police were suspicious of Cubela. Operation Mongoose became the new platform for Cubela.

In July 1962, Cubela met with the CIA in Helsinki and agreed to stay in Cuba, since he "felt that if he could do something really significant for the creation of a new Cuba, he was interested in returning to carry on the fight there."[18]

The following month, however, Cubela refused to take a polygraph test, a standard request at the time for all anti-Castro assets at the Agency.[19] This led some to suggest that he was perhaps a double agent. A cable from CIA headquarters in August 1962 ordered "that no physical elimination missions be given directly to Cubela."[20] The Agency determined that it would be better for them and for the US government if Cuban dissidents began supplying Cubela with weapons, particularly the Belgian FAL rifle with a silencer that he had long requested. They decided that Manuel Artime was perfect for the operation. In 1964, a new plan, facilitated by E. Howard Hunt, was set in motion.

Cubela and Artime met several times in Madrid from December 1964 through early 1965 to discuss equipment and planning.[21] Cubela received a handgun with a silencer and a long-range rifle with a silencer and a scope. He took the devices back to Havana in his diplomatic pouch and began recruiting his coup cabal, but the operation was penetrated by a Cuban security double agent.[22] On June 23, 1965, the CIA sent out cables terminating all contacts with AMLASH (Cubela). It had become obvious that too many people knew about the project and the CIA's association.

In March 1966, Cubela was arrested, tried, and convicted, along with five others. He was sentenced to death by firing squad, but Castro, remembering their collegial days at the University of Havana, personally intervened to save him from execution and later sent him books to read in prison.

When he read about it in the *New York Times*, Secretary of State Dean Rusk asked CIA director Richard Helms what role the Agency might have played. "The Agency was not involved with Cubela in a plot to assassinate Fidel Castro," Helms responded, "nor did it ever encourage him to attempt such an act."[23]

★　★　★

Lansdale's master plan for Mongoose had proposed the use of "gangster elements" for attacks on "key leaders."[24] So the CIA's head of covert action in the late 1950s, William Harvey, a heavy-drinking, two-gun-toting, womanizing secret agent in the James Bond mode, reinforced his contacts with the Mafia, in particular with Johnny Rosselli, for the purpose of reactivating one of their classic assassination schemes, the poison capsule in Castro's food.[25] Harvey had ridden shotgun with Rosselli on earlier attempts to kill Castro, so their relationship was well-established. But Harvey didn't know his Cuban contact, who turned out to be the ubiquitous Tony Varona.

The plan took a while to get off the ground because the Agency decided to improve the poison capsules. Earlier versions had proved problematic. The laboratories were asked to produce some capsules that were easier to manipulate and would dissolve in any liquid.

In April 1962, the improved capsules were ready, but Varona was forced to rely on a CIA agent, a Spanish diplomat named Alejandro Vergara,[26] to get the capsules into Cuba, since the frequent flights between Miami and Havana no longer existed. Vergara agreed to carry them in the name of friendship. He arranged to meet with a member of Varona's insider group, Rescate, by the name of Alberto Cruz Caso. Rescate immediately met to study how they could carry out the plan. They decided to use their contacts at the Havana Libre Hotel. Caso and other members of the group met with some coconspirators who worked there, ultimately selecting two maître d's and a bartender. Rescate explained that the job was to take advantage of any opportunity when Fidel Castro appeared in the cafeteria of the hotel or any of the restaurants and add the poison capsules to his drink.[27]

During the balance of 1962, Castro went to the hotel several times, but apparently his visits never coincided with the working hours of the conspirators. One of them, Santos de la Caridad, carried out a ritual—every day he worked—of placing the capsules inside one of the tubes in the freezer of the cafeteria. In March 1963, Castro entered the cafeteria with some companions, sat down at a table, and ordered a milkshake. The barman on duty that day was Caridad. Seizing the opportunity, he began his preparations for the drink, then hurried to the freezer to retrieve the poison. But due to the effects of a higher refrigeration temperature that day, the capsules had frozen and stuck to the tube. In his efforts to work them loose, Caridad broke them and the poison spilled.[28] Castro had once more dodged a bullet with his incredible luck.

★ ★ ★

Operation Mongoose, as with the earlier Bay of Pigs invasion, is widely acknowledged as an American policy failure against Cuba. According to Noam Chomsky in 1989, Operation Mongoose "won the prize for the largest operation of international terrorism in the world."[29] According to Chomsky, it had a budget of $50 million per year, employing 2,500 people, including about 500 Americans, and still remained secret for fourteen years, from 1961 to 1975. It was revealed in part by the Church Commission in the US Senate and in part "by good investigative journalism." As Chomsky put it, "here is a terrorist operation that could trigger a nuclear conflict," because of operations during the Cuban missile crisis in 1962. He said that "it is possible that the operation is still ongoing [1989], but it certainly lasted throughout all the '70s."

CHAPTER THIRTEEN
THE HITS THAT MISSED

**"THE IMPORTANT THING TO KNOW ABOUT
ASSASSINATIONS IS NOT WHO FIRED THE
GUN, BUT WHO PAID FOR THE BULLETS."**
—ERIC AMBLER, *A COFFIN FOR DIMITRIOS*, 2001

The campaign against Castro had gone on longer than most people knew. On December 11, 1958, two days after William Pawley met with Batista, a blond, ruggedly handsome American stepped off a plane from Key West in Havana and registered at the Commodore Hotel as George R. Collins. His true name was Alan Nye, a naval reserve pilot from Miami who was covertly on the payroll of the Dominican Republic's president, Rafael Trujillo. Trujillo's technicians had customized a sniper rifle for him, and he was offered a $100,000 bounty to bring down Fidel. One of Castro's patrols intercepted Nye on his way up the Sierra Maestra Mountains. After he was captured, Nye was afforded a revolutionary trial and convicted. Castro ordered him released, and Nye returned to Chicago.[1]

Trujillo now went big, forming the Foreign Legion of the Caribbean to defend against Cuban attacks. Interestingly, one of his volunteers was Felix Rodriguez, whose uncle had been Batista's finance minister and who himself had been educated in an exclusive boarding school in Pennsylvania. Rodriguez went on to become a star spook for the CIA. His tour de force was the tracking of Che Guevara in the Bolivian jungle in 1968 that resulted in his capture and execution.[2] Che had struck out into the South American jungle in search of converts. The CIA was trying to corner him and his party, but Che traveled only at night. That gave the Agency a bright idea. The Mark Hurd Aerial Survey company, also based at the Santa Barbara airport, was doing aerial surveys for a new highway

153

in Bolivia. The Agency knew that Che's party emitted body heat, and the ovens they used for cooking emitted heat. The aerial survey planes tracked heat sources on infrared film. Each day, the film would be flown to Santa Barbara, processed, and mounted on a Hurd hangar wall, tracing Che's path through the Bolivian backcountry. At the ideal spot, the Che party was ambushed, and Che was killed on the orders of the CIA. Rodriguez celebrated the hit by lashing Che's body to a helicopter skid like a trophy animal and taking off.[3]

★ ★ ★

Under Trujillo's direction, Johnny Abbes set up several attempts on Castro's life in 1959. Abbes borrowed a swift cabin cruiser, the *Violynn III*, from an interested civilian and landed a squad of eight Dominican commandos on the Cuban shore in predawn darkness. Through a winter downpour, the commandos crept into position beside a road leading to a cemetery where Castro was due to officiate at a burial ceremony. As Castro's motorcade rolled past, a spotter, recognizing Castro's number-one bodyguard, Captain Alfredo Gamonal, gave the signal. Automatic arms fire raked Gamonal's jeep, killing him, the driver, and a local dignitary. But Castro, unaccountably riding in the next-to-last jeep, escaped unharmed. From that day forward, the Cuban leader went to elaborate lengths to avoid precise scheduling. Back in Cuidad Trujillo, Abbes told his aide, "He may have nine lives. But if so, I'll try a tenth time."[4]

Abbes wasted no time in trying again. Through an intermediary, he rented a downtown Havana apartment that overlooked the studios of television station CMQ, where Castro frequently delivered an impromptu speech to the nation. Then he propositioned a *yanqui* who was a former competition sharpshooter to squeeze the trigger for a $25,000 down payment and a cool $1 million upon scoring a clean hit. The rifleman insisted Abbes provide a bench-adjusted carbine with a telescopic sight and non-deflecting muzzle silencer. "Dominican ordnance experts immediately went to work to produce the rifle," recalled General Espaillat. "The weapon was completed and en route to Cuba when Trujillo cancelled the project. . . . He was afraid of Washington's fury. I really think that Fidel would be dead now if the plot had not been called off."[5]

★   ★   ★

In May 1959, a few weeks after Castro's return from his meeting with Nixon in Washington, DC, Frank Sturgis deserted Fidel's cause the instant agrarian reform was enacted.[6] Sturgis was a man of action, but a victim of impulse. One night in the lobby of the Havana Hilton, he spotted Fidel, ringed by bodyguards, talking with a beautiful woman. When the Castro party turned to leave, Sturgis approached the woman and in a low voice told her that he knew who she was, then advised her that he was with the American Embassy. The woman was Marita Lorenz, who met Castro onboard her father's cruise liner *Berlin*. When it docked in Havana harbor, a launch flying the revolutionary flag had pulled alongside the ship, and twenty armed *barbudos* ("bearded revolutionaries") in olive fatigues with hand grenades dangling from their belts boarded. Women in evening gowns and their dinner-jacketed husbands scurried into hiding, thinking it was a bandit raid. But their leader, obviously enjoying the commotion, shouted, "I am a friend. I like Americans."[7] It was Fidel Castro. "My father spoke Spanish and he got along well with Castro," Lorenz recalled to Paul Meskill of the *New York Daily News* (in "Secrets of the CIA," April 20, 1975). Her father took Castro and his men on a tour of the ship, but asked that the Cubans leave their guns outside before sitting down to dinner. Castro sat between the captain and his daughter and, before the meal was over, offered Marita a job as his secretary. She declined because she was planning to return to Germany to finish her education.

Two weeks later, when Lorenz arrived in New York aboard the *Berlin*, two Cuban officers sent her a message, saying that Castro was in desperate need of a translator, and urged her to take the job offered. A plane was standing by ready to take her to Havana. As Marita explained to Sturgis, "I made a big mistake, I got on that plane."[8]

Fidel occupied a suite in the Hilton, and Marita did some office tasks for him, then shortly became his mistress.[9] One day, when the premier was gone, his aides drove Marita to the prison on the Isle of Pines to show her the cell where Castro had been incarcerated years before. Once she was inside, they shut the door and locked her in. Apparently rumors had been sweeping Havana that the premier was keeping a foreign girl at the Hilton, and this was their way of keeping a lid on the story. After a week, Marita was brought back to the Hilton under virtual house arrest.

Sturgis heard of her predicament and approached her in hopes of recruiting an agent in close proximity to Castro.[10] He asked for her collaboration in return for help getting out of Cuba. Marita began reporting to Sturgis on conversations Castro had with visitors and stealing confidential documents. "Fidel had papers strewn all over," Lorenz recalled in conversation with Sturgis, "one filing cabinet was never locked. It was full of money, papers, documents and maps."

The romance ended soon and unhappily when Marita became pregnant, though not with Fidel's child.[11] With the American Embassy's help, she returned to New York. Sturgis, in concert with Alexander Rorke, a confidant of William Pawley, pressured her to return to Cuba armed with two poison capsules.[12] Her mission was to slip them into Castro's coffee. The plotters told her that the poison was odorless and tasteless and that Castro would die quickly. To the surprise of no one involved in these melodramatic attempts on Castro, the operation went wrong when Lorenz hid them in a jar of cold cream to avoid discovery at the airport. When she reunited with Castro at the Hilton, Marita dug the capsules out of the jar in the bathroom only to find them glutinous and greasy, in no state to be used in coffee. She flushed them down the toilet and subsequently returned to Miami the next day.[13] Fidel, unaware that Lorenz had betrayed him, lived on.

★ ★ ★

Poison capsules destined for Fidel became the chosen assassination scenario for a completely different group.[14] As part of the Bay of Pigs invasion planning, the CIA ordered an assassination attempt for Castro. Richard M. Bissell contacted the Mafia to handle the case, but had them coordinate with the Security Office, rather than with his office directly. An official of the Security Office, Jim O'Connell, was given the liaison job. He called in Robert Maheu, an old CIA collaborator and member of the FBI in his youth, because he knew that Maheu had an established relationship with the Mob. O'Connell asked him whom he would recommend for the job of killing Fidel Castro. Maheu recommended Johnny Rosselli. "Then we'll give him the job,"[15] replied O'Connell.

John Rosselli was linked to Sam Giancana, head of the Chicago Mafia, and Santos Trafficante of the Florida Mafia. In the 1950s, the three had used Cuba as a base and route for the drug trade, as an abortion center, and as a place for other illegal activities. Rosselli was linked to the labor unions and government officials in Cuba before and during the Batista administration. When Maheu asked him to take care of Castro, Rosselli asked who was behind the plot. Maheu replied that a US economic group that had suffered losses in Cuba was the sponsor. Rosselli demurred, "Well, if it isn't an official matter, I'm not going to offer my services."[16] Only when Maheu introduced the hit man to O'Connell did the operation get a green light.

After several meetings in New York and Miami between O'Connell, Rosselli, Giancana, and Trafficante, the Mafia was offered a contract of $50,000 for the hit.[17] Now the brainstorming began. Giancana suggested an ambush on a street corner in Havana, using a machine-gun to bring Castro down. The CIA accepted the idea and began looking for recruits in Cuba. But they soon realized that Castro's security system would make it impossible to pull off.

Rosselli suggested that the CIA had to develop a clever way to pull off the assassination and still give the assassin a minimum time to escape. Thus, the famous poison capsules came into play. The agency turned over the request to the head of their laboratories, Joseph Schreider, to prepare a suitable poison with the desired properties; it would kill but with a sufficiently delayed action to give the person administering it time to escape. In a few weeks, Schreider had new capsules ready in the form of little nylon bags which contained a synthetic botulism, a very active substance that dissolved only in cold liquids and only began to have an effect two to three hours after ingestion. The synthetic botulism would produce no symptomology of poisoning and also leave no traces. There was a significant problem with the capsules, however, in that handling them was dangerous. If the assassin touched them or didn't wash his hands well, he could be contaminated.[18]

Despite that caveat, and apparently throwing caution to the winds, Rosselli took the capsules to Florida in March 1961 to meet with Santos Trafficante, who arrived at the meeting with an unsmiling Cuban with close-cropped gray hair and sunglasses in his fifties.[19] This turned out to be Tony Varona, planner of the pending Bay of Pigs invasion and an old collaborator of the Florida Mob boss. Varona and the other planners of the invasion believed that if Castro was taken simultaneously, a leaderless nation would be more vulnerable to attack. So he was delighted to join the Rosselli/ Maheu plot. His counterrevolutionary organization in Cuba, Rescate, would take responsibility for the delivery of the capsule mission. At the meeting in Miami, Varona took possession of the poison capsules from Rosselli and $10,000 cash from Maheu. The CIA insisted that the action not be carried out until they gave the signal. This was to be their downfall.

At the end of March 1961, Varona called the Havana home of one of the Rescate leaders, Alberto Cruz Caso, and asked him to send a courier of absolute confidence to Miami.[20] The courier arrived quickly from Havana, since there were still flights every forty-five minutes at that time, and Varona gave him the capsules and complete instructions for Caso, explaining that timing was important due to the nature of the lethal botulism. It was critical that Castro's death would be attributed to natural causes, so the United States would not be implicated. Rescate began to look for the right time and place to carry out the mission, making arrangements with two of their cells; employees of casinos belonging to Trafficante and the Pekin Restaurant, occasionally patronized by Castro.

Members of Rescate continued making their arrangements with the understanding that they needed a go-ahead signal from Varona but unaware that the deadline for the invasion was approaching. A few days before D-Day, April 14, 1961, CIA officer E. Howard Hunt, who was in charge of security for Varona and the other five members of the provisional government for Cuba, became suspicious of one member, Manolo Rey, a Kennedy liberal. Hunt viewed Rey as embodying "Fidelism without

Fidel," which made him a security risk who might "inform the enemy" of the invasion details.[21] To preclude such treachery, Hunt proposed that all the provisional government members be summoned to New York on a pretext then told that invasion day was near and that "for personal and operational security those who wanted to learn the assault plans—and be flown to the beachhead—would have to agree to isolation from that time on."[22] So the six members were herded into the confines of the Lexington Hotel in New York City. From there, a blacked-out CIA plane flew the six men to the Opa-locka airfield near Miami, where they were held incommunicado awaiting the call to take off for the beachhead.

Varona could only pace back and forth inside the isolated hut. His Rescate hit squad was ready in Havana, where Castro was due to show up at the Pekin Restaurant on busy Twenty-Third Street at the target time. Santos Trafficante had an asset employed at the restaurant, actually the dishwasher. But the signal to activate the assassination could not be sent because Maheu couldn't reach Varona. It wouldn't have mattered in any event. Cuban G-2 General Fabian Escalante told me when we met in Rio de Janeiro, Brazil, that the order was never given, but even if it had been, the criminal plans of the would-be assassins would not have been successful.[23] Apparently, news of the upcoming invasion had leaked, but it was not known exactly where the landing would take place. Escalante said the G-2 had already taken the necessary precautions and the security of the head of the revolution was assured. The dishwasher was a double agent.

Around the middle of April, G-2 increased its arrests of Havana-based counterrevolutionaries. Several members of Rescate were detained, and the poison capsules apparently ended up in the toilet. A fitting end for such a tragic comedy.

★ ★ ★

Nixon had demonstrated his approval of assassination as a political tool; he never saw a proposal he didn't like. In October 1960, Nixon played golf with exiled leader Mario Garcia Kohly, who laid claim to having a formidable guerilla force inside Cuba. When he became an exile in 1959,

Kohly fell into the social set of Charles "Bebe" Rebozo and, ergo, Nixon. The proposal was nothing less than premeditated murder. According to an affidavit executed several years later by Kohly's son, during his golf game with Kohly, Nixon agreed "to the elimination of the leftist officials."[24]

Kohly fully expected that Nixon would be the next president of the United States, and he saw himself as the next president of Cuba. He bragged to Nixon that his organization was the de facto government of Cuba in exile, and that he had an invasion plan in place. It was a risky move for Nixon, since he was locked into a tight contest with JFK for the presidency. Kennedy had been using the Cuba situation on the campaign trail, saying that he would have treated Cuba very differently during the last years of the Batista regime, "but that now we must make clear our intention . . . to enforce the Monroe Doctrine . . . and that we will not be content till democracy is restored to Cuba. The forces fighting for freedom . . . in the mountains of Cuba should be sustained."[25] Nixon, of course, knew about the training of Cuban exiles underway, but he could not sound too vehement in defending the Eisenhower administration's role: "We must recognize that there is no 'quick and easy solution' to Castro's threat; but given the opportunity and time the people of Cuba will find their way back to freedom."

What Nixon seemed not to know was that Kohly was engaged in a counterfeiting operation that would flood the Cuban economy with $50 million of counterfeit pesos, bringing chaos to the financial markets.[26] It was, unfortunately, a sting operation set up by the CIA to discredit Kohly. An agent who said he wanted to help overthrow Castro for patriotic reasons contacted Kohly to provide assistance in getting the counterfeit peso plates engraved. He assured Kohly that it was perfectly legal to manufacture counterfeit Cuban money as long as it was used for the subversion of the Castro regime. The agent introduced him to "Bill Martin," an alleged printer who turned out to be a Secret Service special agent working undercover. Kohly was given the counterfeit-peso engraving plates that he was supposed to turn over to Bill Martin. When he met Martin in a hotel room in New York, Kohly was promptly arrested by the Secret Service and charged with conspiring to counterfeit Cuban currency. He was tried, convicted, and sentenced to two years in prison.[27]

Carlos Prío Socarrás. (*Libro De Cuba: Una Enciclopedia Ilustrada Que Abarca Las Artes, Las Letras, Las Ciencias, La Economia, La Politica, La Historia, La Docencia, y El Progreso General De La Nacion Cubana; Edicion Conmemorative del Cincuentenario de la Republica de Cuba, 1902–1952*)

Colonel Fulgencio Batista, Cuba's dictator, arrives in Washington, DC, and is met at Union Station by General Malin Craig, chief of staff of the United States Army, November 10, 1938. (*Photograph by Harris and Ewing, Prints & Photographs Division, Library of Congress, LC-H22-D-4912*)

General Dwight D. Eisenhower, the Republican nominee for president, at Washington National Airport with his running mate, Senator Richard M. Nixon of California, Nixon's family, and other well-wishers, September 10, 1952. (*Photograph by Abbie Rowe; Photographs and Other Graphic Materials, Audiovisual Collection, Collection HST-AVC; Harry S. Truman Library, Independence, Missouri [online version available through the Archival Research Catalog (ARC identifier 200395) at www.archives.gov; February 13, 2013])*

Hotel Nacional de Cuba, center of Meyer Lansky's gambling operation in Havana. *(Photograph by Jongleur100)*

Meyer Lansky, 1958. *(Photograph by Al Ravenna, New York World-Telegram and the Sun Newspaper Photograph Collection, Library of Congress, LC-USZ62-120718)*

William D. Pawley. *(Photographer unknown)*

Vice President Nixon and President Arturo Frondizi of Argentina in 1958. (From Los Nombres del Poder: Arturo Frondizi. Photographer unknown)

Castro meets the press on his arrival in Washington for his speaking tour and meeting with Vice President Nixon, April 15, 1959. (U.S. News & World Report Magazine Collection, Prints & Photographs Division, Library of Congress, LC-DIG-ppmsc-03256)

Fidel Castro greets Nixon in the Senate Office Building prior to their pivotal meeting in which Nixon's hostility turns the tide of Cuban-American relations. Castro planned to proffer a strategic alliance with the United States against the Soviets but put it back in his pocket when Nixon shamelessly humiliated him. (Copyright Bettmann/Corbis / AP Images)

Frank Sturgis. *(Photographer unknown)*

President Trujillo and Mrs. Trujillo host Eleanor Roosevelt in the Dominican Republic, March 7, 1934. *(Photographs and Other Graphic Materials; Franklin D. Roosevelt Library Public Domain Photographs, Collection FDR-PHOCO; Franklin D. Roosevelt Library, Hyde Park, New York [online version available through the Archival Research Catalog (ARC identified 195944) at www. archives.gov; February 13, 2013])*

William Alexander Morgan with the Second National Front of the Escambray in 1959. As Fidel Castro told this author, "Remember that Morgan in reality was always an official of the North American security forces." *(Copyright Associated Press)*

Gerry Patrick Hemming, leader of Interpen, at training base in No Name Key. *(Image courtesy of E. Carl McNabb)*

March 5, 1960, in Havana, Cuba. Fidel Castro *(far left)*, Che Guevara *(center)*, and Juan Almeida Bosque *(far right)* at a memorial service march for victims of the La Coubre explosion. *(From Museo Che Guevara (Centro de Estudios Che Guevara en La Habana, Cuba). Photographer unknown)*

December 1962, Miami, Florida. Address to the 2506 Cuban Invasion Brigade at the Orange Bowl. Mrs. Kennedy speaks informally with Brigade leaders Erneido Oliva, "Pepe" Perez San Román, Manuel Artime, former Cuban president Jose Miro Cardona, and others after the ceremonies. *(Cecil Stoughton, White House Photographs, John F. Kennedy Presidential Library and Museum, Boston)*

Manuel Artime (saluting), former Cuban president Jose Miro Cardona, President Kennedy, and Mrs. Kennedy in Miami, Florida, at the Orange Bowl. *(Cecil Stoughton, White House Photographs, John F. Kennedy Presidential Library and Museum, Boston)*

Nixon visiting the CIA building, March 7, 1969. *(Photograph by Robert L. Knudsen; Photographs and Other Graphic Materials, White House Photo Office Collection (Nixon Administration), Collection RN-WHPO; Richard Nixon Library, Yorba Linda, California [online version available through the Archival Research Catalog (ARC identifier 194612) at www .archives.gov; February 13, 2013])*

Juan Almeida Bosque wearing insignia of the 26th of July movement. *(From Diario Granma. Photographer unknown)*

FIDEL CASTRO

OPENING SPEECH

DISCOURS D'INAUGURATION

DISCURSO INAUGURAL

Program from Fidel Castro's speech addressing the 68th Conference of the Inter-Parliamentary Union, September 15, 1981. In the speech, Castro says, "William W. Turner, former agent of the Federal Bureau of Investigation, and journalist Warren Hinckle state that the United States used biological warfare against Cuba during the Nixon administration. According to them, Nixon's tricks included introduction of swine fever to destroy Cuba's swine population, atmospheric modification to bring about instant flooding to destroy crops. The authors argue that the CIA has committed the United States to a secret, undeclared and illegal war against Cuba for more than twenty years. The so-called Cuba project is the largest and least known of the projects operated by the CIA outside the legal limits of the statutes, they say. Biological warfare, murders and forgeries were elements tried by the CIA with varying degrees of success, according to Turner and Hinckle."(Fidel Castro: Opening Speech, *program issued at the delivery of Castro's speech to the 68th Conference of Inter-Parliamentary Union, September 15, 1981*)

This photo was taken at the Jockey Club on August 31, 1991, in Rio de Janeiro during a conference on the JFK assassination sponsored by the Supreme Court of the State of Rio de Janeiro. Presiding Justice Dr. Edaristo DaMoraes Filho opened the conference by stating, "We already know there was a conspiracy and it remains to find out who was involved." *Left to right*: John Newman, author of *Oswald and the CIA*; William Weyand Turner, author of *Deadly Secrets* and *The Cuban Connection*; Gaeton Fonzi, investigator for House Committee on Assassination and author of *The Last Investigation*; Wayne Smith, attaché to US Embassy, Havana; Arturo Rodriguez, sergeant, Cuban G2 Security. *(Author's photo)*

But Nixon stuck with him, as evidenced by the letter over his signature sent to the judge in the case, Edward Weinfeld, from his law firm, Nixon, Mudge, Rose, Guthrie, and Alexander. In the letter, he gives a personal commendation of Kohly's character and offers Kohly's patriotism as a reason for his actions. Nixon explains that "the complexities of United States policy toward the Castro regime . . . might well have created an atmosphere in which a person such as Kohly could honestly . . . believe that actions such as those for which he was convicted were not contrary to the interests of the United States."[28] Nixon asks the judge for "consideration of the defendant's application for suspension or reduction of the sentence imposed."

★　★　★

As the White House action officer in the war against Castro, Richard Nixon was a failure. Now in 1961, a superannuated Nixon had one more shot at success, in fact a double one. A lieutenant commander in the Office of Naval Intelligence (ONI) at the Guantanamo Naval Base who had known Nixon since World War II rallied to his cause and placed him in civilian charge of twin assassination plots scheduled for the revolutionary holiday of the 26th of July, barely three months after the Bay of Pigs.[29] Both Fidel and Raul Castro would be appearing in public on that day, Fidel in Havana, leading a celebration for Soviet space hero Yuri Gagarin; and Raul in Santiago, speaking at ceremonies marking the anniversary of the Moncada Barracks attack.

One of the assassins, Luis Balbuena, had long been under ONI control and was considered valuable because of his personal friendship with Fidel and Raul Castro. Balbuena, a thickset man called El Gordo ("the Fat One") had joined the 26th of July Movement in the struggle against Batista, but, as reported by a Miami police detective who interviewed him, "Early in 1959, he, with other top members of the revolution, started conspiring against the government. He was the contact between the US Naval Intelligence and the Oriente underground."[30] Balbuena was an elected official of an anti-Castro council of Cubans employed at Guantanamo Naval Base, promoting counterrevolutionary actions.

The second marksman was Alonzo Gonzales, about whom little is known other than that he was an Episcopalian priest who had designs on becoming bishop of Cuba once Castro was deposed. He claimed to have been trained at the CIA Academy in Virginia, known as the Farm. Balbuena admitted to a US Senate investigator that he had worked with Gonzales out of Guantanamo in 1961 and confirmed that the ambitious priest was proficient with firearms.[31]

Gonzales slipped out of Guantanamo, heading for Havana, but vanished without a trace. Balbuena told the Miami police that he "was involved in an attempt to assassinate Raul Castro," which was "discovered by the Cuban government," forcing him to take sanctuary inside the naval base.[32]

Two weeks after the 26th of July holiday passed without incident, Industry Minister Che Guevara read off a list of American aggressive acts against Cuba at the hemispheric nations' conference in Uruguay.[33] Among them was the charge that the United States had mounted an assassination attempt of Raul Castro (no mention was made of Fidel) from the Guantanamo Naval Base on July 26. Guevara said the plot was for the killing to be followed by a mortar shelling of the base, giving the impression that enraged Cubans were taking revenge for Raul's death at the hands of counterrevolutionaries. The shelling would give the United States a "clear-cut case" of Cuban aggression and provide a pretext for armed intervention—the old Guantanamo shell game.[34]

★ ★ ★

In September 1960, Fidel Castro journeyed to New York to attend the annual General Assembly of the United Nations.[35] The CIA apparently viewed this as an opportunity to do him in that would render all the other clandestine operations moot. Castro himself sensed the danger. After taking off from Havana, he asked his security chief, Ramiro Valdes, if a Cuban Air Force plane would escort them to New York. Valdes hadn't considered it. "If I was running the CIA," Castro remonstrated, "I'd shoot down this plane over water and report it was an accident."

While Castro bear-hugged Khrushchev and pumped the hand of Egypt's Abdal Nasser on the floor of the United Nations, the Agency was hosting a hospitality suite in the Waldorf-Astoria to entertain New York policemen assigned to protect the Cuban leader. As David Wise and Thomas B. Ross tell it in *The Espionage Establishment*, "Chief Inspector Michael J. Murphy wandered into the suite and was approached by a CIA man with a chilling story. The agency had a plan, the CIA man recounted casually, to plant a special box of cigars at a place where Castro would smoke one. When he did so, the agent said, the cigar would explode and blow his head off. Murphy, who could scarcely believe his ears, was appalled, since his responsibility was to protect Castro, not inter him. If the CIA man was pulling Murphy's leg, it was a shockingly foolish subject to joke about."[36] But, much worse yet, the agent seemed completely in earnest. This was obviously such a Rube Goldberg scheme that it is not surprising that it didn't work.

★ ★ ★

As one of the well-known "soldiers of fortune," in 1963 Ed Arthur was approached by Sam Benton, well-known in Miami as a commission broker for Cuban exile groups and coincidentally a former lieutenant for Mike McLaney at the Casino Internacional, for an assassination attempt on Castro.[37] He was taken to a mansion on the canal in Miami and interviewed by a swarthy businessman. He did not know whom he was meeting, but he did know that despite his desire to ouster Castro, he did not want to be involved in murder. So Ed declined the honor.

When I interviewed him in 1974, Arthur recognized a photograph of Mike McLaney as the swarthy man who had propositioned him. From his description I identified the location of the property and visited it on a trip to Miami. I went to the assessor's office and established the address for the property. When I visited the property, I spoke with the caretaker, and he identified the absent owner as Mike McLaney, ex-proprietor of the Hotel Nacional casino in Havana. The house was currently occupied by the ex-dictator of Venezuela, Perez Jimenez, and his mistress, Marita Lorenz, who had earlier been involved with Fidel Castro.[38] Perez Jimenez was later extradited to Venezuela for alleged crimes there. We can only assume that Lorenz moved on to greener pastures.

CHAPTER FOURTEEN

DECISIONS, DECISIONS: INVASION NO. 2

"VIOLENCE FIRST."

—Motto for the Cuban Student
Revolutionary Directorate (DRE)

After the Bay of Pigs failure, as the chief of the CIA Miami Division, Ted Shackley was in charge of the new second invasion, with Manuel Artime as field commander.[1] Artime had been a member of the provisional government of Cuba in the Bay of Pigs invasion. He was currently running an anti-Castro action group called the Second Naval Guerrilla ("Guerrilla," for short), based in Nicaragua, where strongman Luis Somoza was the beribboned honcho. The Guerrilla had been drilled at the CIA base Isolation Tropic in North Carolina.

Attorney General Robert Kennedy had made personal connections with Manuel Artime, including weekend skiing at a New Hampshire resort. The weekend wasn't just about skiing: it also concerned ways and means of getting rid of "that guy with the beard," as Bobby referred to Castro.[2] The result was that Artime was set up with a CIA retainer of $1,500 per month, and his Movimiento de Recuperación Revolucionaria (MRR), now based in Nicaragua, was slated to receive $250,000 a month to launch the Second Naval Guerrilla, aimed at Cuban shipping. Artime's requests and demands carried a whiff of blackmail, as he exploited the Kennedys' guilt over his time in prison after the Bay of Pigs.

It had been like old times in Little Havana.[3] Artime's regimental battle flag, a gold trident on blue, hung outside recruiting headquarters. Volunteers banged on the door, and Bay of Pigs veterans were sought out as war fever spread through the exile colony. Recruits holding field maneuvers proudly told quizzical Miami police they were "training for the next invasion of Cuba."

Arturo Rodriguez was a powerfully built man who liked his martinis. He was also a sergeant in the Cuban counterintelligence arm G-2 under General Escalante. I had a drink with Rodriguez in a bar in Rio de Janeiro, Brazil, over the 1991 Labor Day weekend. He said G-2 had infiltrated Artime's camp in Nicaragua, recorded his radio transmissions, and tapped the phones.[4] The plainclothes sergeant was bursting with pride as he told his story. The Somoza family had thrown the country open to units aiming for Castro. They operated out of Monkey Point, just south of Nicaragua's chief Caribbean port, Bluefields.

Rodriguez related that he managed to infiltrate the Monkey Point complex, tap telephones, and intercept some of the short-wave radio communications. Most were not encoded but composed in a deceptive way. The messages indicated that Artime intended to "double-up" the assassination of Fidel with the invasion.[5]

★ ★ ★

There was another effort in play to support Artime with an amphibious force sailing from the Dom Rep, landing in the east when Artime and the MRR landed on the south-side beaches. The leader of this invasion was Enrique "Harry" Ruiz-Williams, a personal favorite of Bobby Kennedy, who had been severely wounded at the Bay of Pigs. I interviewed Ruiz-Williams on November 28, 1973 in his Floralina Exploration Company office in Fort Lauderdale. I asked him why he was willing to risk getting his ass shot off. He retorted, "But I was also the red ass—I was mad at Castro and I also had a guilty complex [sic]."[6] In Cuba, Ruiz-Williams had remained passive during the debauchery of the Batista regime.

Ruiz-Williams was recruited by Attorney General Bobby Kennedy, who arranged for him to deal directly with Cyrus Vance, the undersecretary of the army, in working out the details for the training of volunteers in the Dom Rep and for the invasion.[7] In our interview, Harry pointed out the location of his base in the Dom Rep, at Montecristi in the northwestern part of the country. From there his expedition was supposed to shove off for a landing in the Oriente Province in eastern Cuba.

It became apparent that Bobby Kennedy was hands-on with the new plan to bring Castro down. Captain Bradley Ayers was an army ranger on detached duty to train the Cuban exiles. He recalled one evening in 1963 when he encountered RFK at a CIA base.[8] Ayers was there to train exile underwater demolition teams and was taken to a CIA base deep in the Everglades. He could sense something big was in the works when he was attracted by the flapping sound of helicopter rotor blades, a rare intrusion to the dead silence of the Everglades. The pilot landed the craft in a small clearing, illuminated by lanterns. On the door was a logo of the Palm Beach Helicopter Service. Two men emerged from a Quonset hut to board the helicopter. One was Gordon Campbell, the JM/WAVE (the major CIA station in Florida) deputy chief, and the other was Robert Kennedy, attorney general of the United States, who presumably had 'coptered over from the family compound at West Palm Beach. Kennedy grasped Ayer's hand firmly and wished him good luck on his mission. In a hut, Campbell spread out maps and charts, explaining that RFK had just given the go-ahead for Ayer's underwater demolition teams to blow up ships in Cuban harbors.[9]

This invasion effort was seriously endangered when a Swift Boat from Artime's attack vessel, the *Santa Maria*, disabled a Spanish flag ship, the *Sierra Aranzazu*, which they had mistakenly identified as the pride of the Cuban fleet.[10] They had poured a stream of fire into the ship until she went dead in the water, and they managed to kill three sailors, including the captain, and injure seventeen others. After an initial celebration, Artime was contacted with intelligence placing the *Santa Maria* far from the scene. He ordered the Swift Boat to take a closer look at the name of the ship and discovered its true identity. This incident caused such international repercussions that Artime had to fly to Madrid to try to placate Generalissimo Francisco Franco with a story naming Castro as the perpetrator of the incident. Franco didn't believe a word of his story.

★ ★ ★

After the Bay of Pigs invasion flopped, Pawley plotted on, his pocketbook still open to exile causes.[11] His pet action group was the Cuban Student

Revolutionary Directorate (DRE), the same outfit that Rolando Cubela hoped would be his vehicle to the Presidential Palace. The DRE had been founded in 1956 by Eddie Chibás, a volatile figure who struck a dramatic note in Cuban politics by committing suicide while on the air. From its inception, the motto of the DRE had been "Violence first." It was widely regarded as an unruly group of hotheads, and their action-oriented agenda attracted substantial funding from the CIA, although they didn't bow to agency supervision.[12] Among the many celebrities dropping coins into the DRE's tin cup in admiration of its violent proclivities was Claire Booth Luce, the wife of *Life* magazine publisher Henry Luce and a Nixon-appointed ambassador to Italy.[13]

In August 1962, two armed motorboats slipped under the Havana Bay radar screen, past two Czech-built patrol craft. Their target was the Hotel Icar on the water's edge in suburban Miramar. The DRE underground inside Cuba had reported that often on late Friday nights, Fidel Castro and high-ranking officials went there for drinks and dinner. If all went well, Fidel and the officials would die in the gunning. As members of the DRE drew into position on the flat waters of the bay, the crews could make out uniforms moving back and forth in front of the Icar's picture windows. They opened fire. A Czech physician strolling on the hotel grounds saw the tracer bullets coming. "Their marksmanship was poor and they were pretty far out," he later told newsmen.[14] "But soon pandemonium ensued. Guests in nightgowns raced through the hotel. Panic seemed more dangerous than the effect of the raid." The Icar was pockmarked with bullet holes, and its lobby was in shambles, but no one was seriously injured.

The pilot of one of the speedboats held a press session in New York, in which he identified himself as Mario Salvat of the DRE.[15] He claimed that the strike was the first of many the action group had planned for the future. The *New York Times* printed the story, and the DRE was on its way. The attack on the Icar could easily have been reported as a terrorist action, which would have been closer to the truth.

★ ★ ★

DRE was the most militant of the exile groups. The rambunctious DRE was acquiring weapons for an invasion of Cuba in conflict with the CIA's own plans to launch a second try.[16] Both were in violation of the Neutrality Act, which was under the jurisdiction of the FBI. The DRE's second invasion was privately funded, as opposed to the CIA/MRR effort headed by Artime. In November 1963, Ted Shackley, CIA chief in Miami, signaled headquarters that he disapproved of the DRE's invasion plan. For one thing, the plan called for a supply line too long for a covert operation, and for another, the DRE hotheads—who were on the agency payroll—were too unruly. But those were excuses: the actual reason was that the DRE stood to mess up the invasion plans of Artime and Ruiz-Williams, which didn't include the DRE. Shackley recommended red-lighting the DRE and cutting off its funds.[17]

The DRE was training and accumulating weapons out of a privately-owned resort property in Lake Pontchartrain, Louisiana, because the heat was on in Miami.[18] Unfortunately for them, the FBI was tipped about an arms cache at the property, and the subsequent raid netted more than a ton of dynamite, twenty 100-pound aerial bomb casings, fuses and striker assemblies, a 50-pound container of plastic explosives and materials to make napalm. FBI chief Harry Maynard announced the results of the raid to the newspapers but declined to say if arrests were imminent. This was not surprising, since the FBI had already released the men they grabbed at the raid when they realized they had stumbled on a CIA operation involving Cuban nationals. The released men included Sam Benton; John Kock Gene, a DRE officer from Miami; several of Gene's paramilitaries; Rich Lauchli, a bomb maker for the Minute Men; and Victor Espinosa Hernandez, an exile paymaster and childhood friend of Rolando Cubela.[19]

The resort property was owned by Bill McLaney, brother to Mike McLaney, the former operator of the Casino Internacional in Havana. The Cuban bombing campaign discovered at Lake Pontchartrain was apparently funded and supported by Mike McLaney.[20] After Castro closed the casinos in 1960, McLaney became the air marshal of a fleet of surplus B-26 light bombers in Florida. Coincidence or not, the original plans for the Bay of Pigs included five bomb raids on three refineries that were now processing Russian crude oil from the Baku region. Mike McLaney was all set to go when he received an urgent teletype from the Justice Department ordering him to call off the air strike. It turned out that the oil companies' executives had gotten wind of his intent and used their clout to preserve their facilities. They were sure Castro would not last long.

After the Bay of Pigs debacle, Mike McLaney submitted another plan to the Agency to firebomb oil refineries in Cuba because he believed that the destruction of these facilities would paralyze the Castro war machine in weeks.[21] Instead of getting his plan approved, McLaney received an urgent phone call warning him not to attempt such a thing under any circumstances. So he decided to ignore channels and set up his own campaign.

McLaney's contact with the exile action groups was Sam Benton. Tall, with horn-rimmed glasses offsetting sharp features and packing a pearl-handled revolver, he was a kind of commission broker to the groups. "Sam would never get near anything that might explode," McLaney told me. "He lined up actions, arranged to fund and supply them, and took a cut off the top." One Benton client was the Chicago-based Junta of the Government of Cuba in Exile (JGCE), headed by the shadowy Paulino Sierra Martinez, with Carlos Prío as its presidential designate. Sierra had been actively raising money for a Cuban invasion for several years, using a smokescreen by naming major national corporations. In fact, most of the funds came from the gambling syndicates eager to reopen in Havana, and from a conglomeration of private interests including McLaney.

★ ★ ★

The 30th of November Cuban exile group headed by Rolando "El Tigre" Masferrer was involved in an invasion attempt in 1963 that took some strange turns.[22] According to a memo from Detective Sergeant C. H. Sapp of the Miami Police force, Masferrer arrived in Miami in August 1963 with a group of approximately sixty Cuban exiles from the New York City area. They were supposed to be joined by approximately forty more Cubans from the Miami area. Some of these Cubans sold their homes, sold their belongings, and quit their jobs in order to finance the invasion and follow Masferrer to Miami, and ultimately Cuba.

Upon arriving in Miami, the group began preliminary training in guerilla warfare but soon came to the attention of the local authorities.[23] So Masferrer moved them to No Name Key for advanced training with Intercontinental Penetration Force, code name Interpen, a paramilitary group based in the Everglades. The training was more intense, but provisions were short, which created discontent among the exiles. Some of the Cubans grew tired of the delays and of being moved from place to place, so they began to pressure Masferrer about getting the invasion launched. He now told them that the original plans had been changed.

The original plan was for the group to make a commando raid on the northeast coast of Cuba, and then proceed to Manuel Artime's training camp in Nicaragua.[24] Now Masferrer informed them that they were to invade Haiti and overthrow the government of François "Papa Doc" Duvalier. With that accomplished, they could use Haiti as a jumping-off point to invade Cuba. The majority of the trainees were furious with this change in plans, so they defected from Masferrer's group and returned to Miami. Masferrer himself allegedly returned to New York City, taking a large amount of arms and ammunition with him.

After the Miami police raided a series of addresses in Miami (given to them by the Cuban defectors) that were supposed to be storage places for the supplies for the invasion and discovered nothing, they assumed that Masferrer had taken the materiel with him.[25] The police concluded that the entire operation was nothing more than a fraud perpetrated by Masferrer to obtain funds from the Cuban exiles for his own use.

CHAPTER FIFTEEN

THE *FLYING TIGER* AND THE PHONY RESCUE

"MARTINO . . . ASKED [LORAN] HALL IF HE
MIGHT BE INTERESTED IN SOMETHING
BIGGER THAN A RAID, BACKED BY 'PEOPLE'
FROM CHICAGO AND MIAMI."
—DAVID KAISER, HISTORIAN AND PROFESSOR,
NAVAL WAR COLLEGE[1]

In early 1963, almost two years after the disastrous Bay of Pigs mission, William Pawley was at the center of arguably one of the most bizarre episodes of the secret war, one that ended so tragically and mysteriously that he was very reluctant to discuss it with me in our 1974 interview.

The new mission began when a flamboyant anti-Castro fighter with the war name Eddie Bayo passed around exile circles a smuggled letter supposedly written by a cell inside Cuba. It stated that three Soviet missile technicians stationed on the island wanted to defect, offering to reveal the location of hidden offensive missiles in exchange. Frank Sturgis thought it was the genuine article, while Gerry Patrick Hemming urged caution: "The Russians might have made some remark about wanting to see the night life of Miami that was overinterpreted," he said.[2] "And it might be an elaborate trap."

As it was backdoored through Senator James O. Eastland, chairman of the Senate Internal Security Subcommittee and leading troglodyte of the era, the plan was for anti-Castro Cuban commandos to be smuggled into Cuba using Pawley's yacht, the *Flying Tiger*, to rescue the two Russian technicians.[3] The techs would then be transported to Eisenhower's estate in Gettysburg and exhibited at a press conference to embarrass Kennedy by proving that Soviet missiles were still located on Cuba. According to David Kaiser, historian and professor at the Naval War College, Nixon's friend Pawley "immediately recognized that this information would utterly discredit the Kennedy administration,"[4] thus helping Nixon's political future in the 1964 election.

It was beyond belief that people who were normally levelheaded could ring themselves in on a venture as wild as this one. But the overpowering hatred of Fidel could overcome one's common sense. In late February or early March 1963, an FBI memo reports that Pawley met with Richard Nixon and Charles "Bebe" Rebozo, just as Pawley was planning a new Cuban operation with Johnny Rosselli.[5] This was probably Nixon's attempt to secure inside information that could help in his quest for the White House. The question of whether all the Soviet missiles had been removed from Cuba was already a hot topic in Republican circles and would be a major issue for the 1964 presidential campaign. If Nixon had the inside story on Soviet missiles still in Cuba, he would have an edge over his Republican rivals.

For this operation, Pawley would be working closely with Rosselli and Trafficante's operative John Martino,[6] an electronics expert who had been imprisoned for transporting counterrevolutionaries out of Cuba and had been released from a Cuban prison only five months earlier. John Martino was extremely bitter over his imprisonment and what he felt were inadequate efforts by the Kennedy administration to win his release. A pilot who first met Rosselli in the late 1950s told the FBI that he flew into Tampa, where he met Rosselli, and then flew him and John Martino from Tampa to Rivera Beach, Florida. The pilot said that during the flight "he learned that one Ambassador Pawley . . . was trying to arrange a raid to remove (Soviet) missile technicians from Cuba."[7] He was under the impression that Pawley was organizing the raid through Rosselli and Martino.

Pawley was in radio contact with his good friend Marshall "Pat" Carter,[8] a CIA deputy director, who saw to it that there were three CIA men along for the ride, including Eugenio Martinez, the future Watergate burglar. The CIA's premier "boat man," Martinez had most recently been the chief pilot for the Operation Mongoose infiltration missions, and he would be the navigator and coastal guide for the invasion team.[9] Carter supplied weather data en route to Cuba. *Life* magazine got wind of the caper and paid $15,000 for a piece of the action, sending reporter Richard Billings along to document the story for later publication[10] The scenario sounded plausible to CIA officials and *Life* because thousands of Soviet technicians and troops remained in Cuba. Fidel had never allowed the UN weapons inspections, so there was no way to prove with absolute certainty that some missiles weren't hidden in caves or underground.[11]

The anti-Castro commandos were part of the anti-Castro network of paramilitaries, led by Eddie Bayo, named for a famous Spanish commando well known in counterrevolutionary circles. When the *Flying Tiger* reached the drop-off coordinates off Baracoa, Eddie Bayo asked Pawley for his watch, saying he would be back "the day after tomorrow."[12] His watch was a Rolex, identical to those issued to all CIA operatives. Pawley gave it to him and never got it back.

The team of ten armed Cuban exiles headed off toward Cuba without Eugenio Martinez, who wisely declined the mission at the last minute as Pawley watched from his yacht.[13] *Flying Tiger* waited for two days off Baracoa for Bayo and his men to return. At this point, Pawley radioed Miami and hired aerial surveillance to search for the missing men. After five days of fruitless searching, Pawley sadly ordered the *Flying Tiger* to set sail. The yacht returned to Pawley's home in Miami, carrying embarrassed CIA operatives, *Life* magazine staff, and John Martino, the man from the Mob.

But there was a strange twist to the *Flying Tiger* saga. I was contacted by Loran "Skip" Hall, head of the anti-Castro Committee to Free Cuba, who ran guns to Interpen in No Name Key. I interviewed Hall at the VA Hospital in Los Angeles in 1968. It was clear that he knew practically everyone linked to the anti-Castro activities in Florida. Hall said that in February 1963 he attended a meeting in Miami called by Santos Trafficante and Martino to exploit a legendary commando named Eddie Bayo. It turned out to be an assassination scheme. Sam Giancana, the Chicago Mafia capo, showed up and offered a $30,000 "prize" for killing Castro, and Trafficante pledged $15,000 in advance to Bayo for equipment. Most of the money was used to buy explosives and the components for electronic devices to detonate them from a distance. The kidnapping of Russian technicians was a con job to get the use of Pawley's yacht.

Apparently, all Bayo wanted the *Flying Tiger* for was a ride to Cuba with his equipment, with which he planned to "blow all to hell" buildings like the Ministry of Agriculture and the Presidential Palace—with the president in it.[14] It would be up to Martino, an electronics expert, to rig the explosive devices. It wasn't until I ran a story in Francis Ford Coppola's *City of San Francisco* magazine that I was able to correct the Pawley version of the *Flying Tiger* story. Hall was relieved that I took action on the information he provided, as most journalists wouldn't blow the whistle on the Mob. He had been slightly peeved with me because in a previous discussion he had in no uncertain terms advised that the Mafia was behind the death of John F. Kennedy and I had not acted.[15]

I asked Fabian Escalante, chief of the Cuban security agency G-2 at the time, about the ill-fated voyage. He said the only thing he knew about it was that the small shore boat from the *Flying Tiger* was found swamped near Baracoa.

Hall provided a conclusion of sorts to the Eddie Bayo saga.[16] He said that Bayo's brother-in-law, Luis Castillo, eventually received word from a source in Cuba that the Bayo group had been ambushed by Cuban militia after landing. Bayo and two of his men managed to get away and arrived in Havana, where they were captured and imprisoned in La Cabaña Fortress. The report seems credible because Castillo had once been a guard at La Cabaña. Hall claimed that he and several of the Interpen Cubans decided to break Bayo out of La Cabaña and blow up Castro while they were there. The mission of mercy came to an inglorious end when Customs agents stopped Hall near the Interpen base at No Name Key and seized his trailer full of munitions.

Pawley probably put the fiasco behind him, at least until he was sued by the Cuban commandos' families for negligence.[17] In 1987, I met with Rolando Salup in Havana.[18] Salup was Third Secretary to the Cuban United Nations Mission. During our lunch, I told him the *Flying Tiger* saga and asked him if he could find out about any survivors of the mission who had been captured. I requested their release on humanitarian grounds and mentioned that this would bring closure to the family members. Salup promised that he would look into it, but I never received any more information from him.

CHAPTER SIXTEEN

THE NAVY THAT NOBODY KNEW

"WE ARE INVESTIGATING THE FACTS IN THE CASE TO SEE WHETHER A US PROTEST WILL BE MADE ON THE BASIS OF THIS VIOLATION AND THE US OWNERSHIP OF THIS VESSEL. [J. LOUIS]"

—US State Department, Washington, DC,
October 1963

It might have been called "the Navy That Nobody Knew." Late one night in 1973, sitting in the back room of a small grocery store on Flagler Street in Miami's Little Havana, I heard a story that unlocked a Pandora's box of secrets of the recondite period following the abortive Bay of Pigs invasion. The narrator was a grizzled Cuban exile who, when I asked, gave the name "Pepe." His graphic account of the 1963 naval raid gone terribly wrong suggested that the Bay of Pigs two years earlier was merely the end of the beginning. After the debacle, the campaign had been stepped up, and it was to be capped by a second invasion by exile forces. But what Pepe had to say also revealed how close John and Robert Kennedy came to precipitating a second superpower crisis with the Soviet Union.[1]

On the night of October 21, 1963, Pepe was a crewmember of the disguised raider *Rex* when it launched a sabotage attack on a shore installation in Pinar del Rio Province. It was a CIA operation. Under a bare light bulb hanging from the ceiling, Pepe diagrammed that attack with a thick pencil on a brown paper grocery sack.

The *Rex* was not listed in *Jane's Fighting Ships*. It was a World War II subchaser pulled out of the mothball fleet at Green Cove Springs, Florida. Painted a classy dark blue, the 174-foot vessel could cut through the waves at twenty knots. It flew the blue-and-white flag of Nicaragua, whose strongman, General Luis Somoza, had hosted the Bay of Pigs invasion brigade. Registration papers showed that the owner was an oil company whose business was fueling cruise ships. In turn, the oil company leased it to a major defense contractor for electronic and oceanographic research.[2] There were oversized searchlights, elaborate electronic gear that towered amidships, and a large crane on the aft deck capable of raising or lowering twenty-foot speedboats.[3] When I asked Pepe what his position was on this impressive craft, he replied, "gunner's mate," the same rank he enjoyed in Batista's navy. He explained that after the *Rex* put to sea, its guns were brought up from below decks and secured in their topside mounts: two 40-mm. naval cannon, a 57-mm. recoilless rifle, and two 20-mm. cannon.

According to Pepe, the forty seamen—all Cubans—were paid $300 a month by the CIA, but their checks were drawn on the cover account of a commercial fisheries company. They were subjected to periodic polygraph tests to ensure their political loyalty. They lived at home, commuting to the secret war. When a mission was scheduled, they received a phone call, then a nondescript CIA van picked them up and took them to the West Palm Beach berth, where the *Rex* was tied up. The dockage fees were paid by a CIA front, Sea Key Shipping Company, which operated out of a postal box. When the *Rex* left port, it usually gave its destination as the Caicos Islands in the outer Bahamas, and when it returned it was "from the high seas." Customs and immigration clearances were waived.

On that October day in 1963, the vans deposited the crew at the berth in midafternoon. Captain Alejandro Brooks paced nervously on the bridge as he awaited the arrival of Gordon Campbell, the CIA's director of naval operations, to arrive with the orders for the night's mission. As the wait stretched into hours, Brooks had to twice admonish the crew, which was chattering loudly in Spanish, to quiet down. Only two months earlier, President Kennedy had become furious when he found out that the *Rex* had been at its West Palm Beach dock, just a stone's throw from the family compound, while he was vacationing there, because he apparently did not want evidence of CIA clandestine activities within his sight.

It was dusk when a black Cadillac pulled up and Campbell emerged. A tall man with a military bearing, he carried a soft leather briefcase up the gangplank and handed the captain a sealed packet. After Campbell disembarked, the *Rex* cast off, quickly cleared the harbor, and swung south. Its lights were completely blacked out.

At this point, Pepe's voice became edgy as he recalled Brooks opening the packet and reading the orders by flashlight. Normally Brooks stood off the Cuban shore a mile and a half and sent in landing parties by launch. But this night the orders were different and dangerous: go within a half mile of shore. The *Rex* slid by the bright lights of Miami and slowed to a crawl off isolated Elliott Key. Brooks strained to spot the rafts in the inky darkness: two black rubber rafts with six men each, wearing black clothes and black-stocking masks. The men belonged to the Commandos Mambises, named after the guerilla fighters in Cuba's war of liberation from Spain. The Mambises were the CIA's elite, the Green Berets of the secret war. They were led by Major Manuel Villafana, a spit-and-polish officer who had commanded the Bay of Pigs air force. Villafana insisted that his men be low paid because he wanted them driven by hate, not money.[4] The target on this mission was the giant Matahambre copper mine near Cape Corriente on the boot heel of Pinar del Rio Province. By blowing it up, the Mambises would put a substantial dent in the Cuban economy.

Pepe recounted that when the *Rex* arrived at the landing zone, there was a sense of foreboding; the Cape Corriente light, normally flashing its warning to marine traffic, was dark. But Brooks decided not to abort the mission. As the vessel came to a stop, two specially designed fiberglass speedboats, called Moppies, slid down high-speed davits on the afterdeck. The commandos clambered into them with backpacks full of C-4 explosives, and M3 Grease Guns slung over their shoulders. The Moppies stopped at the mouth of a river, where the Mambises inflated their rubber rafts, hopped in, and signaled ashore with an infrared blinker. They were supposed to link up with two commandos who had infiltrated a week earlier to reconnoiter the target. The answer came back in the wrong code; it was a trap. The commandos fired at the riverbank, only to be raked by return fire from heavy machine guns. One raft was torn apart by tracer bullets, spilling the dead and dying into the water. The remaining raft wheeled about and tried to reach the Moppies, but they had fled. The commandos then turned toward shore, where Castro's militia awaited them. When one of the escaping Moppies was framed in the searchlight of a Russian-built P-6 patrol craft, the *Rex* quartermaster piloting it surrendered. The other Moppie sped into international waters and was later rescued.

When Captain Brooks saw the firefight erupt, he ordered the *Rex* to turn tail and make a run for it. He was under standing orders to avoid capture at all costs. Pepe was now moving his pencil furiously over the grocery bag. Brooks made a feint toward the open sea, then doubled back and hugged the coastline, hoping to elude radar detection. The move paid off. Minutes later, a pair of Cuban helicopters made a beeline for the zone a mile and a half offshore, where the *Rex* ordinarily waited for the commandos to return. They dropped flares, illuminating a vast expanse of sea. Pepe's excitement rose as if he were reliving the moment. "As we cleared the head, I saw the running lights of a freighter," he said. "I knew right away what was going to happen. The freighter ran right into the light of the flares. The Cubans thought it was us and opened up on her."

The ship was the 32,500-ton *J. Louis*, flying a Liberian flag of convenience but owned by an American billionaire. It was carrying a cargo of bauxite from Jamaica to Texas. Five Cuban MiGs began strafing and rocket-launching runs. Aboard the *J. Louis*, Captain Gerhard Krause radioed an international distress call. At Key West, US Navy Phantom jets took off and headed for the scene. But just before arriving, the Phantoms were called back. Pepe could only guess why. The CIA base in Miami had a huge rhombic antenna that blanketed the Caribbean, and the controllers may have assumed from the jumble of radio traffic that it was actually the *Rex*, maintaining radio silence, that was under attack. If that was the case, the raider, which was "plausibly deniable" under its civilian cover, was expendable. Or the CIA controllers may have realized that the MiGs had the wrong vessel but wanted the attack to continue so that the *Rex* could slip away.

Escape it did. For more than an hour, the MiGs made fourteen passes on the *J. Louis*, and large-caliber bullets chewed holes in the deck and hull, then fire broke out in the forecastle and superstructure. Miraculously, none of the crew was injured. But in the meantime, the *Rex* slunk out of Cuban waters, breaking radio silence to report to the CIA command post that the Cubans had realized their mistake and had sent two gunboats in pursuit. "Do what you have to do," was the noncommittal response. Outgunned, Brooks opted to try a seventy-mile sprint for Mexican waters off Cozumel Island. He made it. For two more days, the gunboats played cat and mouse with the *Rex*, then withdrew. On October 26, the raider skulked into West Palm Beach, first making sure that JFK was not in residence.

While the sea chase was going on, the State Department seized the initiative by announcing, "We are investigating the facts in the case to see whether a US protest will be made on the basis of this violation and the US ownership of this vessel," referring to the *J. Louis*.[5] But it was not until the return of the *Rex* that official Washington knew that crewmen and commandos were missing in action. Two days later, the other shoe dropped when Fidel Castro appeared on Havana television to describe the *Rex*, right down to its distinguishing electronic gear and blue paint. To cap his act, Castro brought on stage two of the missing men, *Rex* quartermaster Luis Montero Carranzana, who had piloted a Moppie, and Dr. Clemente Inclan Werner, a Mambise. Both disclosed that they had been recruited by the CIA, Montero at $250 a month and Inclan at $400. They described previous missions they had carried out. Said White House press secretary Pierre Salinger, "We have nothing to say."[6]

When I heard Pepe's account of the *Rex* incident, I realized that this was a story with momentous sweep and international impact. In October 1962, only a year before the *Rex* was ambushed, JFK had promised Russian premier Khrushchev, as part of the missile-crisis settlement, to prevent aggressions against Cuba mounted from American soil. And only six weeks before, after an attack by Alpha 66, a militant group linked to the Miami exile community, the Soviet Union warned that the United States was "offering Cuban counterrevolutionaries its territories and material needs," causing a "dangerous aggravation" of the situation in the Caribbean.[7] By continuing to authorize missions like that of the *Rex*, Kennedy was playing with matches in a Caribbean tinderbox.

CHAPTER SEVENTEEN

THE CIA'S UNRULY STEPCHILD

"HE [OSWALD] TOLD US YOU DON'T
HAVE ANY GUTS, YOU CUBANS, BECAUSE
PRESIDENT KENNEDY SHOULD HAVE BEEN
ASSASSINATED AFTER THE BAY OF PIGS. IT IS
EASY TO DO."
—LEOPOLDO, WAR NAME FOR CUBAN EXILE WHO
INTRODUCED SYLVIA ODIO TO "LEON OSWALD"
IN DALLAS, OCTOBER 1963[1]

Through the 1960s and mid-1970s, David Sánchez Morales was involved at top levels in a variety of covert projects, including the ZR/RIFLE plot to assassinate Fidel Castro, and the Bay of Pigs invasion operation. According to House Select Committee on Assassinations investigator Gaeton Fonzi in *The Last Investigation*, "Morales was a hit man for the CIA. He was a killer. He said so himself." Morales was prone to erupt at the mere mention of President John F. Kennedy's name, shouting obscenities, flinging pieces of furniture about the room, and pounding his fist into the pillows. His friend Ruben Carbajal claimed that in 1973 Morales opened up about his involvement with the Bay of Pigs invasion operation and stated that "Kennedy had been responsible for him having to watch all the men he recruited and trained get wiped out."[2]

His attorney, Robert Walton, said the worst outbreak of his pathology was in a Washington hotel suite rented by the CIA as a safe house one night in 1961.[3] Morales, also known as Indio, was a big, bronze Mexican from Phoenix. Fueled by rum, he first boasted that he had been in on the hunt for Che Guevara, then, ignited by Walton's favorable remark about Kennedy, Morales raged on for over four minutes, defying logic that this unstable character should be on the Agency's payroll. Morales not only was on the payroll, he was chief of operations for the Miami station of the CIA, code named JM/WAVE, the nerve center for anti-Castro activists. Only a water-ski run away from JM/WAVE was Point Mary, isolated by the maze of waterways from any casual discovery.[4]

★ ★ ★

At this time, Rolando Cubela of the Student Revolutionary Directorate (DRE) was still operating as a functionary for the Cuban government. The CIA had lost contact with him after the missile crisis in 1962, but reconnected with him in 1963. The mercurial Cubela kept chasing his tail, perhaps reluctant to kill someone he had known from his student days. In September 1963,[5] when the CIA encouraged him to implement his coup and couple the murder of Fidel with it, Cubela insisted that a person of "equal value" be involved in the planning, and he named Robert Kennedy. The meeting was out of the question because only a month before, the CIA had assured the attorney general that all assassination plots were defunct. But Director Richard Helms had a solution: Desmond FitzGerald, the chief of the Western Hemisphere division, would go, posing as Kennedy's "personal representative." There was no need to ask Kennedy; he had already said to pull out all the stops.

They met in Paris in October 1963, where the Cuban was tending to International Federation of Students business. Cubela asked for a high-powered rifle with a scope and a silencer so he could take out Castro from a distance without sacrificing his own life. But FitzGerald distrusted this scheme and developed the now-famous "poison pen" option specifically for Cubela.[6]

The plan was to use a common, easily-obtainable insecticide containing about 40 percent nicotine sulphate, a deadly poison, in a plot to kill Castro. In November 1963, the CIA's Technical Service Division rigged an ordinary-looking ballpoint pen with a syringe whose needle was so fine that it delivered doses of poisonous chemicals without the victim feeling a thing. On November 22, Cubela met with his CIA handler, again in Paris, and accepted the device without any poison, along with instructions for the use of the lethal poison. It would be easy for him to get the poison when he returned to Havana. As they stepped outside after their meeting, they heard the news: President Kennedy had been shot down in Dallas.

The fallout from JFK's assassination effectively shut down the DRE's invasion plans for Cuba.

★ ★ ★

Kennedy's murder had been preceded by five days by a warning received by the FBI in New Orleans.[7] The night clerk who later reconstructed it for District Attorney Jim Garrison was William S. Walter, who said it came in from headquarters at 1:45 a.m. on November 17. It was marked "Urgent." It read:

> INFO HAS BEEN RECEIVED BY THE BUREAU THAT A CUBAN FACTION MILITANT REVOLUTIONARY GROUP MAY ATTEMPT TO ASSASSINATE PRESIDENT KENNEDY ON HIS PROPOSED TRIP TO DALLAS, TEXAS, ON NOVEMBER TWENTY-TWO–TWENTY THREE.[8]

I find this teletype similar in all respects to an FBI teletype, with which I was familiar as a special agent for over ten years. I say this because the Bureau, rather than conducting a full field investigation, tried to discredit Walter and the teletype, but he turned out to be an exemplary young man who went into banking. Offices receiving the teletype were instructed to contact their informants for any information. Although the teletype didn't specify the DRE, the facts fit like a tailored suit.

One day before the assassination, a reliable informant for the Secret Service office in Chicago named Thomas Mosley told one of the Secret Service agents that a Cuban exile with whom he had been negotiating a sale of arms boasted that his group now had "plenty of money" and would make the buy "as soon as we take care of Kennedy." The exile, Homer Echevarria, had been outspokenly critical of President Kennedy.[9]

The acting special agent in charge of the Secret Service office in

Chicago, Maurice Martineau, sent an urgent communication to headquarters advising that he was undertaking a top-priority investigation. In subsequent meetings surveilled by the Secret Service, Mosley found out that Echevarria was affiliated with an associate named Juan Francisco Blanco Fernandez, who was the military director of the DRE. Martineau was prepared to place an undercover agent inside the Echevarria group, but the FBI effectively choked off the investigation. After President Johnson ordered it to assume primary jurisdiction in the JFK case, the Bureau "made it clear that it wanted the Secret Service to terminate its investigation," as the House Select Committee on Assassinations phrased it.[10]

★ ★ ★

The Cuban exile community blamed Kennedy for the failure at the Bay of Pigs because he had cancelled the air strikes that were supposed to provide cover for the invasion force. They laid the death and imprisonment of so many in their community at his door. They were also disappointed in his failure to militarily confront the Soviet Union during the Cuban missile crisis. In 1963, when the CIA sliced one of his infiltration operations down to one five-man crew, Orlando Bosch of the Insurrectional Movement for the Recovery of the Revolution (MIRR) rebelled. He published an angry pamphlet, *The Tragedy of Cuba*, charging the Kennedy administration with betraying the exile cause.[11]

After the exchange of prisoners from the Bay of Pigs, including Manuel Artime, for medical supplies to Cuba, Kennedy appeared at a rally in the Orange Bowl and announced that "this flag will fly in a free Havana," referring to the provisional government flag carried by Artime at the rally.[12] The exiles translated that statement into a promise to invade Cuba.

After a Cuban commando group attacked and sank a Russian freighter in a Cuban harbor, the Kremlin bellowed in outrage, charging that the United States was "offering Cuban counterrevolutionaries its territories and material needs."[13] Kennedy immediately issued conciliatory statements to the Soviets and ordered a crackdown to prevent the exiles from further attacks. The commando group responsible was restricted to Dade

County in Florida. Coast Guard air and sea patrols were intensified, and the FBI, Customs, and other federal agencies were instructed to actively seek out violations of the Neutrality Act.

The Cuban exile community saw this as further betrayal. First the Bay of Pigs, then the missile crisis, and now this. Jose Miro Cardona of the Cuban Revolutionary Council (CRC) in Miami charged that Kennedy had switched to a policy of "peaceful coexistence" with Cuba.[14] He subsequently resigned from the CRC, accusing JFK of "breaking promises and agreements" for a second invasion. The mood of the more militant exiles turned increasingly bitter. Many began to hate Jack Kennedy almost as much as Castro, and some wanted to kill them both.

★ ★ ★

Kennedy's crackdown proved to be troublesome for some of the soldiers of fortune who came to Miami to get some of the action against Castro.[15] One particular group called itself the Intercontinental Penetration Force, code name Interpen. Its leader was Gerry Patrick Hemming, the tall, dashing former fighter for Castro who had been a Marine, qualified as both a parachutist and underwater swimmer, and an enlistee at the US Naval Academy Preparatory School with an eye to an Annapolis appointment. He abandoned his military career to join Castro's revolution, and signed up in the rebel army. He became a paratroop instructor and platoon leader. After Hemming soured on the revolution in 1960 and left Cuba, he expected to be recruited by the CIA for reinfiltration into Cuba. But the Agency snubbed him, so he formed Interpen. The group began training several of the anti-Castro paramilitary groups in Miami, particularly the 30th of November Movement led by Rolando "El Tigre" Masferrer, the DRE, and Triple A—an action group formed by Carlos Prío's former education minister, Aureliano Sanchez Arango, at their base in No Name Key.

There has been much written about a connection between Hemming and Lee Harvey Oswald, and it appears to stem from their links to the DRE. Some researchers believe that Interpen members were involved somehow in Kennedy's assassination, but nothing has ever been proven.[16]

★ ★ ★

In 1963, Lee Harvey Oswald, who would become the FBI's lone suspect in the JFK murder, was a PSI (Potential Security Informant) for the Dallas FBI.[17] As such, he was infiltrating the Cuban-exile action group DRE in both New Orleans and Dallas. He was also playing a dual role, having been recruited by the CIA's W. Guy Banister for the same purpose because the DRE was a thorn in the Agency's side in their competing efforts to launch a second strike.

On August 5, 1963, Oswald walked into a downtown clothing store in New Orleans and presented himself to the proprietor, one Carlos Bringuier, the local DRE head.[18] Oswald identified himself as an ex-Marine and offered Bringuier his Marine manual as an inducement to gain entry to anti-Castro training sites. The DRE rep was suspicious of Oswald. He became doubly suspicious when Oswald showed up again the next day and claimed he knew how to blow up the Huey P. Long Bridge, which was part of the guerrilla warfare course he proposed to teach. Imagine Bringuier's surprise when, four days later, he spotted Oswald handing out pro-Castro literature in front of the World Trade Center New Orleans. They scuffled, and both were hauled off to jail. How did Oswald know the DRE had a training ground in the vicinity? He read it in the newspapers, of course. On August 1, a story in the *Times-Picayune* about the FBI raid in Lake Pontchartrain was headed: "Explosives Cache Property Lent to Cuban, Owner's Wife Says." With his cover blown and his inability to infiltrate the DRE in New Orleans, Oswald was probably reassigned to the Dallas DRE operation.

After staying in Dallas a few days, Oswald suddenly bussed down to Mexico City. On his bus trip down, Oswald chatted with two Australian tourists and told them that he planned to go to Cuba to contact Castro. When he showed up at the Cuban Consulate, he demanded an instant visa to Havana as a friend of the revolution. The consulate chief was too suspicious of these demands and turned Oswald down.[19]

Oswald had no sooner left for Mexico City than three men showed up at the residence of Silvia Odio, a supporter of liberal anti-Castro causes whose parents in Cuba were imprisoned for aiding a sniper plot against

Castro. Two of the men were Cuban self-styled exile-action types, and the other Anglo man was introduced to her as Leon Oswald. One of the exiles, who gave the war name "Leopoldo," appealed for funds to buy weapons to overthrow Castro. The following day, Leopoldo phoned Odio to sing the praises of Oswald as an ex-Marine and crack shot. "He is great. He is kind of nuts. He told us you don't have any guts, you Cubans, because President Kennedy should have been assassinated after the Bay of Pigs. It is easy to do."[20]

★ ★ ★

In November 1963, Loran "Skip" Hall, a member of Hemming's Interpen, was transporting weapons from Los Angeles to No Name Key in the Everglades.[21] He was stopped by police in Dallas and turned over to the FBI. The agent handling the matter was W. Harlan Brown, who was teamed with James Hosty in enforcing the Neutrality Act and preventing gunrunning to Cuba. But Brown let Hall go, which raises some question as to the FBI's dedication to the Neutrality Act. Hosty was named to me through an FBI source as being the agent handling Lee Harvey Oswald as a PSI, which meant the Neutrality Act was under his purview. FBI agents were required to contact their informants at least every forty-five days. It may have been this statistical pressure on Hosty that made his search for Oswald so frantic that he contacted Marina Oswald several days before the assassination. Oswald was at that time registered under an alias at a boarding house in the Oak Cliff section of Dallas, close to the DRE safe house. In order to forestall any more drop-ins by the FBI, Oswald quickly dropped off a note to the FBI office, telling them not to visit his apartment again.[22]

In Dallas, Deputy Sheriff Buddy Walthers sent a "Supplementary Investigative Report" in which he advised the Secret Service that "for the past few weeks at a house at 3128 Harlendale some Cubans have been having meetings on the weekends and were possibly connected with the 'Freedom for Cuba Party' of which Oswald was a member."[23] Walther's informant subsequently told him that "Oswald had been to this house before," and that the Cubans had suddenly moved out.

★   ★   ★

Mob boss Sam Giancana knew more about Oswald's role in the assassination than he ever let on to his Mob underlings. In May 1966, he told his younger brother Chuck that he was about to leave Mexico to internationalize his rackets operations with the CIA as his partner.[24] The Agency, he said, had partnered with him on a number of deals over the years when there were mutual profits to be made. To emphasize how close the relationship was, he brought his cigar to his lips and boasted, "We took care of Kennedy . . . together."

Giancana explained that Oswald was no Castro sympathizer but "CIA all the way," a co-opted Marine trained to speak Russian in order to infiltrate the Soviet Union.[25] When the decision to knock off Kennedy was made in the spring of 1963, Oswald was instructed by his pro tem CIA handler, Guy Banister, to advertise himself "as a Commie nut." This made him, Giancana said, the perfect "fall guy" for the assassination.

The Mafia kingpin told his brother the plot went right to "the top of the CIA," numbering some of the Agency's former and present leaders. He said major funding for the hit came from "millions in oil"— wealthy Texas oilmen he had known over the years.[26]

Giancana added that both the CIA and the Mob had supplied personnel for the hit, but there was no need to worry about J. Edgar Hoover's going all out for the truth. "He hated the Kennedys as much as anybody and he wasn't about to help Bobby find his brother's killers."

★   ★   ★

John F. Kennedy's plans for détente with Castro had been developing. In September 1963, the Guinean ambassador to Havana told William Attwood, Kennedy's special adviser for African Affairs at the United Nations, that Castro was unhappy with Cuba's Soviet-satellite status and was looking for a way out. The report coincided with hints Attwood had received from other sources that Castro was growing restive and was ready to make "substantial concessions" to achieve an accommodation with the United

States. It was the first American overture Castro had made since being rebuffed by Nixon in 1959. At this point, Kennedy didn't want to deal with the Cuba problem in a way that would bring in the Soviet Union, yet polls showed Cuba would be a factor on the 1964 elections. He didn't want to get into the same predicament as Nixon in the 1960 election, which may explain why, when Castro offered an olive branch, Kennedy grabbed it. Attwood suggested that discreet contact be made with the Cuban Mission in the United Nations to determine "if in fact Castro did want to talk on our terms." JFK approved of Attwood's conferring with Dr. Carlos Lechuga, the Cuban chief of mission, as long as it was clear "we are not soliciting discussions."[27]

The negotiations were held in the strictest secrecy on both sides.[28] Acting as an intermediary was ABC newswoman Lisa Howard, who had interviewed Castro the previous May and was trusted by him. While Attwood and Lechuga talked at the United Nations, Howard and Dr. Rene Vallejo, Castro's personal aide and confidant, were in touch by telephone. The discussions went smoothly, to the point where Vallejo told Howard that Castro would like Attwood to come to Cuba. An unmarked Cuban plane would fetch him at Key West and fly him to Varadero Beach, where talks could be held in seclusion. On November 18, Attwood, acting on the president's instructions, phoned Vallejo to propose that preliminary negotiations be held at the United Nations after an agenda was worked out. Vallejo agreed.

Everything was now building toward a climax. Attwood was told that the president wanted to see him about the next move "after a brief trip to Dallas."[29]

CHAPTER EIGHTEEN
NIXON'S VENDETTA

"I'D FIND A PROPER LEGAL COVER AND GO IN. THERE ARE SEVERAL JUSTIFICATIONS THAT COULD BE USED LIKE PROTECTION OF AMERICAN CITIZENS LIVING IN CUBA AND DEFENDING OUR BASE AT GUANTANAMO."[1]
—RICHARD NIXON TO JOHN F. KENNEDY, MEETING AT THE WHITE HOUSE, APRIL 1961

At midday on December 15, 1971, the radio in the Miami offices of the Bahamas Line blared out a distress call from one of the company's ships. It was Captain Jose Villa, a Cuban exile who was the skipper of the 1,400-ton *Johnny Express*. He was being pursued by a Cuban Navy gunboat and was turning north to elude it. The ship was en route to Miami after discharging cargo at Port-au-Prince, Haiti. Its position was not far from Little Inaua Island in the lower Bahamas.

At 12:55 p.m., Captain Villa reported that the gunboat was closing in. At 1:00 p.m., he said he had been ordered to heave to. "Don't stop," Bahamas Line official Francisco Blanco radioed. "You are in international waters."[2]

At 1:30 p.m., Villa, his voice urgent, reported *Johnny Express* under fire and himself wounded. Nine minutes later, he screamed into the microphone, "They are shooting at us from close range."

At 2:00 p.m., Blanco, after hurried consultation with other company officials, advised Villa to try to beach his ship. "We are going to keep going until they sink us," the captain defiantly replied. Then radio contact was lost. Finally, at 2:20, p.m., Villa came back on the air, saying the gunboat was firing at his radio mast. He begged for help. Ten minutes later, he began his final transmission: "The deck is covered with blood. I am dying, *chico*. Tell the Coast Guard to come quickly. Tell them there are dead and wounded here."

The gunboat rammed and boarded the *Johnny Express*, then took it in tow to a Cuban port. Villa and two wounded crewmen were rushed to a hospital. Although it appeared to be an outrageous act of piracy, the initial reaction from the Nixon White House was strangely subdued. Press Secretary Ron Ziegler deplored the attack as "a violation of international practice" but said that since the *Johnny Express* flew the Panamanian flag, it was a matter for Panama to deal with. In fact, a sister ship of the *Johnny Express* had been bloodlessly seized by the Cubans twelve days earlier, with scarcely a whisper of protest.

The uncommon quiet in Washington was necessitated by the fact that the barrage of accusations being laid down by Havana Radio to justify the seizure was essentially true. The Cubans charged that the *Johnny Express* was owned by CIA front men, had landed "agents, arms and explosives" in Cuba for the CIA on three occasions in 1968 and 1969, and had been used as a mother ship two months earlier to launch and retrieve a fast motorboat that had raked the seaside town of Boca de Sama with machine-gun fire, killing and wounding civilians. That night, Miami television station WTVJ broadcast an editorial, "James Bond May Be Needed," which asserted that the *Johnny Express* might have been more than an innocent noncombatant. The station showed a Coast Guard "intelligence photo" of the ship with what appeared to be a 20-foot inboard boat with a fast hull design sitting on the cargo deck.

The *Johnny Express* was operated by the brothers Santiago and Teofilo Babun, the American success stories of a large family that had emigrated from Lebanon a generation earlier. Others of the Babun family had settled in Haiti, where they became influential in governmental affairs. Still others had gone across the Windward Passage to Oriente Province in Cuba, where they prospered in commerce. Santiago and Teofilo belonged to the Oriente branch of the family, all of whom hopscotched to Miami when Castro took power. When Santiago Jr. joined Brigade 2506, the proud father prepared his own contribution—a 173-foot vessel that he fitted with guns at his own expense. His generosity was cruelly thwarted when the invasion occurred before the work on the boat was complete.

In 1964, Santiago's cousin, Rudolph Babun, the Haitian consul in Miami, was implicated in the smuggling of T-28 airplanes to Haiti and was forced to leave the United States. In 1968, the year that Havana Radio claimed the *Johnny Express* was first used to drop off arms and agents in Cuba, Santiago Jr. and Teofilo were arrested by Miami police after a huge cache of explosives was found in the Bahamas Lines yards. The Babun family was clearly not unfamiliar with military devices.

If Washington was playing down the incident because of the potential CIA angle, Richard Nixon, at his Florida White House on Key Biscayne, was playing it up. He had Captain Villa's wife and three children brought to the compound and was photographed with a comforting arm around her shoulders while branding the seizure as an unconscionable act and demanding Villa's immediate release. Perhaps taking a cue from the commander in chief, the Pentagon and State Department warned Cuba that all measures allowed by international law would be taken to prevent a recurrence, and air and sea patrols would be doubled. Havana Radio answered that gunboats would not hesitate to capture any vessel believed engaged in "counterrevolutionary activities."

The record of history is unclear as to what Nixon, standing with his arm around Isabel Villa, told the poor woman to comfort her. Nor is it known whether he told her the truth behind her husband's fate or the story of his own role in it. If he did, she got an earful. For Nixon was rekindling the secret war from the cold coals of the Kennedys.

And yet Nixon's revisionist toasting of communist leaders in the faraway halls of Moscow and Beijing was marked by the absence of even a tip of the hat to the communist in neighboring Havana. The signal was clear enough to the CIA and the Miami exiles. The secret war against Castro was to take some new shots. Some of them were Dr. Strangelove dirty.

During 1969 and 1970 the CIA deployed futuristic weather modification technology to ravage Cuba's sugar crop and thus undermine the economy. Planes from the China Lake Naval Weapons Center in the California desert, where high tech was developed, overflew the island, seeding rain clouds with crystals that precipitated torrential rains over non-agricultural areas and left the cane fields arid. The downpours even caused killer flash floods in some areas.

In March 1970, a US intelligence officer passed a vial of the African swine fever virus to a terrorist group. The vial was taken by a fishing trawler to Navassa Island, which had been used in the past as an advance base by the CIA, and was smuggled into Cuba. Six weeks later, Cuba suffered the first outbreak of the swine fever in the Western Hemisphere. Pig herds were decimated, causing a serious shortage of pork, the nation's dietary staple. The United Nations Food and Agricultural Organization called it the "most alarming event" of the year and futilely tried to track down "how the disease had been transmitted."

The Nixon administration saw a renewed series of CIA-supported attempts on Castro's life. Gerry Patrick Hemming's exile group was involved in a triple-play assassination plot when Castro was the guest of Salvador Allende in Chile in October 1971. Castro was to be shot with a trick gun inside a camera upon his arrival in Santiago. The camera-gun plot was confirmed by Antonio Veciano, who had been a financier for the anti-Castro underground in Cuba for many years. Veciano said he was instructed by his case officer, Maurice Bishop, to organize the shoot.[3] "It was very similar to the assassination of Kennedy," Veciano stated, "because the person Bishop assigned to kill Castro was going to get planted with papers to make it appear he was a Moscow Castro agent who turned traitor, and then he himself would be killed." The forged papers were supplied by a former Batista security agent named Luis Posada Carriles, who had enlisted for the Bay of Pigs and later was afforded intelligence training by the CIA.[4]

The assassination attempt misfired by the merest chance. "We had TV cameras with machine guns mounted inside to kill Castro during his speech," Veciano said, "but one agent had an appendicitis attack and we had to rush him to the hospital. The other agent said he wouldn't do it alone."[5] The plotters had a backup plan to kill Castro when he toured a mountain copper mine near Antofagasta in Chile's north country. This only failed because of Castro's nine-lives type luck. The premier was driven up a narrow winding road to the mine site. Halfway up, a disabled car blocked the road, forcing Castro's vehicle to stop. There were four hundred pounds of dynamite in the car, wired to an electric detonator. The plunger was pushed, but the dynamite failed to explode.

The third attempt was made when Castro stopped off in Peru on his way home from Chile. It was planned for the moment when Castro appeared at the door of his Ilyushin jet upon landing at the Lima airport for a state dinner with President Juan Velasco Alvarado. A Beechcraft Baron with a 20-mm cannon behind its door was positioned on an apron where it could blast away at Castro then make a quick getaway. However, the Ilyushin unexpectedly pulled into a special security area, blocking it from the Beechcraft. The pilot of the assassination plane perhaps understandably refused to taxi it to another position because it would blow his chance of escape.

By Gerry Hemming's account, the fall of 1970 saw a scheme so fantastic that it seemed to plagiarize pulp novels.[6] It began when the Cuban exile crews of Florida fishing boats decided to suspend hostilities long enough to make a quick buck. In a kind of floating-commodities exchange, they swapped staples with their Cuban counterparts—coffee and flour, in short supply in Cuba, for lobsters and fish that brought a premium price on the American market. The bootlegging became so lucrative that a Cuban P-4 patrol boat began escorting the Florida boats in and out of the small port of Cayo Bahia de Cadiz to expedite the trading.

The crew of one fishing boat, the *Linda*, became friendly with Fidel's P-4 crewmen, who eventually talked about going to the United States. A plan was proposed in which the P-4 would escort the *Linda* out of port and keep going all the way to Key Biscayne—at a time when Nixon was in residence in his compound—and, with its Cuban markings plainly visible, open fire on *Chez Nixon*. It was meant to be a provocation sufficient to touch off an invasion of Cuba. If Nixon were killed or injured, that would be too bad, but also more provocative: a perfect specimen of the Caribbean plot mentality. "What do you think Spiro Agnew would have done about six hours later," Hemming said, "thinking it was a Castro operation?"[7]

The plan had reached the stage at which two planes had been acquired to fly the conspirators out of the country when it was aborted by an insider's tip to the Secret Service for the usual reward. A few days later, the *Linda* was tied up on the Miami River, the crew aboard under house arrest, when Nixon floated by on Charles "Bebe" Rebozo's houseboat, the *Coco Lobo*. Unaware that he had been deemed expendable by the unhappy Cuban exiles glaring out of the portholes at him, the president yelled greetings while Rebozo obligingly pulled the *Coco Lobo* over so his friend could shake some Cuban hands. Hemming was nervous because the crew was drunk and had automatic carbines on their bunks, but they wouldn't even give Nixon the time of day.

CHAPTER NINETEEN

THE COUP THAT NOBODY KNEW

"THOUSANDS OF CUBANS PAY TRIBUTE TO
CASTRO'S RIGHT-HAND MAN, JUAN ALMEIDA
BOSQUE."

—HEADLINE FOR ALMEIDA'S OBITUARY
IN THE *DAILY MAIL*, SEPTEMBER 14, 2009

When I interviewed Enrique "Harry" Ruiz-Williams, he conveyed a great deal of information about the existence of a second invasion under the auspices of the United States. Ruiz-Williams had laid out the invasion as a war of attrition including economic sabotage, assassination, and destruction of Cuban infrastructure, among other techniques. In this manner, for example, John V. Martino of the Mafia/CIA collaboration was an expert in residence for demolition of selected targets. During the course of this phase of the campaign against Cuba there was considerable information gathering being done on the second invasion and when it could be pulled off. With Warren Hinckle, I published data from Ruiz-Williams about the second invasion in *Deadly Secrets: The CIA/Mafia War against Castro and the Assassination of JFK*, and then I went on to other things. Years later, an intrepid journalist named Lamar Waldron took an interest in the second invasion as an intriguing suggestion that there was more to the story than had appeared in my book.

After dinner at a local Chinese restaurant, during which I briefed Waldron on what was known thus far, Lamar went forth on his Holy Grail quest for Harry Ruiz-Williams. Eureka! He found him back at the Colorado School of Mines, where he was an alumnus. In the course of Waldron's long interview of Ruiz-Williams about the second invasion, he discovered that Ruiz-Williams had not revealed all of his knowledge to me. He learned that

Ruiz-Williams had deliberately withheld critical intelligence. Why? Ruiz-Williams explained, "I was protecting someone, and it was their safety I had in mind."[1] Lamar later called me to advise that Ruiz-Williams had revealed the identity of a high-level military leader in Cuba who had led a coup against Castro. Waldron revealed the name of this defector but swore me to secrecy until the news of his death was announced. Waldron called me to verify that the individual had died of a heart attack on September 9, 2009, and he confirmed that the embargo on the information was lifted. Now we are able to identify this individual as Juan Almeida Bosque.

> Juan Almeida Bosque was a Cuban politician and one of the original commanders of the Cuban Revolution. After the 1959 revolution, he was a prominent figure in the Communist Party of Cuba; at the time of his death in 2009, he was a Vice-President of the Cuban Council of State and was its third ranking member. He received several decorations, and both national and international awards, including the title of "Hero of the Republic of Cuba."[2]

So reads Almeida's official story. If he hadn't existed, he would have been invented. Commander Juan Almeida Bosque was a towering figure in the Cuban Revolution, a man noted for finishing what he started. And what he started was a coup that would overthrow Fidel, his brother Raul, and Che Guevara, the triumvirate of power in the new government.

Almeida was Hollywood-handsome in his olive, drab fatigues and foraging cap flanked by the gold epaulets of a commander, the loftiest rank in the rebel army. A one of few, the only black man to ascend so high, Almeida was there from the start, enlisting in Fidel's service in its staging area in Mexico. He left the life of a bricklayer to join the fight against Batista. In 1953, he joined Fidel and his brother Raul Castro in the assault on the Moncada Barracks in Santiago, and was arrested and imprisoned with the Castro brothers in the Isle of Pines prison. During the Batista amnesty of May 15, 1955, he was released and transferred to Mexico. Almeida sailed to Cuba with the Castro brothers, Che Guevara, and seventy-eight other revolutionaries aboard the *Granma* to start the guerilla struggle against the Batista regime, and he was one of the few who survived the initial landing on the shores of the Oriente Province, during which Cuban government forces killed most of the rebels, mostly strafed by Batista's air force. During the battle, Almeida shouted, "No one here gives up!" (alternatively, "Here, nobody surrenders!") to Guevara, which would become a long-lived slogan of the Cuban Revolution.[3]

One of the ironies of the Castro revolution occurred after the dictator sent his warplanes to strafe the *Granma*. E. Howard Hunt was visiting Cuba to size up the political situation. To his colleagues having drinks at the US Embassy, he announced that all aboard the *Granma* had been wiped out. His count was a bit high. Fidel, Raul, Che, and Almeida were among the men who escaped into the Sierra Maestra. There they planted the Cuban flag, and the revolution was on its way.

Almeida continued to fight Batista's government forces in the guerilla war in the Sierra Maestra mountain range. In 1958, he was promoted to commander and head of the Santiago Column of the Revolutionary Army. His units broke through on the central front in the final drive to victory. Raul Castro broke out of the Sierra Cristal salient to cover the rear of Almeida's thrust. During the revolution, as a black man in a prominent position, Almeida served as a symbol to Afro-Cubans of a change from Cuba's discriminatory past in response to the flow of immigrants from Jamaica and Africa as cheap labor for the cane fields.

He became top heavy with medals, and his popularity was so widely spread that he was given his own radio program. He also became a best friend of Che and another comrade-in-arms, Harry Ruiz-Williams. Ruiz-Williams had been instrumental in providing aid to Castro in the revolution by using his geology company as a cover for moving weapons. "I thought he was the man to back," Ruiz-Williams told me in our 1973 interview in Fort Lauderdale. "I was a liberal," he said, "so I was for Fidel's liberal projects of rural electrification and land reform."

Harry's break with Castro came when socialism became the order of the day. Harry became a bitter enemy and signed on with Brigade 2506 at the Bay of Pigs, fully intending to drive out the Castro regime in short order. Despite the unhappy outcome of that effort, Ruiz-Williams retained his sense of purpose.

As the doors opened on the plane of the charter flight from Havana bearing the walking wounded from Brigade 2506, the crowd of thousands waiting at the Miami airport roared.[4] The band struck up "The Colonel Bogey March," and the last man down the steps was Harry Ruiz-Williams. If he thought he was going to return to his geology business, he was wrong. Bobby Kennedy, acting on the advice of Pepe San Román, Brigade field commander, that Ruiz-Williams was an outstanding leader, called him to his office. As a result of the interview, which both men later said was a bonding experience, Bobby Kennedy asked Harry to be his number-one man in the second invasion, then on the drawing board. When Bobby and his aides decided on the final battle plan for the invasion, Harry was assigned a major role in support of the main thrust by Manuel Artime. Ruiz-Williams related that he got on fine with Bobby and was a frequent guest at his Virginia estate, dubbed Hickory Hills. But he told Ethel Kennedy that he wouldn't like her husband if Bobby didn't start the invasion. At Fort Jackson in North Carolina, Ruiz-Williams began working with E. Howard Hunt on training the cream of the crop of the Brigade 2506 veterans for the invasion.

In the spring of 1963, Robert Kennedy became frustrated by the constant bickering of the Cuban exile groups receiving CIA support. He turned to his friend Harry Ruiz-Williams, telling him that all requests from the exile groups should now go through him, and Harry could then identify the select few he thought were serious and deserved backing.[5] Soon word spread through the exile community that Ruiz-Williams was essentially the gatekeeper for the Kennedys when it came to their support for the exiles.

Robert Kennedy and Ruiz-Williams attempted to operate away from the glare of publicity, so they were surprised when an Associated Press article about their efforts appeared on May 10, 1963, in the *New York Times*, among others, identifying both Harry Ruiz-Williams and Robert Kennedy as "seeking to put together a junta."[6]

The two men were furious about the leak, and they were further enraged when a similar article appeared nine days later in the *Miami News*, noting Ruiz-Williams's trips to Washington, New York, and Puerto Rico, and his meetings with exile leaders. Harry struggled to stop the unwanted press coverage, but it caught the attention of his old friend in Cuba, Commander Juan Almeida, still head of the Cuban Army.[7]

Almeida had become disillusioned with Castro. Almeida's first deviation was snatching away from Raul a role in a TV documentary produced in Cuba; then he published criticism of the regime over its civil-rights policies. He was the only prominent black man in Cuban politics despite the fact that the majority of Cuba is black. At the same time, Che was becoming disillusioned. He and Almeida believed that Fidel had become too unstable to carry out with any authority the dictates of communism in Cuba, and that he had become ideologically adrift. Che's response to his dissatisfaction was to part from Fidel and Raul Castro on good terms and move on to other revolutionary movements in the poverty-stricken hinterlands of South America to build his own forces. Almeida's response was to reach out to Ruiz-Williams, telling him that Castro was becoming nothing more than a dictator, betraying the revolution they had all fought so hard for. So Almeida offered to stage a coup against Fidel, if President Kennedy would back him.[8] Harry took the offer to Bobby immediately. Telephone records show that RFK contacted the president quickly, and then called Ruiz-Williams to tell him that Almeida's offer was accepted and that the US government would give him their full backing. Thus began the JFK/Almeida coup plan.

Ordinarily, the coup planning would have been the purview of Bobby Kennedy. However, because of the absolute importance of the Almeida defection, the case was filed under "JFK/Almeida." Jack Kennedy had run into this situation before. When his brother was going to be appointed attorney general, there was considerable criticism of his youthfulness inside the Kennedy administration. At that time, there was much ado over the desire of Jack Kennedy to force J. Edgar Hoover to retire.[9] But the decision was made not to fire him, despite his liabilities, because JFK thought it would stir up a hornet's nest about his younger brother's appointment to a critical post.

In 1963, Almeida began making covert visits to several foreign embassies, possibly trying to develop a refuge plan for his family in the event of the impending invasion. He stayed in contact with Harry Ruiz-Williams, who had been assigned by Bobby Kennedy as Almeida's handler for the coup effort, simultaneous to the second invasion.[10]

In the summer and fall of 1963, E. Howard Hunt became involved in some of the most sensitive aspects of the JFK/Almeida coup plan. Hunt's responsibilities were to assist Harry Ruiz-Williams with delicate matters involving Commander Almeida and his family.[11]

Williams said that there were "dozens [of meetings] from May to November 1963" with Hunt and other CIA security staff assigned to the operation.[12] Hunt was involved in the payment of the initial installment of $50,000 to Almeida, part of the agreed-upon total of $500,000 authorized by Robert Kennedy. In the event the coup was unsuccessful and Almeida had to flee Cuba, or if he was killed, the money would provide for his wife and children.[13]

In addition to handling the payment to Almeida, Hunt was also part of a covert operation in which Almeida's wife and two children left Cuba on a seemingly innocent pretext prior to the date set for the coup.[14] Almeida's family was supposed to wait out the coup in another country under CIA surveillance. Bobby Kennedy had also authorized Ruiz-Williams to assure Almeida that his family would be taken care of in case something happened to him. In addition to providing for their safety, having the family in another place under the eye of the CIA would ensure that Almeida didn't double-cross the CIA and the Kennedys.

As part of the planning, there was consideration to framing the Soviet Union for the coup if it was discovered. Perhaps it would be an individual Russian of the one thousand technicians remaining in Cuba after the missile crisis. The problem was that the planners couldn't figure out how to do it. They solicited others on the coup-planning group as to their contacts with the Russian community in Cuba for likely candidates to take the fall. To no one's surprise, they were unsuccessful.

Another player in the JFK/Almeida coup plan was James McCord, later arrested for his part in the Watergate break-in. According to published accounts by *Vanity Fair* and this author, and interviews with Harry Ruiz-Williams, McCord was one of the two main officials—along with E. Howard Hunt—assigned to assist Ruiz-Williams and the JFK/Almeida coup.[15] There was a huge budget assigned to this operation, at least $7 million, but it offered no temptation to Ruiz-Williams. When propositioned by McCord about making some money out of the operation, Ruiz-Williams replied, "Look, when I want to make money I will go back to my profession [as a mining engineer]. I am not here to make money."[16] This was apparently just a test of Ruiz-Williams by McCord because he himself was in the operation strictly for patriotic reasons.

The coup was running on a parallel track with the CIA/Artime second invasion, yet only a small number of US officials and Kennedy aides knew about Commander Almeida. But a player from a different sphere managed to learn some details of the coup plan. This was Carlos Prío. According to CIA files, he used his influence with Artime and Tony Varona, former Cuban senator and leader in the Bay of Pigs debacle, to uncover the plot that he named "Plan Judas." Fidel had often told a story of how he and twelve "disciples"—including Juan Almeida, Raul Castro, and Che Guevara—had gone into the mountains of Cuba to start the revolution. It was clear that Prío knew one of those disciples was going to betray Fidel to the US government.[17]

The assassination of President Kennedy in November 1963 put a stop to the JFK/Almeida coup plan, and Almeida apparently put it behind him. He continued his prominent role in Cuban politics. He was promoted to general of the army and was chosen as a member of both the central committee and the political bureau. Over the years he has held a number of other government positions, rising to the office of vice president. Almeida was honored with the title of commander of the revolution, and at the time of his death was one of just three living holders of that title. In 1998, he was named a "Hero of the Republic of Cuba" by Fidel Castro.

On September 11, 2009, Juan Almeida Bosque died of a heart attack at the age of eighty-two. On September 13, a memorial ceremony was held in the Plaza de la Revolución in Havana, with several other memorials occurring across Cuba. A national day of mourning was declared, with flags flown at half-mast. The memorial service was attended by tens of thousands of his countrymen, who queued across the plaza to view a large photograph of Almeida. President Raul Castro attended the service and placed a pink rose in front of the photograph. Fidel Castro, who at the time had not been seen in public since he resigned as president in 2008, did not attend the ceremony, but in a letter dated September 13, 2009, and published at *monthlyreview.org*,[18] Castro honored Almeida and mourned him:

> I have been watching for hours now on television the tribute that the entire country is paying to Commander of the Revolution Juan Almeida Bosque. I think that facing death was for him just another duty as so many others he discharged throughout his life. He did not know (neither did we) how much sadness the news of his physical absence would bring to us.
>
> "I was privileged to know that young black militant worker who would successively be the leader of a revolutionary group, a combatant at the Moncada, a comrade in prison, a platoon captain at the time of the *Granma* landing, an officer with the Rebel Army—held back by a shot on his chest during the violent combat at Uveroâ, the Commander of a column marching on to create the Third Eastern Front, and the comrade sharing the leadership of our forces in the last successful battles to overthrow the tyranny.
>
> I was an exceptional witness to his exemplary conduct for over half a century of heroic and victorious resistance in the struggle against the bandits, during the Girón counteroffensive, the missile crisis, the internationalist missions and the resistance to the imperialist blockade.
>
> It was a pleasure to listen to some of his songs, especially the one particularly emotional where he bade farewell to human dreams in response to the homeland's call to "win or die." . . . He defended principles of justice that will be defended at any time and age while human beings breathe on Earth. Let's not say that Almeida is dead! Almeida lives today more than ever!

We have no idea whether Castro knew of Almeida's treasonous efforts in Plan Judas, but in the end he took the high road and maintained the myth of this "Hero of the Republic of Cuba." It is surprising that neither Castro nor his Security Service G-2 was privy to the Almeida defection and his service as an agent in place directly for the president of the United States. If they did know, what would be their motive for not acting on this blockbuster? To act would be to destroy the formidable image Almeida had acquired, which rendered him the third most powerful figure in Cuba. His reputation on the part of the people of Cuba was unassailable. He was a hero of the Cuban republic and a military legend on the order of Simón Bolívar. In other words, in destroying Almeida, Castro would be damaging his own mythical stature.

Almeida was survived by his two sons, both prominent businessmen in Cuba. An echo of *l'affaire* Almeida came in August 2012, when one of Almeida's sons, named Juan Juan, went on a hunger strike in Havana to pressure the Castro regime into giving him an exit visa. The visa was forthcoming in a record one day. Juan Juan and his family relocated to Miami, where he remains bitterly critical of the lack of freedom in Castro's Cuba.[19]

HAVANA REDUX

Dwight Eisenhower rode in a limousine with US flags flying on the fenders and golf clubs in the trunk. Richard Nixon had an enameled American flag pin on the lapel of what appeared to be an off-the-rack suit. Fidel Castro Ruz was a rumpled revolutionary with a wardrobe of fatigue uniforms and paratrooper boots.

Four months after his revolution had militarily succeeded, Castro was invited to Washington, DC, by the American Society of Newspaper Editors for a lecture tour of the Washington vicinity. The editors knew a good story when they saw one. Fidel Castro was the Robin Hood of the hills, who had sped out of the hills on New Year's Day 1959 and assumed control of the Cuban government by taking over the baroque Presidential Palace in Havana. It was clear from his rapport with the people that he was the world man of the hour.

The Eisenhower White House recoiled at the idea of giving such a cultural disaster a full reception. They were in a quandary as to how they could trivialize Castro's visit. Eisenhower, in his last term as president, opted for a golfing trip to North Carolina, where no one could count his mulligans. The task of playing host to Castro defaulted to Vice President Nixon, who saw it as an opportunity to enhance his reputation as the scourge of all things left-leaning. Early in his career, the vice president had acquired a political handle as a Red-baiter.

The White House staff dug up information on Castro that revealed his call for agrarian reform at the start of his revolution. I suspect that they probably didn't include the fact that Castro saw this as a way of relieving the abject poverty of rural Cuba. The chimera of agrarian reform set off a conservative backlash that was based on the faulty premise that land would be confiscated in the Chinese example, but Fidel was referring only to surplus acreage.

Nevertheless, the White House staff placed Castro on its communist-sympathizer list. If they had bothered to check, they would have found that the Cuban leader was actually a member of the Cuban Ortodoxo Party, which was in no way affiliated with any radical group.

Before boarding his flight to Washington, Castro paid an impromptu visit to Carlos Prío, a former president of Cuba. Prío was a member of a rival mainstream party, the Autenticos, but he willingly offered advice on how Fidel should comport himself with the American officials he would be dealing with.

The meeting with Nixon was designed as an insult to Castro. Instead of receiving the prime minister in the White House, Nixon steered the Cuban leader to one of the offices in the Senate Office Building. The door was shut to the press. According to Fidel, Nixon waved around what he said was an FBI report indicating he had communist leanings. Castro knew immediately that Nixon was out to sabotage him. The meeting, toxic in content, went on for three hours.

In the breast pocket of his fatigues jacket, Castro had a proposal to form a strategic alliance with the United States in which Cuba would come to the aid of the United States in the event of hostilities with the Soviet Union. It was his feeling in the current state of world affairs that third-world countries should select one of the two superpowers and align with them. But he never got to run his proposal by government officials because of Nixon's hostile behavior. He was, in short, humiliated.

When I interviewed ex-president Prío in retirement, he confirmed that Castro did have such a proposal but kept it in his pocket when Nixon's behavior became more than obnoxious.

That night at the Cuban Embassy, Fidel was heard to curse Nixon's treatment of him. Since he had no promises from Nixon to provide aid for the poor in Cuba, Fidel was caught in a vise. When he left the meeting with Nixon, he had the feeling that the Eisenhower administration was already planning to overthrow him. At the same time, he had to return empty-handed to Havana and face his brother Raul and Che Guevara, who were putting the heat on him to obtain aid from the United States. This lack of support gave the pair considerable leverage to pursue a more stringent agenda. Fidel underwent an epiphany that led him down the path to socialism.

It is not difficult to conceive what might have happened had Fidel not been spurned by Ike and Dick. There would have been no need for the self-crippling Bay of Pigs and no missile crisis because Cuba would not have become communist.

The darker side of United States policy toward Cuba is that it became obvious that assassination had developed into an instrument of American foreign policy. Even before Castro had won the revolution, the dictator of the Dominican Republic, Rafael Trujillo, paid an American naval reservist named Alan Nye a hundred thousand dollars to go into the hills and kill Fidel.[1] He was fortunately intercepted by a patrol. A later CIA attempt to assassinate Castro took place when he visited the United Nations the year after the Nixon debacle. In that scheme, the CIA tried to involve the New York Police Department in poisoning the Cuban at a reception. The NYPD responded that they were there to protect Castro, not to kill him.[2]

The fabric of a society rests on the moral compunctions of its people. The attitude of the majority of Americans seems to be to pass the responsibility on to government officials. It is perhaps revealing of organizations like the CIA that have no compunctions in using the most horrendous of crimes, like narcotic trafficking, and criminals, like the Mob, to further their agenda. What this creates can be an evil worse than the one they are trying to eliminate. The Mob has never failed to exact a prize for cooperating in an operation, and it never will.

It is impossible to scan the criminal horizon today and not realize so much of it was proliferated in the heyday of the Mob in the open city of Havana. The fact that Fidel Castro shut down the gambling casinos was reason enough for Meyer Lansky, the "chairman of the board" of organized crime, to issue a bounty of one million dollars for Castro's demise.[3]

In the light of assassination as a political tool, there has always been speculation that the assassination of President Kennedy in Dallas on November 22, 1963, was planned and executed right out of the covert CIA base at Point Mary in the Everglades. When asked by his son about who fired the rifles at the Kennedy assassination, John V. Martino, who frequented the Point Mary complex, responded, "They were just a couple of Cubans, it doesn't matter."[4]

Finally, there has come to light a defector operation at the highest level in the Cuban government. The components that came together to produce the JFK/Almeida coup plan comprise some of the best and worst attributes of the American intelligence services and their tendency to use the most corrupt elements in highly sensitive cases. This situation, as described by Lamar Waldron in *Watergate: The Hidden History*, employed risky personnel, namely E. Howard Hunt (of later Watergate infamy), in two of the most sensitive aspects of the highly secret plan involving Almeida and his family.

As a famous folk song claims, the roads of Cuba never run straight. In the case of the CIA secret war against Castro, the roads of Cuba led to a dead end. The agency set up a secret city on the South Campus of the University of Miami from which it directed the second invasion of Cuba and its various attendant assassination plots. The station included dummy front companies created for gathering supplies and managing personnel for the invasion like Zenith Technical Enterprises and Ace Cartography Incorporated. It was a huge operation with a budget of well over $500 million, employing six hundred to seven hundred American personnel.[5] Yet it ground to a halt with the assassination of JFK. Lyndon Johnson considered the operation "Bobby's thing" and ordered it shut down so that the intelligence services could move on to Vietnam. Today it is a latter-day Stonehenge, a reminder of the extraordinary resources the US government can expend in the pursuit of futility.

DOCUMENT—CIA PLOTS TO KILL CASTRO

his document, "CIA Inspector General's Report on Plots to Assassinate Fidel Castro," was approved for release in 1993 under the CIA Historical Review Program. This document has been edited to remove extraneous information about the administrative functions of the report and information not pertinent to this book, *The Cuban Connection*. The editor retained the original page numbering and left the remaining original text unaltered, including misspellings, typos, and the like. The text includes many acronyms which are not explained. Prior to the release in 1993 under the CIA Historical Review Program, the CIA removed many names that proved too sensitive to release.

23 May 1967
MEMORANDUM FOR THE RECORD
SUBJECT: Report on Plots to Assassinate Fidel Castro
This report was prepared at the request of the Director of Central Intelligence. He assigned the task to the Inspector General on 23 March 1967. The report was delivered to the Director, personally, in installments, beginning on 24 April 1967. . . .
The one stayback burn copy, all notes, and all other derived source materials were destroyed on 23 May 1967.
This ribbon copy is the only text of the report now in existence, either in whole or in part. Its text has been read only by:
Richard Helms, Director of Central Intelligence
J.S. Earman, Inspector General
K.E. Greer, Inspector (one of the authors)
S.D. Breckinridge, Inspector (one of the authors)

. . . .

Filed with the report are:

Office of Security file used as source material

Memorandums concerning William Harvey

Certain MONGOOSE papers

Drew Pearson columns

[Signed]

J.S. Earman

Inspector General

. . . .

OUTLINE

Introductory Section

Miscellaneous Schemes Prior to August 1960

Aerosol Attack on Radio Station

Contaminated Cigars

Depilatory

The Gambling Syndicate Operation

Phase 1 (August 1960 - May 1961)

Phase 2 (Late 1961 - June 1963)

. . . .

Schemes in Early 1963

Skin Diving Suit

Sea Shell

Project AMLASH - Rolando Cubela (March 1961—March 1966)

Discussion of Assassination at High-Level Government Meetings

Special Group (Augmented) Meeting of 10 August 1962

Special Group Meeting of 30 July 1964

The Ramifications of the Gambling Syndicate Operation

23 April 1967

MEMORANDUM

This reconstruction of Agency Involvement in plans to assassinate Fidel Castro is at best an imperfect history. Because of the extreme sensitivity of the operations being discussed or attempted, as a matter of principle no official records were kept of planning, of approvals, or of implementation.

The few written records that do exist are either largely tangential to the main events or were put on paper from memory years afterward. William Harvey has retained skeletal notes of his activities during the years in question, and they are our best source of dates. Dr. Edward Gunn of the Office of Medical Services, has a record of whom he met and when and cryptic references to the subjects discussed. [deletion] of TSD, has a record of two or three dates that are pertinent. Gunn and [deletion] were involved in only the technical aspects of operational planning, and their participations were short-lived. Although fragmentary, their records are a help in establishing critical time frames. Operational files are useful in some instances, because they give dates of meetings, the substances of which may be inferred from collateral information.

For the most part, though, we have had to rely on information given to us orally by people whose memories are fogged by time. Their recollections of dates are particularly hazy, and some of them

-1-

are no longer able to keep the details of one plan separate from those of another. We interviewed everyone whom we could identify as likely to be knowledgeable, with the exceptions of Mr. Dulles and General Cabell. A complete list is attached at Tab A. We did not go on fishing expeditions among the mere possibles. To have done so would have risked making witting a number of employees who were previously unwitting and, in our estimate, would have added little to the details available from those directly involved. There are inconsistencies among the various accounts, but most of them can be resolved by collating the information furnished by all of the identifiable participants in a particular plan and by then checking it against specific dates that can be fixed with fair certainty. We believe that this reconstruction of what happened and of the thinking associated with it is reasonably sound. If there are significant inaccuracies in the report, they are most likely to occur in faulty ordering of the sequence of events. People still remember much of what happened, but they can no longer recall precisely when.

It became clear very early in our investigation that the vigor with which schemes were pursued within the Agency to eliminate Castro personally varied with the intensity of the U.S. Government's efforts to overthrow the Castro regime. We can identify five separate phases in Agency assassination planning, although the transitions from one

-2-

to another are not always sharply defined. Each phase is a reflection of the then prevailing Government attitude toward the Cuban regime.

a. Prior to August 1960: All of the identifiable schemes prior to about August 1960, with one possible exception, were aimed only at discrediting Castro personally by influencing his behaviour or by altering his appearance.

b. August 1960 to April 1961: The plots that were hatched in late 1960 and early 1961 were aggressively pursued and were viewed by at least some of the participants as being merely one aspect of the over-all active effort to overthrow the regime that culminated in the Bay of Pigs.

c April 1961 to late 1961: A major scheme that was begun in August 1960 was called off after the Bay of Pigs and remained dormant for several months, as did most other Agency operational activity related to Cuba.

d. Late 1961 to Late 1962: That particular scheme was reactivated in early 1962 and was again pushed vigorously in the era of Project MONGOOSE and in the climate of intense administration pressure on CIA to do something about Castro and his Cuba.

e. Late 1962 until well into 1963: After the Cuban missile crisis of October 1962 and the collapse of Project MONGOOSE, the

-3-

aggressive scheme that was begun in August 1960 and revived in April

1962 was finally terminate in early 1963. Two other plots were originated in 1963, but both were impracticable and nothing ever came of them.

We cannot overemphasize the extent to which responsible Agency officers felt themselves subject to the Kennedy administration's severe pressures to do something about Castro and his regime. The fruitless and, in retrospect, often unrealistic plotting should be viewed in that light.

Many of those we interviewed stressed two points that are so obvious that recording them here may be superfluous. We believe, though, that they are pertinent to the story. Elimination of the dominant figure in a government, even when loyalties are held to him personally rather than to the government as a body, will not necessarily cause the downfall of the government. This point was stressed with respect to Castro and Cuba in an internal CIA draft paper of October 1961, which was initiated in response to General Maxwell Taylor's desire for a contingency plan. The paper took the position that the demise of Fidel Castro, from whatever cause, would offer little opportunity for the liberation of Cuba from Communist and Soviet Bloc control. The second point, which is more specifically relevant to our investigation, is that bringing about the downfall of a government necessarily requires the removal of its leaders from

-4-

positions of power, and there is always the risk that the participants will resort to assassination. Such removals from power as the house arrest of a [Mossainq?] or the flight of a [Busieca?] could not cause one to overlook the killings of a Diem or of a Trujillo by forces encouraged but not controlled by the U.S. government.

There is a third point, which was not directly made by any of those we interviewed, but which emerges clearly from the interviews and from review of files. The point is that of frequent resort to synecdoche—the mention of a part when the whole is to be understood, or vice versa. Thus, we encounter repeated references to phrases such as "disposing of Castro," which may be read in the narrow, literal sense of assassinating him, when it is intended that it be read in the broader, figurative sense of dislodging the Castro regime. Reversing this coin, we find people speaking vaguely of "doing something about Castro" when it is clear that what they have specifically in mind is killing him. In a situation wherein those speaking may not have actually meant what they seemed to say or may not have said what they actually meant, they should not be surprised if their oral short-hand is interpreted differently than was intended.

The suggestion was made that operations aimed at the assassination of Castro may have been generated in an atmosphere of stress in intelligence publications on the possibility of Castro's

-5-

demise and on the reordering of the political structure that would follow. We reviewed intelligence publications from 1960 through 1966, including National Intelligence Estimates, Special National Intelligence Estimates, Intelligence Memorandums, and Memorandums for the Director. The NTE's on "The Situation and Prospects in Cuba" for 1960, 1963, and 1964 have brief paragraphs on likely successor governments if Castro were to depart the scene. We also find similar short references in a SNIE of March 1960 and in an Intelligence Memorandum of May 1965. In each case the treatment is no more nor less than one would expect to find in comprehensive round-ups such as these. We conclude that there is no reason to believe that the operators were unduly influenced by the content of intelligence publications.

Drew Pearson's column of 7 March 1967 refers to a reported CIA plan in 1963 to assassinate Cuba's Fidel Castro. Pearson also has information, as yet unpublished, to the effect that there was a meeting at the State Department at which assassination of Castro was discussed and that a team actually landed in Cuba with pills to be used in an assassination attempt. There is basis in fact for each of those three reports.

a.   A CIA officer passed an assassination weapon to an Agency Cuban asset at a meeting in Paris on 22 November 1963. The weapon was a ballpoint pen rigged as a hypodermic syringe.

-6-

The CIA officer suggested that the Cuban asset load the syringe with Black Leaf 40. The evidence indicates that the meeting was under way at the very moment President Kennedy was shot.

b. There was a meeting of the Special Group (Augmented) in Secretary Rusk's conference room on 10 August 1962 at which Secretary McNamara broached the subject of liquidation of Cuban leaders. The discussion resulted in a Project MONGOOSE action memorandum prepared by Edward Lansdale. At another Special Group meeting on 31 July 1964 there was discussion of a recently-disseminated Clandestine Services information report on a Cuban exile plot to assassinate Castro. CIA had refused the exile's request for funds and had no involvement in that plot.

c. CIA twice (first in early 1961 and again in early 1962) supplied lethal pills to U.S. gambling syndicate members working in behalf of CIA on a plot to assassinate Fidel Castro. The 1961 plot aborted and the pills were recovered. Those furnished in April 1962 were passed by the gambling syndicate representative to a Cuban exile leader in Florida, who in turn had them sent to Cuba about May 1962. In June 1962 the exile leader reported that a team of three men had been dispatched to Cuba to recruit for the operation. If the opportunity presented itself, the team would make an attempt on Castro's life—perhaps using the pills.

-7-

This report describes these and other episodes in detail; puts them into perspective; and reveals, that while the events described by Drew Pearson did occur and are subject to being patched together as though one complete story, the implication of a direct, causative relationship among them is unfounded.

-8-

Miscellaneous Schemes Prior to August 1960

March to August 1960

We find evidence of at least three, and perhaps four, schemes that were under consideration well before the Bay of Pigs, but we can fix the time frame only speculatively. Those who have some knowledge of the episodes guessed at dates ranging from 1959 through 1961. The March-to-August span we have fixed may be too narrow, but it best fits the limited evidence we have.

a. None of those we interviewed who was first assigned to the Cuba task force after the Bay of Pigs knows of any of these schemes.

b. J.D. (Jake) Esterline, who was head of the Cuba task force in pre-Bay of Pigs days, is probably the most reliable witness on general timing. He may not have been privy to the precise details of any of the plans, but he seems at least to have known of all of them. He is no longer able to keep the details of one plan separate from those of another, but each of the facts he recalls fits somewhere into one of the schemes.

Hence, we conclude that all of these schemes were under consideration while Esterline had direct responsibility for Cuba operations.

c. Esterline himself furnishes the best clue as to the possible time span. He thinks it unlikely that any planning of this sort would have progressed to the point of consideration of means until after U.S. policy concerning Cuba was decided upon about March 1960. By about the end of the third quarter of 1960, the total energies of the task force were concentrated on the main-thrust effort, and there would have been no interest in nor time for pursuing such wills-o'-the-wisp as these.

We are unable to establish even a tentative sequence among the schemes; they may, in fact, have been under consideration simultaneously. We find no evidence that any of these schemes was approved at any level higher than division, if that. We think it most likely that no higher-level approvals were sought, because none of the schemes progressed to the point where approval to launch would have been needed.

Aerosol Attack on Radio Station

[deletion] of TSD, remembers discussion of a scheme to contaminate the air of the radio station where Castro broadcasts his speeches with an aerosol spray of a chemical that produces reactions similar to those of lysergic acid (LSD). Nothing came of the idea. [deletion] said he had discouraged the scheme, because the chemical could not be relied upon to be effective. [deletion], also of TSD,

-10-

recalls experimentation with psychic energizers but cannot relate it to Castro as a target. We found no one else who remembered anything of this plot, with the possible exception of Jake Esterline who may have it confused with other schemes.

Contaminated Cigars

Jake Esterline claims to have had in his possession in pre-Bay of Pigs days a box of cigars that had been treated with some sort of chemical. in our first interview with him, his recollection was that the chemical was intended to produce temporary personality disorientation. The thought was to somehow contrive to have Castro smoke one before making a speech and then to make a public spectacle of himself.

Esterline distinctly recalls having had the cigars in his personal safe until he left WH/4 and that they definitely were intended for Castro. He does not remember how they came into his possession, but he thinks they must have been prepared by [deletion] In a second interview with Esterline, we mentioned that we had learned since first speaking with him of a scheme to cause Castro's beard to fall out. He then said that his cigars might have been associated with that plan. Esterline finally said that, although it was evident that he no longer remembered the intended effect of the cigars, he was positive they were not lethal. The cigars were never used, according to Esterline, because WH/4 could not figure out how to deliver them without danger of blowback on the Agency. He says he destroyed them before leaving WH/4 in June 1961.

Sidney Gottlieb, of TSD, claims to remember distinctly a plot involving cigars. To emphasize the clarity of his memory, he named the officer, then assigned to WH/CA, who approached him with the scheme. Although there may well have been such a plot, the officer Gottlieb named was then assigned to India and has never worked in WH Division nor had anything to do with Cuba operations. Gottlieb remembers the scheme as being one that was talked about frequently but not widely and as being concerned with killing, not merely influencing behaviour. As far as Gottlieb knows, this idea never got beyond the talking stage. TSD may have gone ahead and prepared the cigars just in case, but Gottlieb is certain that he did not get the DD/P's (Richard Bissell) personal approval to release them, as would have been done if the operation had gone that far. We are unable to discover whether Esterline and Gottlieb are speaking of a single cigar episode or of two unrelated schemes. We found no one else with firm recollections of lethal cigars being considered prior to August 1960.

-12-

Depilatory

[deletion] recalls a scheme involving thallium salts, a chemical used by women as a depilatory—the thought being to destroy Castro's image as "The Beard" by causing the beard to fall out. The chemical may be administered either orally or by absorption through the skin. The right dosage causes depilation; too much produces paralysis. [deletion] believes that the idea originated in connection with a trip Castro was to have made outside of Cuba. The idea was to dust thallium powder into Castro's shoes when they were put out at night to be shined. The scheme progressed as far as procuring the chemical and testing it on animals. [deletion] recollection is that Castro did not make the intended trip, and the scheme fell through. [deletion] remembers consideration being given to use the thallium salts (perhaps against Castro) and something having to do with boots or shoes.

[deletion] does not remember with whom he dealt on this plot. We found no one else with firm knowledge of it.

-13-

Gambling Syndicate

The first seriously-pursued CIA plan to assassinate Castro had its inception in August 1960. It involved the use of members of the criminal underworld with contacts inside Cuba. The operation had two phases: the first ran from August 1960 until late April or early May 1961, when it was called off following the Bay of Pigs; the second ran from April 1962 until February 1963 and was merely a revival of the first phase which had been inactive since about May 1961.

Gambling Syndicate – Phase I

August 1960

Richard Bissell, Deputy Director for Plans, asked Sheffield Edwards, Director of Security, if Edwards could establish contact with the U.S. gambling syndicate that was active in Cuba. The objective clearly was the assassination of Castro although Edwards claims that there was a studied avoidance of the term in his conversation with Bissell. Bissell recalls that the idea originated with J.C. King, then Chief of WH Division, although King now recalls having had only limited knowledge of such a plan and at a much later date—about mid-1962.

-14-

Edwards consulted Robert A. Maheu, a private investigator who had done sensitive work for the Agency, to see if Maheu had any underworld contacts. Maheu was once a special agent of the FBI . . . The late Robert Cunningham, of the Office of Security (and also a former Special Agent with the FBI), knew Maheu and knew that his business was having a shaky start financially. Cunningham arranged to subsidize Maheu to the extent of $500 per month. Within six months Maheu was doing so well financially that he suggested that the retainer be discontinued. Over the years he has been intimately involved in providing support for some of the Agency's more sensitive operations. He has since moved his personal headquarters to Los Angeles but retains a Washington office. A more detailed account of Maheu's background appears in a separate section of this report. . . .

. . . Maheu acknowledged that he had a contact who might furnish access to the criminal underworld, but Maheu was most reluctant to allow himself to be involved in such an assignment. He agreed to

-15-

participate only after being pressed by Edwards to do so. Maheu identified his contact as one Johnny Roselli, who lived in Los Angeles and had the concession for the ice-making machines on "the strip" in Las Vegas and whom Maheu understood to be a member of the syndicate. Maheu was known to Roselli as a man who had a number of large business organizations as clients. Edwards and Maheu agreed that Maheu would approach Roselli as the representative of businessmen with interests in Cuba who saw the elimination of Castro as the essential first step to the recovery of their investments. Maheu was authorized to tell Roselli that his "clients" were willing to pay $150,000 for Castro's removal.

September 1960

Shef Edwards named as his case officer for the operation James P. O'Connell (a former Special Agent of the FBI), then Chief, Operational Support Division, Office of Security. O'Connell and Maheu met Roselli in New York City on 14 September 1960 where Maheu made the pitch. Roselli initially was also reluctant to become involved, but finally agreed to introduce Maheu to "Sam Gold" who either had or could arrange contacts with syndicate elements in Cuba who might handle the job. Roselli said he had no interest in being paid for his participation and believed that "Gold" would feel the

-16-

same way. A memorandum for the record prepared by Sheffield Edwards on

14 May 1962 states: "No monies were ever paid to Roselli and Giancana. Maheu was paid part of his expense money during the periods that he was in Miami." (Giancana is "Gold. ")

O'Connell was introduced (in true name) to Roselli as an employee of Maheu, the explanation being that O'Connell would handle the case for Maheu, because Maheu was too busy to work on it full time himself. No one else in the Office of Security was made witting of the operation at this time. Edwards himself did not meet Roselli until the summer of 1962.

At this point, about the second half of September, Shef Edwards told Bissell that he had a friend, a private investigator, who had a contact who in turn had other contacts through whom syndicate elements in Cuba could be reached. These syndicate elements in Cuba would be willing to take on such an operation. As of the latter part of September 1960, Edwards, O'Connell, and Bissell were the only ones in the Agency who knew of a plan against Castro involving U.S. gangster elements. Edwards states that Richard Helms was not informed of the plan, because Cuba was being handled by Bissell at that time.

With Bissell present, Edwards briefed the Director (Allen Dulles) and the DDCI (General Cabell) on the existence of a plan involving members of the syndicate. The discussion was circumspect; Edwards

-17-

deliberately avoided the use of any "bad words." The descriptive term used was "intelligence operation." Edwards is quite sure that the DCI and the DDCI clearly understood the nature of the operation he was discussing. He recalls describing the channel as being "from A to B to C." As he then envisioned it, "A" was Maheu, "B" was Roselli, and "C" was the principal in Cuba. Edwards recalls that Mr. Dulles merely nodded, presumably in understanding and approval. Certainly, there was no opposition. Edwards states that, while there was no formal approval as such, he felt that he clearly had tacit approval to use his own judgment. Bissell committed $150,000 for the support of the operation.

(Comment: In the light of this description of the briefing, it is appropriate to conjecture as to just what the Director did approve. It is safe to conclude, given the men participating and the general subject of the meeting, that there was little likelihood of misunderstanding—even though the details were deliberately blurred and the specific intended result was never stated in unmistakable language. It is also reasonable to conclude that the pointed avoidance of "bad words" emphasized to the participants the extreme sensitivity of the operation.)

During the week of 23 September 1960, O'Connell and Maheu went o Miami where Roselli introduced only Maheu to "Sam Gold" at a meeting

-18-

in the Fontainbleau Hotel. "Gold" said he had a man, whom he identified only as "Joe," who would serve as courier to Cuba and make arrangements there. Maheu pointed out "Gold" to O'Connell from a distance, but O'Connell never met with either "Gold" or "Joe." He did, however, learn their true identities. As Office of Security memorandum to the DDCI of 24 June 1966 places the time as "several weeks later."O'Connell is now uncertain as to whether it was on this first visit to Miami or on a subsequent one that he and Maheu learned the true identities of the two men. Maheu and O'Connell were staying at separate hotels. Maheu phoned O'Connell one Sunday morning and called his attention to the Parade supplement in one of that morning's Miami newspapers. It carried an article on the Cosa Nostra, with pictures of prominent members. The man Maheu and O'Connell knew as "Sam Gold" appeared as Mom Salvatore (Sam) Giancana, a Chicago-based gangster. "Joe, the courier" (who was never identified to either Maheu or O'Connell in any other way) turned out to be Santos Trafficante, the Cosa Nostra chieftain in Cuba.

At that time the gambling casinos were still operating in Cuba, and Trafficante was making regular trips between Miami and Havana on syndicate business. (The casinos were closed and gambling was banned effective 7 January 1959. On 13 January 1959, Castro announced that the casinos would be permitted to reopen for tourists and foreigners

-19-

but that Cubans would be barred. The cabinet on 17 February 1959 authorized reopening the casinos for the tourist trade. Time magazine for 2 March 1959 announced that the casinos had been reopened the previous week. The New York Times issue of 30 September 1961 announced that the last of the casinos still running had been closed.) Trafficante was to make the arrangements with one of his contacts inside Cuba on one of his trips to Havana.

Fall and Early Winter 1960

Very early in the operation, well before the first contact with Roselli, the machinery for readying the means of assassination was set in motion. The sequence of events is not clear, but is apparent that a number of methods were considered. Preparation of some materials went ahead without express approval.

(Comment: It should be noted that TSD maintains a stock of equipment and materials for operational use. When queries are made of TSD technicians about materials or devices that are not stock items, it is not unusual for the technicians to go ahead with the preparation of the materials or devices against the event that there is a formal request for them. Because of this, undue significance should not be attached to advance preparations for this operation. It should also be noted that

-20-

it was not unusual at the time in question for the Chief of TSD to be by-passed in operations involving his people. While Cornelius Roosevelt, then Chief of TSD, has the clear impression that all requests were levied through him, instances were cited in the course of this inquiry where such was not the case. The practices and procedures in existence at the time may account, at least in part, for the differing recollections of what did and what did not happen and for the differing degrees of significance given developments in the minds of the participants.)

Dr. Edward Gunn, Chief, Operations Division, Office of Medical

Services, has a notation that on 16 August 1960 he received a box of Cuban cigars to be treated with lethal material. He understood them to be Fidel's favorite brand, and he thinks they were given to him by Shef Edwards. Edwards does not recall the incident. Gunn has a notation that he contacted [deletion] of TSD, on 6 September 1960. [deletion] remembers experimenting with some cigars and then treating a full box. He cannot now recall whether he was initially given two boxes, experimenting with one and then treating the other; or whether he bought a box for experimentation, after which he treated the box supplied him by Gunn. He does not, in fact, remember Gunn as the supplier of any cigars. He is positive, though, that he did contaminate a full box of fifty cigars with botulinus toxin, a virulent poison that

-21-

produces a fatal illness some hours after it is ingested. [deletion] distinctly remembers the flaps-and-seals job he had to do on the box and on each of the wrapped cigars, both to get the cigars and to erase evidence of tampering. He kept one of the experimental cigars and still has it. He retested it during our inquiry and found that the toxin still retained 94% of its original effectiveness. The cigars were so heavily contaminated that merely putting one in the mouth would do the job; the intended victim would not actually have to smoke it.

Gunn's notes show that he reported the cigars as being ready for delivery on 7 October 1960. [deletion]'s notes do not show actual delivery until 13 February 1961. They do not indicate to whom delivery was made. Gunn states that he took the cigars, at some unspecified time, and kept them in his personal safe. He remembers destroying them within a month of Shef Edwards retirement in June 1963.

[Hand notation in the margin: "We believe (deletion) gave the cigars to Gunn. "]

(Comment: Others recall the cigar scheme, but only as an idea that was considered and then discarded. Roosevelt, Chief of TSD at the time, and O'Connell, the case officer, recall the cigar scheme, but feel that it was never considered seriously. To Gunn and [deletion] who gave it a good deal of time but did not participate in the broader operational discussions, the cigars loom as important.)

-22-

Edwards recalls approaching Roosevelt after Bissell had already spoken to Roosevelt on the subject; Roosevelt recalls speaking to Edwards after Bissell discussed it with Edwards. Bissel does not recall specific conversations with either of them on the technical aspects of the problem, but he believes that he must have "closed the loop" by talks with both Edwards and Roosevelt. Roosevelt recalls his first meeting with Edwards as being in Edwards' office. Edwards remembers asking to be introduced to a chemist. He is sure that he did not name the target to Roosevelt, but Roosevelt says he knew it was Castro. Roosevelt believes that he would have put Edwards in touch with [deletion], then chief of TSD's Chemical Division, but [deletion] has no recollection of such work at that time. [deletion] recalls other operations at other times, but not this one. Roosevelt did say that, if he turned it over to [deletion] [deletion] could have assigned it to [deletion]

Roosevelt remembers that four possible approaches were considered: (1) something highly toxic, such as shellfish poison to be administered with a pin (which Roosevelt said was what was supplied to Gary Powers); (2) bacterial material in liquid form; (3) bacterial treatment of a cigarette or cigar; and (4) a handkerchief treated with bacteria. The decision, to the best of his recollection, was that bacteria in liquid form was the best means. Bissell recalls the same decision,

-23-

tying it to a recollection that Castro frequently drank tea, coffee, or bouillon, for which a liquid poison would be particularly well suited.

January – February 1961

Despite the decision that a poison in liquid form would be most desirable, what was actually prepared and delivered was a solid in the form of small pills about the size of saccharine tablets. [deletion] remembers meeting with Edwards and O'Connell in Edwards' office to discuss the requirement. The specifications were that the poison be stable, soluble, safe to handle, undetectable, not immediately acting, and with a firmly predictable end result. Botulin comes nearest to meeting all those requirements, and it may be put up in either liquid or solid form. [deletion] states that the pill form was chosen because of ease and safety of handling.

(Comment: The gangsters may have had some influence on the choice of a means of assassination. O'Connell says that in his very early discussions with the gangsters (or, more precisely, Maheu's discussions with them) consideration was given to possible ways of accomplishing the mission. Apparently the Agency had first thought in terms of a typical, gangland-style killing in which Castro would be gunned down. Giancana was flatly opposed to the

-24-

use of firearms. He said that no one could be recruited to do the job, because the chance of survival and escape would be negligible. Giancana stated a preference for a lethal pill that could be put into Castro's food or drink. Trafficante ("Joe, the courier") was in touch with a disaffected Cuban official with access to Castro and presumably of a sort that would enable him to surreptitiously poison Castro. The gangsters named their man inside as Juan Orta who was then Office Chief and Director General of the Office of the Prime Minister (Castro). The gangsters said that Orta had once been in a position to receive kickbacks from the gambling interests, has since lost that source of income, and needed the money.)

When Edwards received the pills he dropped one into a glass of water to test it for solubility and found that it did not even disintegrate, let alone dissolve. [deletion] took them back and made up a new batch that met the requirement for solubility.

Edwards at that point wanted assurance that the pills were truly lethal. He called on Dr. Gunn to make an independent test of them. Edwards gave

Gunn money to buy guinea pigs as test animals. Gunn has a record of a conversation with [deletion] on 6 February 1961. It may have related to the tests, but we cannot be sure. What appears to have happened is that Gunn tested the pills on the guinea pigs and found them ineffective.

-25-

[deletion] states that tests of bouillon on guinea pigs are not valid, because guinea pigs have a high resistance to this particular toxin. [deletion] himself tested the pills on monkeys and found they did the job expected of them.

We cannot reconstruct with certainty the sequence of events between readying the pills and putting them into the hands of Roselli. Edwards has the impression that he had a favorable report from Dr. Gunn on the guinea pig test. Gunn probably reported only that the pills were effective, and Edwards assumed the report was based on the results of tests on guinea pigs. Dr. Gunn has a clear recollection, without a date, of being present at a meeting in which Roosevelt demonstrated a pencil designed as a concealment device for delivering the pills. Roosevelt also recalls such a meeting, also without a date. Gunns' notes record that his last action on the operation came on 10 February 1961 when he put Gottlieb in touch with Edwards. Gottlieb has no recollection of being involved, an impression that is supported by Bissell who states that Gottlieb's assignments were of a different nature. O'Connell, who eventually received the pills, recalls that he dealt with [deletion] [deletion] has no record of delivering the pills at this time, but he does not ordinarily keep detailed records of such things.

-26-

In any event, O'Connell did receive the pills, and he believes there were six of them. He recalls giving three to Roselli. Presumably the other three were used in testing for solubility and effectiveness. The dates on which O'Connell received the pills and subsequently passed them to Roselli cannot be established. It would have been sometime after Gunn's notation of 10 February 1961.

Gunn also has a record of being approached about the undertaking by William K. Harvey (former special agent of the FBI) in February in connection with a sensitive project Harvey was working on for Bissell. According to Gunn's notes, he briefed Harvey on the operation, and Harvey instructed him to discuss techniques, but not targets, with Gottlieb. Gunn's notation on this point is not in accord with the recollections of any of the others involved. We are unable to clarify it; the note may have been in another context. O'Connell states that J.C. King was also briefed at this time, although King denies learning of the operation until much later.

Late February – March 1961

Roselli passed the pills to Trafficante. Roselli reported to O'Connell that the pills had been delivered to Orta in Cuba. Orta is understood to have kept the pills for a couple of weeks before returning them. According to the gangsters, Orta got cold feet.

-27-

(Comment: Orta lost his position in the Prime Minister's Office on 26 January 1961, while planning for the operation was still going on in Miami and in Washington. He took refuge in the Venezuelan Embassy on 11 April 1961 and became the responsibility of the Mexican Embassy when Venezuela broke relations with Cuba in November 1961. Castro refused to give him a safe conduct pass until October 1964 when he was allowed to leave for Mexico City. He arrived in Miami in early February 1965.

(It appears that Edwards and O'Connell did not know at the time of Orta's fall from favor. They have made no reference to it—ascribing Orta's failure to cold feet. It would seem, though, that the gangsters did know that Orta had already lost his access to Castro. They described him as a man who had once had a position that allowed him a rake-off on gambling profits, a position that he had since lost. The only job with which we can associate Orta that might have allowed him a rake-off was the one he held in the Prime Minister's Office, which he lost on 26 January 1961. It seems likely that, while the Agency thought the gangsters had a man in Cuba with easy access to Castro, what they actually had was a man disgruntled at having lost access.)

The previously-mentioned 24 June 1966 summary of the operation prepared by the Office of Security states that when Orta asked out

-28-

of the assignment he suggested another candidate who made several attempts without success. Neither Edwards nor O'Connell know the identity of Orta's replacement nor any additional details of the reported further attempts.

March – April 1961

Following the collapse of the Orta channel, Roselli told O'Connell that Trafficante knew of a man high up in the Cuban exile movement who might do the job. He identified him as Tony Varona (Dr. Manuel Antonio de VARONA y Loredo). Varona was the head of the Democratic Revolutionary Front, [1/2 line deletion] part of the larger Cuban operation. O'Connell understood that Varona was dissatisfied [two lines deletion]

(Comment: Reports from the FBI suggest how Trafficante may have known of Varona. On 21 December 1960 the Bureau forwarded to the Agency a memorandum reporting that efforts were being made by U.S. racketeers to finance anti-Castro activities in hopes of securing the gambling, prostitution, and dope monopolies in Cuba in the event Castro was overthrown. A later report of 18 January 1961 associates Varona with those schemes. Varona

-29-

had hired Edward K. Moss, a Washington public relations counselor, as a fund raiser and public relations advisor. The Bureau report alleged that Moss' mistress was one Julia Cellini, whose brothers represented two of the largest gambling casinos in Cuba. The Cellini bothers were believed to be in touch with Varona through Moss and were reported to have offered Varona large sums of money for his operations against Castro, with the understanding that they would receive privileged treatment "in the Cuba of the future." . . .

(There is a record of CIA interest in Moss, but there is no indication that the Agency had any involvement with him in connection with Cuba. [four lines deletion]. . . .

-30-

[one and three-quarters lines deletion]

Trafficante approached Varona and told him that he had clients who wanted to do away with Castro and that they would pay big money for the job. Varona is reported to have been very receptive, since it would mean that he would be able to buy his own ships, arms, and communications equipment.

(Comment: By this time Roselli had become certain that O'Connell was an Agency employee, not a subordinate of Maheu. He told O'Connell that he was sure that O'Connell was "a government man – CIA" but that O'Connell should not confirm this to him. Roselli said that as a loyal American he would do whatever he could and would never divulge the operation.)

Roselli was to deliver money to Varona for expenses. . . . An Office of Security memorandum to the DDCI,

-31-

dated 24 June 1965, sets the amount as $10,000 in cash and $1,000 worth of communications equipment. Jake Esterline, who signed the vouchers for the funds, recalls the amounts as being those stated in the Office of Security memorandum.

(Comment: As a sidelight, Esterline says that, when he learned of the intended use of Varona, steps were taken to cancel the plan. Varona was one of the five key figures in the Revolutionary Front and was heavily involved in support of the approaching Bay of Pigs operation. If steps were in fact taken to end Varona's participation in the syndicate plan, they were ineffective. It is clear that he continued as an integral part of the syndicate scheme.)

When the money was ready, O'Connell took the pills from his safe and delivered them and the money to Roselli. Roselli gave the pills and the money to Varona, whom Roselli dealt with under pseudonym. Little is known of the delivery channels beyond Varona. Varona was believed to have an asset inside Cuba in a position to slip a pill to Castro. Edwards recalls something about a contact who worked in a restaurant frequented by Castro and who was to receive the pills and put them into Castro's food or drink. Edwards believes that the scheme failed because Castro ceased to visit that particular restaurant.

[handwritten note in margin: "Edwards does not recall where he said this. "]

-32-

April—May 1961

Soon after the Bay of Pigs, Edwards sent word to Roselli through O'Connell that the operation was off—even if something happened there would be no payoff. Edwards is sure there was a complete standdown after that; the operation was dead and remained so until April 1962. He clearly relates the origins of the operation to the upcoming Bay of Pigs invasion, and its termination to the Bay of Pigs failure. O'Connell agrees that the operation was called off after the Bay of Pigs but that the termination was not firm and final. He believes that there was something going on between April 1961 and April 1962, but he cannot now recall what. He agrees with Bill Harvey that when the operation was revived in April 1962, Harvey took over a "going operation."

(Comment: As distinguished from Edwards and O'Connell, both Bissell and Esterline place the termination date of the assassination operation as being about six months before the Bay of Pigs. Esterline gives as his reason for so believing the fact that the decision had been made to go ahead with a massive, major operation instead of an individually-targeted one such as this. Whatever the intention in this respect, if the decision to terminate was actually made, the decision was not communicated

-33-

effectively. It is clear that this plan to assassinate Castro continued in train until sometime after the Bay of Pigs.)

O'Connell believes that he must have recovered the pills, but he has no specific recollection of having done so. He thinks that instead of returning them to TSD he probably would have destroyed them, most likely by flushing them down a toilet.

[deletion] has no record of the pills having been returned to him, but he says he is quite sure that they were.

In a memorandum of 14 May 1962 Sheffield Edwards stated that knowledge of this particular operation was limited to six persons. In the course of this investigation, we have identified the following persons who knew in late 1960 or early 1961 of this specific plan to assassinate Castro:

1. Allen Dulles, Director of Central Intelligence
2. General C.P. Cabell, Deputy Director of Central Intelligence
3. Richard Bissell, Deputy Director for Plans
4. Sheffield Edwards, Director of Security
5. James O'Connell, Office of Security, the case officer
6. J.D. Esterline, Chief, WH/4
7. Cornelius Roosevelt, Chief, TSD
8. [deletion] Chemical Division, TSD
9. Edward Gunn, Chief, Operations Division, Medical Services

-34-

10. William Harvey, Chief, FI/D
11. Sidney Gottlieb, Special Assistant to the DD/P (Gottlieb's name was encountered repeatedly in this inquiry, but he denies knowing of the operation in 1960-1961.)
12. Robert Bannerman, Deputy Director of Security
13. J.C. King, Chief, WH Division (He too denies knowing of the operation at the time.)

The following persons outside the government are known to be witting of the operation and either know or strongly suspect the Agency's connection with it:

1. Robert Maheu, a private investigator
2. John Roselli, the Agency's principal contact with the gambling syndicate
3. Sam Giancana, an important figure in the syndicate
4. Santos Trafficante, the courier and man inside Cuba

These additional people were aware of the operation, but their knowledge of CIA's connection with it can only be speculated:

1. Juan Orta, the man originally selected to poison Castro
2. Antonio Varona, a Cuban exile leader
3. The son-in-law of Varona, who is known to have been involved with him closely during this time. (The Varona 201 file makes no reference to Varona having a son-in-law, but he identified this close associate as such.)

-35-

The Agency's General Counsel, Lawrence Houston, and Attorney General Robert Kennedy learned the full details of the operation in May 1962. We do not know the particulars of the report Drew Pearson now has, but it may include many of the details of this operation. If it does, then the circle of those now knowledgeable would be widened to include:

1. Edward P. Morgan, Maheu's Washington attorney
2. Columnist Drew Pearson and probably his partner, Jack Anderson
3. Chief Justice Earl Warren
4. James Rowley, chief of the Secret Service
5. Pat Coyne, Executive Secretary of the PFIAB
6. Attorney General Ramsey Clark
7. Various members of the FBI

-36-

Gambling Syndicate — Phase 2

William Harvey, Chief of FI/D, was briefed in February 1961 (by authority of Richard Bissell) on phase one of the gambling syndicate operation. That briefing was in connection with a sensitive operation that Bissell had assigned to Harvey. Harvey describes it thus: Early in the Kennedy administration, Bissell called him in to discuss what Harvey refers to as an Executive Action Capability; i.e., a general stand-by capability to carry out assassinations when required. Harvey's notes quote Bissell as saying, "The White House has twice urged me to create such a capability." Bissell recalls discussing the question of developing a general capability with Harvey. He mentioned the Edwards/gambling syndicate operation against Castro in that context, but he now thinks that the operation was over by then and that reference to it was in terms of a past operation as a case in point. It was on this basis that Harvey arranged to be briefed by Edwards. Harvey's fixing of the date as February was only after review of events both preceding the briefing and following it. He says now that it might have been as early as late January or as late as March 1961.

After some discussion of the problems involved in developing as Executive Action Capability, Bissell placed Harvey in charge of the effort. Harvey says that Bissell had already discussed certain aspects of the problem with [deleted] and with Sidney Gottlieb. Since [deleted] was already cut in, Harvey used him in developing the Executive Action Capability, although never with respect to Castro. We did not question Gottlieb on his knowledge of the program for creating an Executive Action Capability, but Harvey's mention of him in this connection may explain a notation by Dr. Gunn that Harvey instructed Gunn to discuss techniques with Gottlieb without associating the discussion with the Castro operation.

Harvey states that after the decision was made to go ahead with the creating of an Executive Action Capability, and while he was still discussing its development with Bissell, he briefed Mr. Helms fully on the general concept but without mention of the then ongoing plan to assassinate Castro.

The Executive Action program came to be known as ZRRIFLE. Its principal asset was an agent, QJWIN, who had been recruited earlier by [deleted] for use in a special operation in the Congo [the following line was struck through with a pen, but not redacted—it reads: "the assassination of Patrice Lumumba) to be run by [deleted] [deleted] made a survey of the scene, decided he wanted no part in an assassination attempt, and asked to be released—which Bissell granted.) The project name, ZRRIFLE, first appears in the files in May 1961, although the first recorded approval is dated 19 February 1962. The new DD/P (Helms) on that date authorized Harvey, by

-37 and 38-

memorandum, to handle the project on a special basis. Accounting for expenditures was to be by general category and on Harvey's certification. The initial approval was for $14,700, consisting of $7,200 for QJWIN's annual salary and $7,500 for operational expenses.

Project ZRRIFLE was covered as an FI/D operation (ostensibly to develop a capability for entering safes and for kidnapping couriers). It continued on a course separate from the Edwards/gambling syndicate operation against Castro until 15 November 1961. Harvey has a note that on that date he discussed with Bissell the application of the ZRRIFLE program to Cuba. Harvey says that Bissell instructed him to take over Edwards' contact with the criminal syndicate and thereafter to run the operation against Castro. Harvey adds that, as a completely unrelated development, shortly after this discussion with Bissell he was told by Helms that he was to be placed in charge of the Agency's Cuba task force.

Later 1961 – Early 1962

Harvey recalls that he was very busy with a number of things in the period that followed the discussion with Bissell that led to his taking over Edwards' Castro operation . . . He was reading in on Cuba operations and

-39-

was engaged in daily meetings concerning them. He attended a station chiefs' conference in Panama in late January and early February.

February – March 1962

Harvey recalls a first meeting with Edwards in February 1962 on the subject of the Castro operation. He also recalls working out the details of the takeover during March.

(Comment: After Harvey took over the Castro operation he ran it as one aspect of ZRRIFLE; however, he personally handled the Castro operation and did not use any of the assets being developed in ZRRIFLE. He says that he soon came to think of the Castro operation and ZRRIFLE as being synonymous. The over-all Executive Action program came to be treated in his mind as being synonymous with QJWIN, the agent working on the over-all program. He says that when he wrote of ZRRIFLE/QJWIN the reference was to Executive Action Capability; when he used the cryptonym ZRRIFLE alone, he was referring to Castro. He said that his correspondence would disclose this distinction. We reviewed the correspondence and found it for the most part unrevealing.

. . . .

-40-

. . . .

April 1962

Edwards recalls Harvey contacting him in April and asking to be put in touch with Roselli. Edwards says that he verified Helms' approval and then made the arrangements. Harvey states that he briefed Helms before his first meeting with Roselli, explaining its purpose, and that he also reported to Helms the results of his meeting with Roselli. Harvey states that thereafter he regularly briefed Helms on the status of the Castro operation.

(Comment: Edwards statement that he "verified Helms' approval" is the earliest indication we have that Mr. Helms had been made witting of the gambling syndicate operation against Castro. Harvey added that, when he briefed Helms on Roselli, he obtained Helms' approval not to brief the Director.)

Edwards, Harvey, and O'Connell have differing recollections of the specifics of the turnover from Edwards/O'Connell to Harvey. Not

-41-

all of the differences can be resolved—not even by follow-up interviews in which the information furnished by each was checked with each of the other two. There is no disagreement on the fact that the turnover nor on when it took place. The recollections vary decidedly, though, on the status of the operation at the time of its transfer to Harvey and on just how clean the break was between phase one under Edwards and phase two under Harvey.

a. Edwards believes that the operation was called off completely after the Bay of Pigs and that there was no further operational activity in connection with it until Harvey met Roselli and reactivated the operation in April 1962. O'Connell introduced Harvey to Roselli, and Edwards had nothing further to do with the operation—with the exception of a meeting with Attorney General Robert Kennedy . . . Edwards' records show that on 14 May 1962 Harvey called Edwards "and indicated that he was dropping any plans for the use of Roselli for the future."

b. Harvey's recollections of the turnover tends to support Edwards' summary, but he claims that he took over "a going operation." Some support for this claim is found in his description

-42-

of just how it was planned to get the poison into Castro's food by employing someone with access to a restaurant frequented by Castro. The mechanics were identical with those described by Edwards and as reported in our earlier account of phase one of the operation.

c. O'Connell's account of his own role in the operation in the early weeks following Harvey's supposed takeover makes it evident that there was not a clean break between the Office of Security's responsibility and that of Harvey. Further, O'Connell now believes that there must have been "something going on" between April 1961 (after the Bay of Pigs) and April 1962, but he claims to be unable to remember any of the particulars.

There are other disagreements among the three on facts. They are reviewed here, not because they alter the essential fact of the turnover or of Harvey's sole responsibility for the operation after a certain point in time, but because they suggest that persons who were supposedly unwitting of events after the turnover were in fact witting, because they were not effectively cut off at the instant of turnover.

Harvey's notes show that he and O'Connell went to New York City to meet Roselli on the 8th and 9th of April 1962. O'Connell recalls it as being early in April and that the introduction was made on a

-43-

Sunday, which would make it the 8th. Harvey says that only he and O'Connell met with Roselli; O'Connell says that Maheu was also present at the meeting. Both are positive of the accuracy of their recollections, and each gives reasons for his confidence in his clarity of recall. The significance, for purposes of this inquiry, is whether Maheu did or did not know that the operation continued under Harvey.

a. Harvey is certain that he would have remembered it if Maheu were present. He and Maheu were in the same FBI training class at Quantico in 1940. He does not remember having seen Maheu since he, Harvey, came with the Agency in 1947, although he acknowledges that he may have seen him once or twice socially. He is sure he has not seen Maheu since 1952 when Harvey was assigned to Berlin.

b. O'Connell, who set up the meeting, is just as positive that Maheu was there. . . .

-44-

. . . .

The two differing recollections cannot be reconciled. As a point of interest, Edwards stated that when he briefed Harvey on the operation he deliberately omitted reference to Maheu in order to screen Maheu off from Harvey's takeover of the operation.

The next significant point of difference has to do with what happened after the New York meeting. O'Connell told us that he and Roselli left New York for Miami the next day (presumably 10 April)

-45-

and remained there until Harvey arrived. Harvey, on the other hand, recalls a meeting with O'Connell and Roselli in Washington on 14 April. O'Connell, at first, did not recall the Washington meeting, but, when given Harvey's chronology, he said he did recall returning to Washington to meet Harvey for some purpose but that the details are vague in his mind. Harvey at first thought that the 14 April meeting in Washington was O'Connell's last contact with Roselli during this second phase of the gambling syndicate operation. O'Connell told us that Roselli was apprehensive over the new arrangement (and of Harvey personally) and asked O'Connell to remain on for a time, which O'Connell agreed to do. When told that O'Connell was sure that he had continued on in the operation for some two or three weeks after Harvey's takeover, Harvey agreed that this was correct. O'Connell's carryover was for purposes of continuity. We cannot be sure of the date O'Connell was finally eliminated from the operation . . .

Harvey recalls leaving Washington for Miami by automobile on 19 April. He thought that he took delivery of the pills from Dr. Gunn before leaving. Gunn has no record of any such delivery at that time; his last record concerning pills is dated February 1961. [deletion]

-46-

does have a notation of delivering four pills (one capsule and three tablets) to "J.C." on 18 April 1962. [deletion] reads this as being Jim O'Connell. When told of this, Harvey agreed that it was probably correct. O'Connell also feels that he must have been in Washington for the pill delivery.

Harvey says that he arrived in Miami on 21 April 1962 and found Roselli already in touch with Tony Varona, the Cuban exile leader who had participated in phase one. It is at this point that the final difference in recollections occurs. Harvey described the manner in which the lethal material was to be introduced into Castro's food, involving an asset of Varona's who had access to someone in a restaurant frequented by Castro. We told Harvey that Edwards had described precisely the same plan. When we asked Harvey how Edwards could have known of the mechanics if there had been no activity in the operation for a year, and if Harvey was starting again from scratch, Harvey replied that he took over a going operation— one that was already "in train." Edwards denies that this is so. O'Connell says that Harvey is the one who is right. The operation was going on when Harvey took it over, although O'Connell does not remember when Varona was reactivated or what had been done with him in the meantime.

Along with the change in Agency leadership of the operation, which saw Harvey replacing Edwards/O'Connell, there also were changes

-47-

in the original cast of hoodlum players. Harvey specified that Giancana was not to be brought in on the reactivation of the operation, and he believes that Roselli honored the request. Roselli once reported to Harvey that Giancana had asked if anything was going on, and when Roselli said that nothing was happening, Giancana said, "Too bad." Additionally, Santos Trafficante ("Joe, the courier" from the earlier phase) was no longer involved. With the closing of the last casino in Havana in September 1961, Trafficante presumably no longer had access. Roselli now had a man known to Harvey as Maceo, who also used the names Garcia-Gomez and Godoy.

(Comment: Harvey is unable further to identify Macoe; he describes him as "a Cuban who spoke Italian." . . . This second phase appears to lack the overwhelming, high-level gangster flavor that characterized the first phase. Roselli remained as a prominent figure in the operation, but working directly with the Cuban exile community and directly on behalf of CIA. Roselli was essential to the second phase as a contact with Varona, who presumably still

-48-

believed he was being supported by U.S. businessmen with financial stakes in Cuba. Roselli needed Giancana and Trafficante in the first phase as a means of establishing contacts inside Cuba. He did not need them in the second phase, because he had Varona. However, it would be naive to assume that Roselli did not take the precaution of informing higher-ups in the syndicate that he was working in a territory considered to be the private domain of someone else in the syndicate.)

When the pills were given to Varona through Roselli, Varona requested arms and equipment needed for the support of his end of the operation. Roselli passed the request to Harvey. Harvey, with the help of Ted Shackley, the chief of the JMWAVE Station, procured explosives, detonators, twenty .30 caliber rifles, twenty .45 caliber hand guns, two radios, and one boat radar. Harvey says that the "shopping list" included some items that could be obtained only from the U.S. Government. Harvey omitted those items, because Roselli, posing as a representative of private business interests, would not have had access to such equipment. The cost of the arms and equipment, about $5,000, was T/A'd to headquarters.

Harvey and Shackley rented a U-Haul truck under an assumed name, loaded it with the arms and equipment, and parked it in the parking lot of a drive-in restaurant. The keys were then given to Roselli for

-49-

delivery either to Maceo, to Varona, or to Varona's son-in-law. Evidently Harvey and Roselli had not yet come to trust each other. Perhaps fearing a double-cross, each set about independently to assure himself that the equipment reached the proper hands. After parking the truck, Harvey and Shackley kept the parking lot under surveillance until the pass was completed. Roselli, accompanied by O'Connell, did the same. Neither pair knew that the other was watching. Eventually the truck was picked up and driven away. It was returned later, empty, and with the keys under the seat as prearranged. Harvey returned it to the rental agency. Harvey says that Shackley never knew to whom delivery was made nor for what purpose. Shackley was merely called upon to furnish support for a headquarters operation from which he was otherwise excluded.

May 1962

Harvey and Roselli arranged a system of telephone communication by which Harvey was kept posted on any developments. Harvey, using a pay phone, could call Roselli at the Friars Club in Los Angeles at 1600 hours, Los Angeles time. Roselli could phone Harvey at Harvey's home in the evening. Roselli reported that the pills were in Cuba and at the restaurant reportedly used regularly by Castro.

-50-

June 1962

Roselli reported to Harvey on 21 June that Varona had dispatched a team of three men to Cuba. Just what they were supposed to do is pretty vague. Harvey said that they appeared to have no specific plan for killing Castro. They were to recruit others who might be used in such a scheme. If an opportunity to kill Castro presented itself, they or the persons they recruited were to make the attempt—perhaps using the pills. Harvey never learned their names or anything else about them. From the sequence of the reports, it would seem that the pills were sent in ahead of the three-man team, but this is not now ascertainable.

September 1962

Harvey saw Roselli in Miami on 7 and 11 September. Varona was reported as then ready to send in another team of three men. They were supposedly militia men whose assignment was to penetrate Castro's body guard. During this period the "medicine" was reported as still in place and the three men of the first team safe.

September 1962 - January 1963

Although Harvey received several reports that the militia men were poised to take off, presumably from somewhere in the Florida keys,

-51-

they did not actually leave. First, "conditions inside" were given as the reason for delay; then the October missile crisis threw plans awry. Harvey was in Miami between 22 December and 6 January. He saw both Roselli and Maceo several times during that period. He made a payment of $2,700 to Roselli for passing to Varona for the expenses of the three militia men. Harvey and Roselli had telephone discussions of the operation between 11 and 16 January. Harvey says that Roselli wasn't kidding himself. He agreed with Harvey that nothing was happening and that there was not much chance that anything would happen in the future. As far as Harvey knows, the three militia men never did leave for Cuba. He knows nothing of what may have happened to the three reported to have been sent to Cuba.

February 1963

Harvey was in Miami 11-14 February. He had no contacts with any of the principals, but he left word for Maceo that there was nothing new and that it now looked as if it were all over. . . .

Harvey left Miami on 15 February to meet with Roselli in Los Angeles. They agreed at the Los Angeles meeting that the operation would be closed off, but that it would be unwise to attempt a precipitate break between Roselli and Varona. Roselli agreed that he would continue

-52-

to see Varona, gradually reducing the frequency of contact until there was none.

April - May 1963

Harvey says that he received two telephone calls from Roselli during this period. Harvey decided that it would be best to have one last meeting with Roselli before he left for his assignment in [deletion] He states that he reported this decision to Mr. Helms who gave his approval.

June 1963

Roselli came to Washington to meet with Harvey sometime about the middle of June. Harvey met him at Dulles airport. Harvey remembers having suggested to Roselli that he bring only carry-on luggage so there would be no delay at the airport awaiting baggage. Harvey had by then closed his own home in preparation for leaving the country and was living in the house of a neighbor who was out of town . . . That evening . . . While dining, Harvey received a phone call from Sam Papich who wanted to know if Harvey knew the identity of his dinner guest. Harvey said that he did.

-53-

It subsequently developed that the FBI had Roselli under intensive surveillance at the time, and Harvey speculates that he was picked up as he left the airport parking lot and was identified through his auto license number. Harvey met Papich for breakfast the next morning and explained that he was terminating an operational association with Roselli. Papich reminded Harvey of the FBI rule requiring FBI personnel to report any known contacts between former FBI employees and criminal elements. Papich said that he would have to report to J. Edgar Hoover that Harvey had been seen with Roselli. Harvey said he understood Papich's situation and did not object to such a report being made. Harvey said that he asked Papich to inform him in advance if it appeared that Hoover might call Mr. McCone—Harvey's point being that he felt that McCone should be briefed before receiving a call from Hoover. Papich agreed to do so. Harvey said that he then told Mr. Helms of the incident and that Helms agreed that there was no need to brief McCone unless a call from Hoover was to be expected.

This was Harvey's last face-to-face meeting with Roselli, although he has heard from him since then. The later links between Harvey and Roselli are described in a separate section of this report.

The list of persons witting of the second phase of the operation differs from those who knew of the first phase.

Those we have identified are:

-54-

1. Richard Helms, Deputy Director for Plans
2. William Harvey, Chief, Task Force W
3. James O'Connell, Office of Security (He knows that Harvey took over the operation and delivered the pills, arms, and equipment in April 1962. He does not know of developments after May 1962.)
4. Sheffield Edwards, Director of Security (He knows of the fact of the turnover to Harvey, but states he knows nothing of developments thereafter.)
5. J.C. King, Chief, WH Division (He stated in our interview with him that he knew that Harvey was having meetings with members of the gambling syndicate in 1962.)
6. [deletion] Harvey's deputy in 1962 [deletion] knows that Harvey was meeting with gangsters in Reno (sic) in the winter of 1962.)
7. Ted Shackley, Chief, JMWAVE (He assisted Harvey in the delivery of arms and equipment to Varona in April 1962, but presumably did not know the identities of the recipients nor the purpose for which the material was to be used.)
8. [deletion] TSD [deletion]s participation was limited to furnishing the pills to O'Connell on 18 April 1962.)
9. Antonio Varona, the Cuban exile leader (He presumably was not aware of government sponsorship.)
10. Varona's son-in-law (He too was presumably was not aware of the government's role.)
11. Maceo, Roselli's "man" (Maceo probably knew there was a government connection, but may not have identified CIA as the agency.)

We can only conjecture as to who else may have known at least that the operation was continuing and perhaps some of the details. Sam

-55-

Giancana was supposedly cut out of the second phase, but we cannot be sure that Roselli did not keep him informed. The same may be said of Santos Trafficante. Harvey is sure that Maheu was not involved in Harvey's introduction to Roselli, but O'Connell is equally positive that Maheu participated. The story that Drew Pearson told the President, and which is known in other Government circles, sounds suspiciously like this second phase of the operation. If that is so, then it is unlikely that the operation has leaked—perhaps through these channels:

Roselli to Maheu
Maheu to Edward P. Morgan, Maheu's Washington lawyer
Morgan to Drew Pearson
Pearson to Chief Justice Warren and to the President
Warren to Rowley, chief of the Secret Service
Rowley to Pat Coyne and to the FBI
The FBI to Attorney General Clark

We have a more detailed treatment in a separate section of this report of the channels through which the story may have passed.

-56-

. . . .

-57 to 62-

. . . .

May 1962

The Attorney General obviously was told of CIA's operational involvement with gangster elements, because he requested a briefing on the details. On 7 May 1962 Sheffield Edwards and Lawrence Houston met with Attorney General Robert Kennedy and, as Edwards puts it, "briefed him all the way." Houston says that after the briefing Kennedy "thought about the problem quite seriously." The Attorney General said that he could see the problem. . . . He spoke quite firmly, saying in effect, "I trust that if you ever try to do business with organized crime again—with gangsters— you will let the Attorney General know before you do it." . . . Edwards says that among the points covered was that of Roselli's motivation. The Attorney General had thought that Roselli was doing the job (the attempt at assassination) for money. Edwards corrected that impression; he was not.

-62a-

Houston recalls that during the meeting with the Attorney General the latter asked for a memorandum record of the meeting . . . The memorandum is dated 14 May 1962. It was typed in two copies only, with the original being sent to Attorney General Kennedy and the other copy being retained by the Director of Security. It was typed by Edwards' secretary, Sarah Hall. It does not state the purpose of the operation on which Kennedy was briefed, but it does make it clear that the operation was against Castro and its true purpose may be inferred from the memorandum.

Edwards states that the briefing of the Attorney General and the forwarding of a memorandum of record was carried out without briefing the Director (John McCone), the DDCI (General Carter), or the DD/P (Richard Helms). He felt that, since they had not been privy to the operation when it was under way, they should be protected form involvement in it after the fact. As noted previously, Houston had briefed the DDCI on the fact that there was a matter involving the

-63-

Department of Justice, but Houston had not given the DDCI the specifics. He feels it would have been normal for him to have briefed the DCI in view of the Attorney General's interest, but he also feels quite sure that he would have remembered doing it and he does not. He suggested that Edwards' deliberate avoidance of such briefings may have led him also to avoid making any briefings. He recalls no disagreements with Edwards on this point and concludes that he must have accepted Edwards' decision not to brief.

Houston and Edwards briefed Robert Kennedy on a CIA operation embracing gangster elements, which presumably was terminated following the Bay of Pigs fiasco. Kennedy stated his view, reportedly quite strongly, that the Attorney General should be told in advance of any future CIA intentions to work with or through U.S. gangster elements. From reports of the briefing, it is reasonable to assume that Kennedy believed he had such a commitment form Agency representatives.

In fact, however, at the time of the 7 May 1962 briefing of the Attorney General on "Gambling Syndicate - Phase One," Phase Two under William Harvey was already well under way. Harvey had been introduced to Roselli on 8 April and Varona or his men had received the lethal pills, the arms, and related support equipment in late April. The Attorney General was not told that the gambling syndicate operation had already been reactivated, nor, as far as we know, was he ever told

-64-

that CIA had a continuing involvement with U.S. gangster elements.

When the Attorney General was briefed on 7 May, Edwards knew that Harvey had been introduced to Roselli. He must also have known that his subordinate, James O'Connell, was in Miami and roughly for what purpose (although Edwards does not now recall this). The gambling syndicate operation had been taken from him, and, in retrospect, he probably acted properly in briefing the Attorney General on only that aspect of the operation for which he had been responsible and of which he had direct, personal knowledge.

Harvey states that on 14 May he briefed Mr. Helms on the meeting with the Attorney General, as told to him by Edwards. Harvey, too, advised against briefing Mr. McCone and General Carter and states that Helms concurred in this. On that same date, 14 May, Edwards prepared a memorandum for the record stating that on that day Harvey had told him that any plans for future use of Roselli were dropped. Edwards' memorandum states that he "cautioned him (Harvey) that I (Edwards) felt that any future projects of this nature should have the tacit approval of the Director of

Central Intelligence." Edwards informed us that he has no specific recollection of having told Harvey of Kennedy's warning that the Attorney
General should be told in advance of any future CIA use of gangsters.

-65-

Although the Attorney General on 7 May 1962 was given a full and frank
account of the Agency's relations with Maheu, Roselli, and Giancana in
the Castro operation, . . . , it appears that the FBI was not given anything
like the same detail. The Bureau quite properly was not told about the
assassination operation, . . . Edwards states that to have briefed the Bureau
on the assassination operation would have put it in an impossible bind,
since both Roselli and Giancana were high on the Bureau's "list."

The briefing of Attorney General Kennedy was absolutely restricted to
him, and we can only speculate that the confidence was observed.

. . . .

-66-

. . . .

-67 to 74-

Schemes in Early 1963
    Skin Diving Suit
    At about the time of the Donovan-Castro negotiations for the release
of the Bay of Pigs prisoners a plan was devised to have Donovan present
a contaminated skin diving suit to Castro as a gift. Castro was known to
be a skin diving enthusiast. We cannot put a precise date on this scheme.
Desmond FitzGerald told us of it as if it had originated after he took over
the Cuba task force in January 1963. Samuel

    Halpern said that it began under William Harvey and that he, Halpern,
briefed FitzGerald on it. Harvey states positively that he never heard of it.

    According to Sidney Gottlieb, this scheme progressed to the point of
actually buying a diving suit and readying it for delivery. The technique

involved dusting the inside of the suit with a fungus that would produce a disabling and chronic skin disease (Madura foot) and contaminating the breathing apparatus with tubercle bacilli. Gottlieb does not remember what came of the scheme or what happened to the scuba suit. Sam Halpern, who was in on the scheme, at first said the plan was dropped because it was obviously impracticable. He later recalled that the plan was abandoned because it was overtaken by events: Donovan had already given Castro a skin diving suit on his own initiative. . . .

-75-

. . . .

-76-

Booby-trapped Sea Shell

Some time in 1963, date uncertain but probably early in the year, Desmond FitzGerald, then Chief, SAS, originated a scheme for doing away with Castro by means of an explosives-rigged sea shell. The idea was to take an unusually spectacular sea shell that would be certain to catch Castro's eye, load it with an explosive triggered to blow when the shell was lifted, and submerge it in an area where Castro often went skin diving.

Des bought two books on Caribbean Mollusca. The scheme was soon found to be impracticable. None of the shells that might conceivably be found in the Caribbean area was both spectacular enough to be sure of attracting attention and large enough to hold the needed volume of explosive. The midget submarine that would have had to be used in emplacement of the shell has too short an operating range for such an operation.

FitzGerald states that he, Sam Halpern, and [deletion] had several sessions at which they explored this possibility, but that no one else was ever brought in on the talks. Halpern believes that he had conversations with TSD on feasibility and using a hypothetical case. He does not remember with whom he may have spoken. We are unable to identify any others who knew of the scheme at the time it was being considered.

-77-

Tab A

SOURCES OF INFORMATION

Files were furnished for review by the Director of Security, the Deputy Director for Support, the General Counsel, the Legislative Counsel, the Chief of WH Division, and by Col. J.C. King, former Chief of WH Division. Biographic files and intelligence publications were furnished by the Director of Central Reference. . . .

We called back four officers for interviews: Richard Bissell, Sheffield Edwards from retirement, William Harvey from sick leave, and Nestor Sanchez from his post in [deletion]. Otherwise, our interviews were confined to officers assigned to the headquarters installation. We opened each interview by referring to the Drew Pearson column of 7 March 1967, citing that as the reason for our interest in learning of plots to assassinate Castro. We told those interviewed that we were on a fact-finding mission on behalf of the Director, and that this was not the usual sort of Inspector General investigation. We asked each to name any others who were likely to have knowledge of such plots. We cautioned each not do discuss the subject of the interview with anyone else—even others whom we might interview. This is a complete list of those interviewed:

Desmond FitzGerald
Samuel Halpern
[deletion]
J.C. King
Alfonso Rodriguez
J.D. Esterline
Edward Gunn
Howard Osborn
James O'Connell
Sidney Gottlieb
Sheffield Edwards
Richard Bissell

Lawrence Houston
[deletion]
John Warner
Nestor Sanchez
William Harvey
Cornelius Roosevelt
Robert Bannerman
[deletion]
[deletion]

-77a-

Project AMLASH - Rolando Cubela
    9 March 1961
[deletion] an officer then assigned to the Mexico City Station, met in Mexico City with Rolando Cubela to sound out Cubela on his views on the Cuban situation. Cubela had been attending the leftist-sponsored Latin American Conference on National Sovereignty, Emancipation and Peace held in Mexico City from 5 to 8 March. Cubela was noncommital. The meeting was arranged by [deletion]

. . . .

(Comment: Rolando CUBELA Secades was the secondranking leader of the Directorio Revolucionario (DR) 13 de Marso, which was an elite group of leftist student activists founded in 1956 to organize violence to overthrow the Batista regime. Cubela was believed to have been one of the participants in the assassination in 1956 of Lt. Col. Antonio BLANCO Rico, then the head of Batista's military intelligence service. The DR members considered themselves quite apart from the Fidelista 26th of July Movement, despite the fact that they had reluctantly signed a unity pact. In the final days of the revolution the DR took the Presidential Palace, which they refused to surrender

-78-

to Che Guevara but eventually (and reluctantly) turned over to Fidel Castro. Cubela was a major in the Cuban army, the highest Cuban military rank.

(A CS Information Report with a date of information of March 1959 reported that: "Prior to his appointment to the post of Cuban Military Attache to Spain and his subsequent departure for Madrid on 27 March 1959, Rolando Cubela frankly expressed to Prime Minister Fidel Castro his dissatisfaction over the present situation in Cuba. Cubela .. privately told intimates that he was so disgusted with Castro that if he, Cubela, did not get out of the country soon, he would kill Castro himself."

(Although the March 1961 meeting between [deletion] and Cubela in Mexico City was inconclusive, it led to other meetings out of which grew Project AMLASH. Cubela (AMLASH-1) repeatedly insisted that the essential first step in overthrowing the regime was the elimination of Castro himself, which Cubela claimed he was prepared to accomplish. He repeatedly requested that we furnish him the special equipment or material needed to do the job. Those immediately concerned with the running of the operation now recall it as one in which the Agency was interested primarily in keeping Cubela active in the [deletion] program directed against

-79-

Cuban military leaders, while resisting his pleas for technical assistance in an assassination attempt. The voluminous project files and the information furnished us by [deletion] Cubela's case officer, do not wholly support those recollections. The Agency offered both direct and indirect support for Cubela's plottings.)

28 March 1961

An asset of the Miami Station reported that Rolando Cubela and Juan Orta wanted to defect and needed help in escaping. (Juan Orta was the gangsters' "man inside Cuba" with access to Castro in the lethal pill operation we have called Gambling Syndicate - Phase One.) Headquarters expressed interest in exfiltrating Orta and Cubela. The exfiltration attempt was called off as a result of a report that the Cuban police were aware of Cubela's desire to defect and of his departure plans.

(Comment: This is one of three name-links we found in the AMLASH file between Rolando Cubela and persons involved in the gambling syndicate episodes. The other two links are even more nebulous than this. If Cubela was in fact one of the gangsters' assets inside Cuba, that fact was unknown to either the CIA officers running the gangster episodes or to those handling Cubela.)

-80-

14 August 1961

[deletion] reported that Rolando Cubela was planning to attend the French National Student Union Cultural Festival later in the month. Cubela sent a message to [deletion] saying that he wanted to talk with a "friend of [deletion]'s" in Paris if possible. The message presumably was passed through Cubela's girl friend, an airline stewardess. [deletion] was given approval to approach Cubela, but there is not indication in the file that he was actually contacted.

15 June 1962

The JMWAVE Station cabled that a station asset [deletion] was told by [deletion] that Cubela had left Cuba for Helsinki on 10 June 1962. He was traveling on a Czech airline, by way of Prague, to Helsinki where he planned to attend the World Youth Festival. [deletion]'s mother and father had arrived in Miami on 9 June and had been seen off at the airport by Cubela when they left Cuba. [deletion]'s mother told [deletion] that Cubela wanted to defect and to enter the U.S. Cubela said that on his return from Helsinki he would pass through Paris where he hoped to meet his old friend, [deletion]

-81-

27 June 1962

The FBI forwarded the CIA a report of a meeting with an FBI informant in Miami on 11 June. The informant reported that Cubela was attending the Youth Festival in Helsinki in July-August 1962 and wanted to defect. In a detailed transmittal memorandum, the FBI identified its informant as [deletion] whom the FBI knew to be a long-time contact of CIA. [deletion] offered his services to the FBI to assist in the defection of Cubela. He told the Bureau of [deletion]'s meeting with Cubela in Mexico City in March 1961. The Bureau stated in its memorandum to us that it had told [deletion] that his offer would be forwarded to the proper U.S. agency. The Bureau also stated that it was informing its Paris representative to refer [deletion] to CIA if [deletion] should contact the Paris Legal Attache.

8 July 1962

The JMWAVE Station reported the substance of a telephone conversation between Tepedino and a station officer, which was arranged by [deletion] Tepedino identified the original source of his information on Cubela's desire to defect as being the Echavarrias, from whom the JMWAVE Station had received its report. Tepedino said he had approached the FBI in Miami because of dissatisfaction with the

-82-

way CIA had handled Cubela's "planned defection" in Paris in August 1961. [deletion] agreed to meet with a CIA officer and contact arrangements were made.

13 and 14 July 1962

[deletion] from headquarters, met with [deletion] in New York City on 13 and 14 July 1962. [deletion] agreed to meet [deletion] in Helsinki, and to travel anywhere else necessary, to aid in an attempt to defect Cubela. [deletion] who is a successful Cuban exile [deletion] in New York City, refused an offer to pay his full expenses. He did accept reimbursement for airline tickets and hotel expenses. He was not offered a salary or bonus.

30 July - 6 August 1962

[deletion] arrived in Helsinki on 30 July. [deletion] was already there. Cubela was found, and the first of a series of meetings with him was held on 1 August. The original objective of defecting Cubela was quickly changed to one of recruiting him in place. These are excerpts from [deletion]'s contact report of the first meeting with Cubela: He said he was considering not going back to Cuba, but after talking to [deletion] he felt that if he could do something really significant for the creation of a new Cuba, he was interested in returning to carry on the fight there.

-83-

He said he was not interested in risking his life for any small undertaking, but that if he could be given a really large part to play, he would use himself and several others in Cuba whom he could rely upon.

He said he had plans to blow up an oil refinery, as he felt that the continuing existence of a semblance of normal functioning in Cuba depended upon a continuing supply of petroleum, supplies of which, as we know, are at a critical stage today.

He also wanted to plan the execution of Carlos Rodriguez (a top-ranking Castro subordinate) and the Soviet Ambassador, and also to eliminate Fidel, by execution if necessary.

While we were making no commitments or plans, we pointed out to Cubela that schemes like he envisioned certainly had their place, but that a lot of coordination, planning, information-collecting, etc., were necessary prerequisites to ensure the value and success of such plans.

Cubela stated many times during the course of this and subsequent meetings that he was only interested in involving himself in a plan of significant action, and which was truly designed to achieve rapidly his desire to help Cuba.

7 - 9 August 1962

Because of the security hazard in too frequent meetings in Helsinki, where Cubela was surrounded by his associates in the Cuban delegation, it was agreed that further meetings would be held in Stockholm or Copenhagen. Cubela agreed to meet with a Spanish-speaking case officer in Paris later in the month. Nothing significant came out of the meetings in Stockholm, 7 - 9 August, except Cubela's revelation that he had told four of his Cuban associates of his meetings in Helsinki with [deletion]

-84-

10 - 11 August 1952

[deletion], [deletion], and Cubela met in Copenhagen for further meetings. [deletion] wrote in his contact report:

. ".at one time when we [deletion] always wrote of himself as 'we' were discussing the various aspects of Cubela's future role in Cuba, we used the term 'assassinate.' The use of this term, we later learned from [deletion] and from Cubela himself, was most objectionable to the latter, and he was visibly upset. It was not the act he objected to, but rather merely the choice of the word used to describe it. 'Eliminate was acceptable.'"

. . . .

14 - 23 August 1962

Cubela, [deletion] and [deletion] met in Paris and were joined by [deletion], a Spanish-speaking case officer [deletion] Cubela was given S/W training and was issued appropriate S/W supplies. He was taken to the south of France on 20 August for a demolition demonstration. [deletion] planned to polygraph Cubela and asked for a polygraph operator to be sent to Paris. Cubela indignantly refused to be polygraphed. [deletion] cabled on 17 August:

"Have no intention give Cubela physical elimination mission as requirement but recognize this something he could or might try to carry out on his own initiative."

Headquarters replied by cable on 18 August:

"Strongly concur that no physical elimination missions be given Cubela."

29 August 1962

Cubela left Prague by air for Havana

-85-

5 - 8 September 1963

Cubela attended the Collegiate Games in Porto Alegre, Brazil, as a representative of the Cuban government. He was met there by [deletion] and [deletion] Also participating was [deletion], a Spanish-speaking case officer from headquarters, who thereafter acted as case officer for Cubela.

Cubela claimed that he had written two S/W messages. (Only one had been received.) He said he was reluctant to use S/W because he feared the efficiency of the Cuban postal censorship.

Cubela discussed a group of Cuban military officers known to him, and possible ways of approaching them. The problem was, he explained, that although many of them were anti-Communist, they were either loyal to Fidel or were so afraid of him that they were reluctant to discuss any conspiracies for fear they might be provocations. Cubela said that he thought highly of [deletion] (AMTRUNK-[deletion] who was hiding [deletion]. [deletion] had been sent to Cuba by CIA to recruit [deletion] in place, and had done so. Cubela said he planned to use [deletion] but was concerned about [deletion]"nervous condition" and the fact that he drank heavily. Cubela was told to assist [deletion] in [deletion] intelligence assignments, but not to help [deletion] leave Cuba—as Cubela proposed.

-86-

14 September 1963

From Porto Alegre, Cubela flew to Paris, arriving on 14 September. He was there ostensibly to attend the Alliance Francaise, but actually to take an extended vacation—of which he planned to inform Fidel after the fact.

16 September 1963

Cubela (in Paris) wrote to [deletion] (in New York):"I don't intend to see (be interviewed by) your friend again," which you should tell them, "so they don't make the trip. I want to get away from politics completely.."

3 October 1963

[deletion] arrived in Paris for meetings with Cubela. (The record does not reveal why [deletion] went to Paris in the face of Cubela's stated wish not to see him. The letter may have been written during a spell of temporary depression. [deletion] were already in contact with Cubela when [deletion] arrived.) Also participating in the meetings were [deletion] and [deletion]. [three lines deletion]

11 October 1963

[deletion] cabled that Cubela was insistent upon meeting with a senior U.S. official, preferably Robert F. Kennedy, for assurances

-87-

of U.S. moral support for any activity Cubela under took in Cuba. [deletion] said that the answer Cubela received might be crucial to CIA's relationship with Cubela. [deletion] recommended that "highest and profound consideration be given as feeling drawn by all who in contact Cubela is that he determined attempt op against Castro with or without U.S. support."

13 October 1963

[deletion] cabled: [deletion] ETA LOND 13 Oct. Pending change after 12 Oct meet [deletion] plans return Hqs after LOND stop in order discuss details operation before entering final round discussions with AMLASH."

17 October 1963

[deletion] cabled the results of a meeting with Cubela and [deletion] Cubela, in a private conversation with [deletion], reiterated his desire to speak with a high-level U.S. Government official. [deletion] said that basically Cubela wanted assurances that the U.S. Government would support him if his enterprise were successful.

29 October 1963

Desmond FitzGerald, then Chief, SAS, who was going to Paris on other business, arranged to meet with Cubela to give him the assurances

-88-

he sought. The contact plan for the meeting, a copy of which is in the AMLASH file, has this to say on cover:

FitzGerald will represent self as personal representative of Robert F. Kennedy who traveled to Paris for specific purpose meeting Cubela and giving him assurance of full U.S. support if there is change of the present government in Cuba.

According to FitzGerald, he discussed the planned meeting with the DD/P (Helms) who decided it was not necessary to seek approval from Robert Kennedy for FitzGerald to speak in his name.

The meeting was held in [deletion]'s house in Paris on 29 October

1963. FitzGerald used the alias [deletion] [deletion] [deletion] acted as interpreter. [deletion] was not present during the meeting. [deletion] on 13 November 1963 wrote a memorandum for the record of the meeting. It reads, in part:

FitzGerald informed Cubela that the United States is prepared to render all necessary assistance to any anti-communist Cuban group which succeeds in neutralizing the present Cuban leadership and assumes sufficient control to invite the United States to render the assistance it is prepared to give. It was emphasized that the above support will be forthcoming only after a real coup has been effected and the group involved is in a position to request U.S. (probably under OAS auspices) recognition and support. It was made clear that the U.S. was not prepared to commit itself to supporting an isolated uprising, as such an uprising can be extinguished in a matter of hours if the present government is still in control of Havana. As for the post-coup period, the U.S. does not desire that the political clock be turned back but will support the necessary economic and political reforms which will benefit the mass of the Cuban people.

-89-

(Comment: Those involved now recall the purpose of the meeting as being something quite different from that appearing in written records prepared at about the time of the meeting. FitzGerald recalls that Cubela spoke repeatedly of the need for an assassination weapon. In particular, he wanted a high-powered rifle with telescopic sights or some other weapon that could be used to kill Castro from a distance. FitzGerald wanted no part of such a scheme and told [deletion] to tell Cubela that the U.S. simply does not do such things. When he was told this, Cubela said he wanted confirmation from a senior U.S. official, not a member of the CIA. FitzGerald says that when he met with Cubela in Paris he told Cubela that the U.S. government would have no part of an attempt on Castro's life. Sam Halpern, who was not present at FitzGerald's meeting with Cubela but who was thoroughly familiar with all that was going on, has a recollection identical with that of FitzGerald.)

Be that as it may, the written record tells a somewhat different story. In memorandum of the meeting with Cubela he wrote that:

Nothing of an operational nature was discussed at the FitzGerald meeting. After the meeting Cubela stated that he was satisfied with the policy discussion but now desired to know what technical support we could provide him.

-90-

14 November 1963

[deletion] met with [deletion] in New York City on 14 November. [deletion]'s contact report reveals Cubela's reaction (as told to [deletion]) to his meeting with FitzGerald.

The visit with FitzGerald, who acted in the capacity of a representative of high levels of the Government concerned with the Cuban problem satisfied Cubela as far as policy was concerned, but he was not at all happy with the fact that he still was not given the technical assistance for the operational plan as he saw it. [deletion] said that Cubela dwelt constantly on this point. He could not understand why he was denied certain small pieces of equipment which promised a final solution to the problem, while, on the other hand, the U.S. Government gave much equipment and money to exile groups for their ineffective excursions against Cuban coastal targets.

According to [deletion] Cubela feels strongly on this point, and if he does not get advice and materials from a U.S. Government technician, he will probably become fed-up again, and we will lose whatever progress we have made to date.

19 November 1963

Memorandum for the record prepared by [deletion]:"C/SAS (FitzGerald) approved telling Cubela he would be given a cache inside Cuba. Cache could, if he requested it, include .. high power rifles w/ scopes ... C/SAS requested written reports on AMLASH operation be kept to a minimum."

20 November 1963

Thus far, this account of the Cubela project has been based almost

-91-

wholly on documents found in the project file. Beginning here is an account of an episode in the Cubela operation on which there is no documentary evidence. Dr. Gunn has a record of nine contacts and their dates; otherwise, this summary is drawn from the recollections of those involved.

[deletion] says that, while Cubela was anxious to do away with Castro, Cubela was not willing to sacrifice his own life in exchange for Castro's. What Cubela really wanted was a high-powered, silenced rifle with an effective range of hundreds or thousands of yards. Cubela finally said that, as a doctor of medicine (which he was), he was quite sure that we could devise some technical means of doing the job that would not automatically cause him to lose his own life in the try.

Samuel Halpern and [deletion] approached Dr. Gunn for assistance. Although none of the participants specifically so state, it may be inferred that they were seeking a means of assassination of a sort that Cubela might reasonably have been expected to have devised himself. What they settled upon was Black Leaf 40, a common, easily-obtainable insecticide containing about 40% nicotine sulphate. Nicotine is a deadly poison that may be administered orally, by injection, or by absorption through the skin. It is likely that there also were discussions of means of administering the poison, because Gunn was ready to move when asked.

The plan reached the action stage when Halpern and [deletion] contacted

-92-

Gunn again on the morning of 20 November 1963 and told him that the device for administering the poison (a ballpoint pen rigged as a hypodermic syringe) had to be ready in time for [deletion] to catch a plane at noon the next day. Gunn says that he went immediately to the FI/D workshop and spent the rest of the day and most of that night fabricating the device. Those in FI/D who worked with him knew what he was trying to make but not for whom it was intended. Eventually, after seven or eight failures, he succeeded in converting a Paper-Mate pen into a hypodermic syringe that worked. He said that the needle was so fine that the victim would hardly feel it when it was inserted—he compared it with the scratch from a shirt with too much starch. He delivered the workable device to [deletion] the following morning and retained two of the later prototypes. He states that they are still in his safe. He does not know what happened to the device he gave [deletion] he does not remember its having been returned to him. He believes he was told that Cubela refused to accept the device. He says he would not now be able to differentiate the final pen from the earlier prototypes that are in his safe.

22 November 1963

[deletion] arrived in Paris on the morning of 22 November and met with Cubela late that afternoon. [deletion] states that he

-93-

showed the pen/syringe to Cubela and explained how it worked. He is not sure, but he believes that Cubela accepted the device but said that he would not take it to Cuba with him. [deletion] distinctly recalls that Cubela didn't think much of the device. Cubela said that, as a doctor, he knew all about Black Leaf 40 and that we surely could come up with something more sophisticated than that. It should be noted that Gunn and [deletion] agree that the syringe was not loaded. Cubela was expected to supply his own poison; we merely suggested Black Leaf 40 as an effective poison for use in the syringe.

[deletion] wrote a contact report of the meeting. It makes no mention of a pen or of poison. The following is a summary of the contact report. Cubela said that he was returning to Cuba fully determined to pursue his plans to initiate a coup against

Castro. [deletion] reiterated the assurances given Cubela by FitzGerald of full U.S. support if a real coup against the Castro regime was successful. Cubela asked for the following items to be included in a cache inside Cuba: 20 hand grenades, two high-powered rifles with telescopic sights, and approximately 20 pounds of C-4 explosive and related equipment. Cubela suggested the best place for the cache was on the finca (farm) managed by his friend, [deletion] Since he was returning to Cuba by way of Prague, he did not want to carry S/W or any other incriminating materials with him. As they were coming

-93a-

out of the meeting, [deletion] and Cubela were informed that President Kennedy had been assassinated. Cubela was visibly moved over the news. He asked, "Why do such things happen to good people?" The contact report does not state the time nor the duration of the [deletion]-Cubela meeting, but it is likely that at the very moment President Kennedy was shot a CIA officer was meeting with a Cuban agent in Paris and giving him an assassination device for use against Castro. [deletion] states that he received an OPIM cable from FitzGerald that night or early the next morning telling him that everything was off. We do not find such a cable in the AMLASH file. There is a record in the file that [deletion] was due to arrive back in Washington at 1810 hours, 23 November.

The AMLASH project was probably about as widely known within the Clandestine Services as any other project of a similar nature. However, we can identify only four people who know of the just-described episode involving a hypodermic syringe and Black Leaf 40. [deletion] knew all of the story, Halpern knew most of it, and Gunn knew much of it. FitzGerald did not mention this aspect of the Cubela operation when he first briefed us on it. When we went back to him later with specific questions, he said he remembered something about Black Leaf 40, but nothing whatever about a device for administering it. Gunn said he had the impression that FitzGerald

-94-

knew about the operation "but didn't want to know." [deletion] says that FitzGerald knew that he and Halpern were seeing Gunn. Halpern agrees, but adds that FitzGerald did not know the specifics of the fabricating of an assassination device.

*****

. . . .

-95 to 97-

. . . .

30 August 1964

Manuel Artime received information through Madrid that a group of dissident members of the Castro regime desired to establish direct contact with Artime. On 7 October 1964, an Artime associate went to France for a meeting with an intermediary from the dissident group. The intermediary was named as Alberto BLANCO Romariz.

12 November 1964

FBIS report: "A delegation of the University Student Federation of Cuba arrived in Prague on 11 November to participate in the meeting of the Executive Council of the International Student Union to be held from 14 to 17 November. The delegation is made up of .. Maj. Rolando Cubela, who will attend the event as a special guest of the IUS."

-98-

Contact report of a meeting in Washington with Artime: "Artime agreed to talk to AMLASH-1 if it turns out that he is the contact man for the internal dissident group. Artime thinks that if AMLASH-1 is the chief of the dissident group we can all forget about the operation."

25 November 1964

[deletion] reported Cubela's arrival in Paris.

4 December 1964

[deletion] prepared a memorandum request for $6,500 as an extraordinary budget expenditure for the travel of Artime for maintaining contact with the internal dissident group's representatives in Europe during November and December 1964. There is no direct indication in the file that the request was approved, but indirect evidence indicates that it was. Artime did travel to Europe and maintained the contacts.

6 - 7 December 1964

[deletion] met Cubela in Paris. This is a summary of the details reported by [deletion] Cubela, although unhappy because he was unable

-99-

to carry out his plans during the past year, continued to feel that his solution to the Cuban problem was the only one feasible and that he had to continue trying. Cubela was told that the U.S. Government could not and would not in any way become involved or provide assistance in the task he had planned for himself. Cubela appeared to understand our position and said that if he needed help he would look elsewhere.

10 December 1964

Memorandum prepared by Sanchez and left with [deletion], of the [deletion] as background on the then current status of the AMLASH operation—excerpts:

"Artime does not know and we do not plan to tell him that we are in direct contact with Cubela, [one and one half lines deletion]

"Cubela was told and fully understands that U.S. Government cannot become involved to any degree in the 'fist step' of his plan. If he needs support, the realizes that he will have to get it elsewhere. FYI: This is where Artime could fit in nicely in giving any support Cubela would request."

(Comment: Sanchez explained to us that what had happened was that SAS contrived to put Artime and Cubela together in such a way that neither knew that the contact had been engineered by CIA. The thought was that Artime needed a man inside and Cubela wanted a silenced weapon, which CIA was unwilling to furnish

-100-

to him directly. By putting the two together, Artime might get his man inside and Cubela might get his silenced weapon—from Artime. CIA did not intend to furnish an assassination weapon to Artime to give to Cubela, and did not do so.)

17 December 1964

Headquarters cable to Paris: "When [deletion] contacts Cubela to debrief him, .. please confirm statement by Cubela to [deletion] that only money and a few commo items were retrieved by the fishermen. Cubela and [deletion] unhappy that fishermen had not recovered more from the cache, but it was not possible for Cubela and [deletion] to go to the site of the cache personally. (Cubela had told [deletion] that [deletion] had used some "fishermen" to recover the cache and that not all of it was recovered. This was the cache put down in the AMTRUNK infiltration area, which did not include the FAL rifles.)

27 December 1964

Artime and Cubela met for the first time—in Madrid.

30 December 1964

Artime and Cubela met for a second time in Madrid on 30 December. Artime reported the results in a meeting with [deletion] in Florida on 3 January 1965. Cubela told Artime that he had requested

-101-

a silencer for a FAL rifle from the Americans, which they had not been able to provide. Artime agreed to furnish either a silencer for a FAL or a comparable rifle with silencer. If Artime obtained a silencer for a FAL, Cubela would personally carry it back to Cuba with him. If Artime had to settle for some other type of silenced rifle, he would cache it in Cuba for Cubela.

28 January 1965

[deletion] arrived in Paris for meetings with Cubela.

2 February 1965

[deletion] cabled from Paris: "Cubela and [deletion] returned Paris 31 January. Met 1 February. Cubela states full agreement reached with Artime and he well satisfied with arrangements which he outlined for our information (along same lines as reported by Artime) ... Artime provided package in Madrid which Cubela plans carry back in personal luggage."

[deletion] cabled from Paris: "As of November 1964 when Cubela departed Cuba neither he nor [deletion] had received any part of the Matanzas cache. [deletion] told him fishermen recovered money and parts of communications gear but that money was no good since it was in a series out of circulation."

-102-

11 February 1965

[deletion] cabled: "From Cubela on 10 February: On 10 or 11 February Cubela is to receive one pistol with silencer and one Belgian FAL rifle with silencer from Artime's secretary. Both weapons come from U.S. and now in Madrid." (This is in conflict with the earlier report that Artime would cache a rifle and silencer if that were all he could find. We are unable to resolve the conflict.)

12 February 1965

[deletion] cabled: "Artime reported on final meeting with Cubela: Artime had three packages of special items made up by his technical people and delivered to Cubela in Madrid. Cubela seemed satisfied."

4 March 1965

[deletion] reported receiving a telephone call from a friend in Havana who had seen Cubela back in Havana the previous day.

15 March 1965

[deletion] cabled that one Rafael GARCIA-BANGO Dirube had arrived in Madrid from Cuba on 15 March and had been introduced [deletion] claimed to be in contact with a

-103-

group of Cuban military leaders who were planning to eliminate Castro and take over the government. It quickly became clear that he was referring to Cubela. [deletion] said that he had always been publicly identified as a close friend of Cubela, whom he last saw in Havana on 9 March. [deletion] said that he had been the lawyer [three lines deletion]

(Comment: This is another name-link between Cubela and the gambling syndicate plots reported upon earlier in this report. [deletion] was one of the principals in Shef Edwards' Phase One of the operation. He presumably was not involved in Phase Two under Harvey, but we cannot be sure of that. After all, [deletion] was the man who brought Varona into the operation late in Phase One, and Varona was one of the main players during Phase Two. The three-man team that was sent in by Varona was reported on 21 June 1962 to be in place in Cuba.)

June 1965

Headquarters decided to terminate all contacts with key members of the Cubela group. It had become increasingly apparent that the circle of Cubans who knew of Cubela's plans and of CIA's association

-104-

with them was ever-widening. The last straw came in early June 1965. (Note: There is a discrepancy in dates. The memorandum prepared at the time lists dates of 2, 3 and 4 May. From other evidence in the file, it is apparent that the month was June—not May.) One [deletion], a former MP trainee who was terminated as a malcontent on 20 March 1961, contacted an I&NS agent on 2 June 1965 with a story that [deletion] thought affected U.S. security. I&NS heard him out and then sent him to the FBI. The FBI listened to the story on 3 June and then sent him to CIA. A CIA officer interviewed him on 4 June. [deletion] said that in May he had received a letter from a friend in Paris urging him to meet in Paris with a friend of Cubela. [deletion] went to Paris to meet with [deletion] one of Cubela's closest associates in the supposed plan to assassinate Castro. [deletion] claimed to have a message from Cubela, which Cubela wanted [deletion] to deliver to CIA. The message was that Cubela and the others with him were in a position to kill Castro and others in the regime, but they needed some help and to know whether the CIA and the U.S. Government were with them and willing to support them. If the answer were affirmative, Cubela would send out details on what he needed. From his story it was obvious that [deletion] knew the full details of the Cubela operation.

(Comment: There is no indication in the file that CIA ever

-105-

found out the sort of "help" Cubela thought he needed. At a meeting in Paris on 1 February 1965 he asked for $10,000 "to organize the internal group." CIA refused to give him the money and suggested he try to get it from Artime. Cubela was quite upset over the turn down. A few days later, in Madrid, he approached a Cuban [deletion], claiming he was stranded in Madrid with no money. Headquarters approved a "personal loan" of $200. On 16 February 1965, Cubela asked [deletion] for $1,000, which headquarters approved giving him. In a later meeting with [deletion] in New York City, [deletion] said that he had given Cubela $7,000.)

On 23 June 1965 headquarters sent a cable to the stations concerned directing termination of contact with members to the Cubela group. It read, in part:

". . . convincing proof that entire AMLASH group insecure and that further contact with key members of group constitutes menace to CIA operations against Cuba as well as to the security of CIA staff personnel in Western Europe.

"Under the circumstances headquarters desires that contact with key members of the group or peripherally involved in AMLASH conspiracy be warned of danger implicit in these associations and directed to eliminate contacts ASAP."

-106-

1 March 1966

Reuters reported from Havana that the Cuban security police had arrested two military officers for alleged counterrevolutionary activities involving the U.S. Central Intelligence Agency. They were identified as Maj. Rolando Cubela and Maj. Ramon Guin.

7 March 1966

FBIS quoting Havana Domestic Service: "The trial of the accused Rolando Cubela, Ramon Guin, and others who are linked to the U.S. Central Intelligence Agency, was begun in the revolutionary court of Havana district in La Cabana today at 1500 hours."

8 March 1966

Excerpts from first day's trial proceedings as reported by the Havana Domestic Service and copied by FBIS:

Former Majors Rolando Cubela and Ramon Guin as well as others who are under indictment have confessed their guilt. The defendants are being tried for crimes against the integrity and stability of the nation by having planned the assassination of Maj. Fidel Castro.

The defendants are Rolando Cubela Secades, Ramon Guin Diaz, Jose Luis Gonzalez Gallarreta, Alberto Blanco Romariz, and Juan Alsina Navarro, all of whom confessed their guilt in the imputed facts of the case. Also appearing in the trial were Guillermo Cunill Alvarez and Angel Herrero Veliz.

-107-

The accused Jose Luis Gonzales Gallarreta, who worked as a diplomatic attache in the Cuban Embassy in Spain, betrayed his country for 100,000 dollars given him by CIA agents whom he contacted only a month after his arrival in Spain. (He) met with an official of the aforementioned organization of international subversion named James Noel who covered his activities by appearing as an official of the U.S. Embassy in Spain. Noel demanded that biographic information and information about the Cuban diplomatic mission be furnished him under this arrangement.

Cubela during his stay in Europe makes three trips to Spain, on 26 December 1964, and on 6 and 20 February 1965. The revolutionary ringleader Artime goes to Madrid at the beginning of February 1965. A meeting is held between Cubela and Artime in which they agree on the final plan.

This plan would begin with a personal attack aimed at Maj. Fidel Castro Ruz. This criminal act would be followed by an armed invasion of the country 48 hours later by U.S. troops. The attack against Comrade Fidel Castro would be made using a 7.62 mm. FAL rifle that Cubela owned. This weapon would be fitted with a powerful 4x40 telescopic sight and a silencer.

Artime sent Gallego to the United States to get the telescopic sight and the silencer. Once obtained, this equipment was delivered to Blanco Romariz. He in turn delivered it to Gonzalez Gallarreta who then delivered it to Cubela the day before he left Madrid.

In order to insure the success of his plans, Cubela meets with defendant Guin. Guin had been recruited since September 1963 as a spy for the Yankee CIA. This recruiting was done by CIA agent Miguel Diaz who infiltrated Cuba in order to recruit him, and did so.

Seized in Cubela's residence was a Tasco brand telescopic sight with accessories, the FAL rifle, large quantities of weapons and ammunition for them, fragmentation and incendiary grenades, and other military equipment and materiel.

-108-

The punishment to which the defendants are subject and which this prosecution wishes imposed is as follows: For Rolando Cubela Secades, Ramon Guin Diaz, Jose Luis Gonzalez Gallarreta, and Alberto Blanco Romariz—the death penalty by firing squad. For Juan Alsina Davarro, Guillermo Cunill Alvarez, and Angel Herrero Veliz—30 years imprisonment plus corresponding additional penalties.

9 March 1966

FBIS report from Havana Domestic Service: "Prime Minister Fidel Castro has sent a letter to the prosecutor in the case .. against Majors Rolando Cubela, Ramon Guin, and other defendants. In it, the Prime Minister says that it must be recognized from all this, a bitter but useful lesson may be drawn, adding, 'I suggest that the court not ask the death sentence for any of the accused."

. . . .

-109-

. . . .

11 March 1966

FBIS report quoting Havana Domestic Service of 10 March:

Revolutionary Court No. 1, which has tried case 108 in crimes against the integrity and security of the nation, has pronounced sentences on the accused Rolando Cubela Secades, Ramon Guin Diaz, and others.

According to the sentences, Rolando Cubela and Ramon Guin were sentenced to 25 years imprisonment; Jose Luis Gonzalez Gallarreta and Alberto Blanco Romariz, 20 years; and Juan Hilario Alsina Navarro, 10 years.

Guillermo Cunil Alvarez and Angel Serrero Veliz were absolved of guilt. They were released provided they are not liable to any other charges.

-110-

. . . .

-111-

Discussion of Assassinations at High-Level Government Meetings

Drew Pearson claims to have a report that there was a high-level meeting at the Department of State at which plans for the assassination of Castro were discussed. We find record of two high-level, interagency meetings at which assassination of Castro was raised. The first (and probably the one to which Pearson refers) was at the Department of State on 10 August 1962. It was a meeting of the Special Group (Augmented). The second meeting we have identified was held on 30 June 1964. It was a meeting of the 303 Committee and probably was held in the White House Situation Room. The two meetings are described separately below.

10 August 1962

The Special Group (Augmented) met at the Department of State, either in Secretary Rusk's office or in his conference room. The following are recorded as being present:

State Dean Rusk, Alexis Johnson, Edward Martin, Richard Goodwin, Robert Hurwitch

White House Maxwell Taylor, McGeorge Bundy (Bill Harvey's notes record that Robert Kennedy was absent and that Bundy had his proxy.)

Defense Robert McNamara, Roswell Gilpatric, Lyman Lemnitzer, Edward Lansdale

-112-

CIA John McCone, William Harvey
    USIA Edward Murrow, Donald Wilson
    Secretary Thomas Parrott

Tom Parrott's minutes of the meeting make no mention of the subject of assassination. Both McCone and Harvey recall that McNamara raised the subject. Harvey's notes taken at the meeting show that it was also mentioned by Murrow, but the nature of the comments was not recorded. Mr. McCone states, in a memorandum of 14 April 1967, that he recalls meetings on 8 or 9 August in the JCS Operations Room in the Pentagon and on 10 August 1962 in Secretary Rusk's conference room.

At one of these meetings (and McCone now recalls it as being at the JCS) the suggestion was made that top people in the Cuban regime, including Castro, be liquidated.

(Comment: As it will later be seen, Mr. McCone's recollection is probably faulty. It is quite clear that assassination came up for discussion at the 10 August meeting at State.)

Mr. McCone says that he took immediate exception to the discussion and promptly after the meeting called on Secretary McNamara personally to emphasize his position. According to McCone, McNamara "heartily agreed." McCone states in his memorandum that at no time did the suggestion receive serious consideration by the Special Group (Augmented)

-113-

or by any individual responsible for policy. McCone adds that through the years the Cuban problem was discussed in terms such as "dispose of Castro," "remove Castro," and "knock off Castro," etc., but that these phrases were always construed to mean the overthrowing of the communist government in Cuba. Harvey recalls that, when McCone told him of the McCone-McNamara conversation, McCone said that if he,

McCone, were to be involved in such a thing he would be excommunicated.

Following the 10 August meeting, and without reference to the reported exchange between McCone and McNamara, Lansdale addressed a memorandum on 13 August to William Harvey (CIA), Robert Hurwitch (State), General Harris (Defense), and Don Wilson (USIA). The memorandum assigned responsibility for drafting papers on various subjects related to the Cuban operation. Harvey's assignment included:

"Intelligence, Political (splitting the regime, [portion excised from the CIA file copy]).

On 14 August, Harvey submitted a memorandum to the DD/P (Helms) reporting the Lansdale communication and what Harvey had done about it. Harvey's memorandum to the DD/P states that the excised portion had consisted of the phrase: "including elimination of leaders." Harvey wrote that he had phoned Lansdale's office and had spoken with Frank Hand in Lansdale's absence. Harvey said he had protested the use of the phrase and had proposed that steps be taken to have it

-114-

excised from all copies. This was agreed to. Harvey deleted the phrase from his own copy and assumes that instructions were given to other recipients to do the same. Harvey told us that Lansdale repeatedly tried to raise the matter of assassination of Castro with Harvey over the next several weeks. Harvey says that he always avoided such discussions. Harvey estimates that five persons in Lansdale's office were generally aware of the sensitive details of Project MONGOOSE and of Lansdale's interest in assassination as an aspect of it.

30 July 1964

The 303 Committee met in regular session, probably in the Situation Room of the White House. (Desmond FitzGerald recalls that such meetings were generally held there.) The following are recorded as being present:

McGeorge Bundy, Cyrus Vance, John McCone, Thomas Hughes

Desmond FitzGerald for the discussion on Cuba

Col. Ralph Steakley was present for another item on the agency, but it is not shown if he was present when the Cuba item was discussed.

Peter Jessup as secretary

The minutes of the meeting record this in the context of the discussion of Cuba:

-115-

"It was agreed that Mr. FitzGerald would contact Mr. Sam Papich of the FBI in regard to the earlier report of an alleged plot with Mafia overtones to assassinate Castro and which the Attorney General agreed to handle as a matter of law enforcement."

The reference is clearly to a 10 June 1964 memorandum information report from the DD/P to the Director. The following additional "elite" dissemination was made of it:

Special Assistant to the President for National Security Affairs

Assistant Secretary, Inter-American Affairs, Department of State

Director of Intelligence and Research, Department of State

Director, Defense Intelligence Agency

The Attorney General

Director, Federal Bureau of Investigation

Deputy Director of Central Intelligence

Deputy Director for Intelligence

The report related a proposal for the assassination of Castro that was made to prominent Cuban exiles. The Mafia appeared to be involved in the scheme. The asking price for doing the job was $150,000, with a guarantee of $10,000 for expenses. A wealthy Cuban exile, [one line deletion] was reported ready to contribute $50,000. [deletion] approached the Chief of Station, JMWAVE, and suggested that the U.S. Government also contribute funds. The suggestion was rejected out of hand. The record indicates the CIA's only involvement in the plot was to report information of its existence. The last record we find of the incident

-116-

is a memorandum from DCI (McCone) to Bundy, dated 19 August, 1964, reporting the results of FBI interviews with the alleged participants. Obviously, nothing came of the plot.

. . . .

-117-

. . . .

-118-

The Possible Ramifications of the Gambling Syndicate Operation

The earlier sections of this report describe all of the CIA schemes aimed at the assassination of Castro that we have been able to discover. The accounts of the two phases of the gambling syndicate operation are factual to the extent that they are based on what those interviewed recall or believe the facts to have been. It is evident that some of these facts have leaked, are being talked about, or are being peddled. On the opposite page is a list of the main details of the story Drew Pearson has, as they are known to us, together with a brief comment on the apparent accuracy of each. There is support in fact for most of the details in Pearson's story. He has a garbled account of the role played by Robert Kennedy, and he errs in telling the story as if all of the details are part of a single story, which they are not. For the most part, though, his facts are straight and he has the truly important aspects of the gambling syndicate operation.

. . . .

-119-

. . . .

-120 to 127-

. . . In the following paragraphs we explore some of the ramifications and discuss what might be done about them.

Should we try to silence those who are talking or might later talk?

It appears to us that this tactic offers little chance of success. For one thing, the story is already out and probably in about as full detail as it will ever be. The only participant on whom we have any real leverage is Maheu, and he has already done all of the talking he is likely to do (to his lawyer, Morgan). We have no hold on any of the others who might furnish confirmation for Roselli's story.

a. Varona is almost certainly not a friend of the Agency. As the Bay of Pigs operation developed, Varona was one of the most critical of the lack of Cuban control of the operation and of the people involved in it. He was bitter over termination of Agency support of his exile group (and the consequent loss of his own income). The last we know of him he was in New York living a hand-to-mouth existence as a part-time auto salesman.

-128-

b. Roselli, Giancana, and Trafficante have fallen on "evil" days. Giancana is reported (in a Chicago newspaper of recent date) to have been deposed as the Mafia head in Chicago and was rumored to be hiding in Mexico. Maheu reports that Trafficante is in jail in Tampa. Roselli is persona non grata in Las Vegas, being required to register with the police any time he is in town. None of them would have compunctions about dragging in his CIA connection when he was being pushed by law enforcement authorities. Giancana has already done it when the FBI was crowding him in 1963. Roselli appears to be doing it in his conversations with Morgan and Garrison.

(Comment: The cover story used with Roselli, Giancana, Trafficante, Varona, and presumably with Orta was that the sponsors were U.S. businessmen with interests in Cuba. Roselli soon concluded that CIA was the true sponsor and so told O'Connell. In Roselli's subsequent dealings with Harvey and Edwards he came to know this for sure. Giancana named CIA in 1963. We must assume that the others, with the possible exception of Orta and perhaps Varona, are equally sure that CIA was the true sponsor.)

c.   Morgan may always retire behind the screen of an attorney/client relationship, as he reportedly did when the FBI approached

-129-

him on the Pearson story.

d.   Pearson, Anderson, and Greenspun (in Las Vegas) are newspapermen with a newsworthy story. Pearson has already published much of it.

e.   Maheu does have good reason for not wanting the story aired further. Unfavorable publicity might cause him to lose his lucrative client, Howard Hughes. There might be some value to be gained from endorsing his suggestion that he approach Morgan and perhaps Roselli and urge discretion.

What do other components of Government know about this operation? Former Attorney General Robert Kennedy was fully briefed by Houston and Edwards on 7 May 1962. A memorandum confirming the oral briefing was forwarded to Kennedy on 14 May 1962. The memorandum does not use the word "assassinate," but there is little room for misinterpretation of what was meant. Presumably the original of that memorandum is still in the files of the Justice Department. It should be noted that the briefing of Kennedy was restricted to Phase One of the operation, which had ended about a year earlier. Phase Two was already under way at the time of the briefing, but Kennedy was not told of it.

As far as we know, the FBI has not been told the sensitive

-130-

operational details, but it would be naive to assume that they have not by now put two and two together and come out with the right answer. They know of CIA's involvement with Roselli and Giancana as a result of the Las Vegas wiretapping incident. From the Chicago newspaper stories of August 1963, and from Giancana's own statement, it appears that they know this related to Cuba. When Roselli's story reached them (Roselli to Morgan to Pearson to Warren to Rowley to the FBI), all of the pieces should have fallen into place. They should by now have concluded that CIA plotted the assassination of Castro and used U.S. gangster elements in the operation.

There is some support for this thesis in the conversation I had with Sam Papich on 3 May 1967 when I told him of the expected meeting between Roselli and Harvey. Sam commented that Roselli and Giancana have CIA "over a barrel" because of "that operation." He said that he doubted that the FBI would be able to do anything about either Roselli or Giancana because of "their previous activities with your people."

Can we plausibly deny that we plotted with gangster elements to assassinate Castro?

No, we cannot. We are reasonably confident that there is nothing in writing outside of the Government that would confirm Pearson's

-131-

story of the gambling syndicate operation, but there are plenty of non-gangster witnesses who could lend confirmation.

    a. Maheu can confirm that Shef Edwards told Roselli that Edwards had told the Attorney General of Roselli's activities on behalf of the Government.

    b. Varona and Varona's son-in-law can confirm the pill and three-man team elements of the story.

    c. Orta can confirm the pill element of Phase One.

d. If an independent investigation were to be ordered, the investigators could learn everything that we have learned.

Such an investigation probably would uncover details unknown to us, because it would have access to the non-CIA participants.

Can CIA state or imply that it was merely an instrument of policy?

Not in this case. While it is true that Phase Two was carried out in an atmosphere of intense Kennedy administration pressure to do something about Castro, such is not true of the earlier phase. Phase One was initiated in August 1960 under the Eisenhower administration. Phase Two is associated in Harvey's mind with the Executive Action Capability, which reportedly was developed in response to White House urgings. Again, Phase One had been started and abandoned months before the Executive Action Capability appeared

-132-

on the scene.

When Robert Kennedy was briefed on Phase One in May 1962, he strongly admonished Houston and Edwards to check with the Attorney General in advance of any future intended use of U.S. criminal elements. This was not done with respect to Phase Two, which was already well under way at the time Kennedy was briefed. The Pearson story, which is now causing us so much distress, includes one detail that is found only in Phase Two: the three-man team.

What measures might be taken to lessen the damage?

We see little to be gained from personal approaches now to Maheu, Morgan, or Roselli. Maheu has much to lose and might be able to prevail upon Morgan and Roselli not to spread the story further. It is questionable whether any such urging would be effective with Roselli, because Roselli stands only to gain from having the story of his CIA connection known and accepted. We cannot now suppress the story, because it is already out and may boil up afresh from the Garrison case. If we were to approach any of the participants and urge discretion upon him, and if this became known, it would merely lend credence to a tale that now sounds somewhat improbable.

-133-

[End of CIA report on Plots to Assassinate Castro.]

NOTES

ACKNOWLEDGMENTS

1. From FBI personnel files of William Weyand Turner acquired by author August 1980 through the Freedom of Information Act.

PREFACE

1. Carlos Prío Socarrás, interview with the author, Miami, Florida, November 1974.

2. Lyman Kirkpatrick, interview with the author, Rhode Island, April 1974.

3. Alfonso Chardy and Michael Sallah, "Yanqui Rebel William Morgan's Saga in Cuban Revolution Is Revived," *Miami Herald*, January 6, 2009.

4. Frank Sturgis, interview with the author, Miami, Florida, April 1974.

5. Prío, interview.

6. Ibid.

7. Speech delivered in Ciudad Libertad, January 9, 1959, available at the Castro Speech Data Base, Latin American Network Information Center, lanic.utexas.edu.

8. Prío, interview.

9. Ibid.

10. William Pawley, interview with the author, Miami, Florida, November 1963.

11. Sturgis, interview.

12. *Wikipedia*, s.v. "Cuban Project," wikipedia.org/wiki/Cuba_Project (accessed February 25, 2013).

13. Warren Hinckle and William W. Turner, *Deadly Secrets* (1981; repr., New York: Thunder's Mouth Press, 1992), p. 285.

14. Saul Landau, "The Jeb Connection—Part I: At Our Expense; The Costly Relationship between Jeb Bush and Right Wing Cuban Exiles," *Radio Progreso Weekly*, July 25, 2002, available at the Transnational Institute, tni.org//archives/archives_landau _jeb1 (accessed February 25, 2013).

15. "Cuban Linked to Terror Bombing Is Freed by Government in Miami," *New York Times*, July 18, 1990.

16. Andres Viglucci, "Miami-Dade Recount Protest by GOP called 'Fascism,'" *Miami Herald*, November 26, 2000.

CHAPTER 1: THE VIOLENT PAST IS PROLOGUE

1. Fidel Castro, "History Will Absolve Me" speech, 1953, transcribed by Andrew Paul Booth and Brian Baggins, translated by Pedro Álvarez Tabío and Andrew Paul Booth (La Habana, Cuba: Editorial de Ciencias Sociales, 1975), available online at the Castro Internet Archive, 2001, www.marxists.org/history/cuba/archive/castro/1953/10/16.htm (accessed February 25, 2013).

2. Castro Internet Archive, "On the Promulgation of the Agrarian Law," a speech delivered by Fidel Castro, May 17, 1959, http://www.marxists.org/history/cuba/archive/castro/1959/05/17.htm (accessed February 15, 2013).

3. Georgie Anne Geyer, *Guerrilla Prince: The Untold Story of Fidel Castro*, Kindle ed. (New York: Garrett County Press, 2010), loc. 1099–1101.

4. Ibid., loc. 1101–1102.

5. Hugh Thomas, *Cuba or the Pursuit of Freedom* (New York: DaCapo Press, 1971), p. 769.

6. Ibid., p. 755.

7. Carlos Prío Socarrás, interview with the author, Miami, Florida, November 1974.

8. Frank Sturgis, interview with the author, Miami, Florida, April 1974.

9. Ibid.

10. Ibid.

11. Thomas, *Cuba or the Pursuit of Freedom*, p. 1022.

12. E. Howard Hunt, *Give Us This Day* (New York: Popular Library, 1973), p. 85.

CHAPTER 2: THE EAGLE HAS LANDED

1. Former State Department officer in Havana, interview with the author, Rio de Janeiro, Brazil, August 31, 1991.

2. Douglas Kellner, *Ernesto "Che" Guevara: World Leaders Past & Present* (London: Chelsea House Publishers, 1988), p. 48.

3. Tim O'Meilia, "Cuban Dictator's Wife Gave Quietly," *Palm Beach Post*, October 5, 2006.

4. Hank Messick, *Lansky* (New York: Berkeley, 1971), p. 123.

5. Warren Hinckle and William W. Turner, *Deadly Secrets* (1981; repr., New York: Thunder's Mouth Press, 1992), p. 344.

6. Hugh Thomas, *Cuba or the Pursuit of Freedom* (New York: DaCapo Press, 1971), p. 947.

7. William Pawley, interview with the author, Miami, Florida, November 1963.

8. Ibid.

9. Ibid.

10. Ibid.

11. Thomas, *Cuba or the Pursuit of Freedom*, p. 1196.

12. Pawley, interview

13. Thomas, *Cuba or the Pursuit of Freedom*, p. 1204.

14. Pawley, interview.

15. E. Howard Hunt, *Give Us This Day* (New York: Popular Library, 1973), p. 102.

16. Pawley, interview.

17. Ibid.

18. Testimony by Ambassador Earl E. T. Smith before the US Senate Hearing on the "Communist Threat to the United States through the Caribbean," August 27–30, 1960.

19. Ibid.

20. Arturo Espaillat, *Trujillo: The Last Caesar* (Chicago: Henry Regnery, 1963), p. 142.

21. Pawley, interview.

22. Carlos Prío Socarrás, interview with the author, Miami, Florida, November 1974.

23. Ibid.

CHAPTER 3: HAVANA SYNDICATED

1. Gerry Patrick Hemming, interview with the author, Miami, Florida, April 1974.

2. FBI legal attaché to the Havana Embassy, interview with the author, Carmel Valley, California, 2004.

3. Hugh Thomas, *Cuba or the Pursuit of Freedom* (New York: Da Capo Press, 1998), p. 1029.

4. Ibid.

5. T. J. English, *Havana Nocturne: How the Mob Owned Cuba, and Then Lost It to the Revolution* (HarperCollins ebooks), loc. 1700 of 7796.

6. Ibid., loc. 1880 of 7796.

7. Ibid., loc. 2381 of 7796.

8. Ibid., loc. 4338 of 7796.

9. *Wikipedia*, s.v. "Walter Annenberg," wikipedia.org/wiki/Walter_Annenberg (accessed February 25, 2013).

10. English, *Havana Nocturne*, loc. 256 of 7796.

11. Ibid., loc. 810 of 7796.

12. Harry J. Anslinger and Will Oursler, *The Murderers: The Shocking Story of the Narcotics Gangs* (New York: Farrar, Straus and Cudahy, 1961), p. 185.

13. Dennis Eisenberg, Uri Dan, and Eli Landau, *Meyer Lansky: Mogul to the Mob* (New York: Paddington, 1979), p. 288.

14. Frank Sturgis, interview with the author, Miami, Florida, April 1974.

15. William W. Turner, *Hoover's FBI* (New York: Thunder's Mouth Press, 1993), p. 160.

16. Confidential source.

17. Turner, *Hoover's FBI*, p. xxi.

18. Sturgis, interview.

19. Ibid.

20. Ibid.

21. Ibid.

22. Ibid.

23. Ibid.

24. Mike McLaney, interview with the author, Miami, Florida, December 1974.

25. Sturgis, interview.

26. Gerry Patrick Hemming, interview with the author, Miami, Florida, April 1974.

27. FBI legal attaché, interview.

28. Steve Wasserman and William W. Turner, *Ramparts Magazine*, submitted interrogatory for Fidel Castro to Cuban official in 1978. The reply from Castro came through the same channel.

29. Sturgis, interview.

30. E. Howard Hunt, *Give Us This Day* (New York: Popular Library, 1973), p. 122.

31. Murray Kempton, *America Comes of Middle Age: Columns 1950–1962* (New York: Penguin Books, 1972), p. 135.

32. Sturgis, interview.

33. Ibid.

34. Ibid.

35. Claudia Furiati, *ZR Rifle: The Plot to Kill Kennedy and Castro* (Melbourne, Australia: Ocean Press, 1994), p. 18.

36. Warren Hinckle and William W. Turner, "How the CIA and the Mafia Tried to Kill Castro," *Boulevard Magazine*, October 1981.

CHAPTER 4: SIDEBAR: JACK RUBY

1. James Hepburn and William W. Turner, *Farewell America: The Plot to Kill JFK* (Liechtenstein: Frontiers Publishing, 1968), p. 271.

2. "The Warren Commission Report," National Archives, 1964, p. 796, archives.gov/research/jfk/warren_commission_report/appendix_16.html.

3. Ibid., p. 780.

4. The report is no longer available; it was discovered by the author in the course of his work with District Attorney Garrison on the JFK assassination in 1967.

5. Ibid.

6. Warren Hinckle and William W. Turner, *Deadly Secrets* (New York: Thunder's Mouth Press, 1981), p. 246.

7. "Warren Commission Report," p. 802.

8. FBI memorandum to the Warren Commission, March 26, 1964.

9. Thayer Waldo, interview with the author, San Rafael, California, September 1967.

10. Gerry Patrick Hemming, interview with the author, Miami, Florida, April 1974.

11. FBI memorandum to the Warren Commission, March 26, 1964.

12. William W. Turner, *Hoover's FBI* (New York: Thunder's Mouth Press, 1993), p. 170.

13. Bernard Gavzer and Sid Moody, "The Warren Report and Its Critics," *Joplin Globe*, June 29, 1967.

14. Ibid.

15. FBI Report of Mary Thompson's testimony provided to the Warren Commission, 1964.

16. Ibid.

17. Alan J. Weberman and Michael Canfield, *Coup d'Etat in America* (San Francisco: Quick American Archives, 1992), p. 157.

18. FBI interview with Edward Browder, January 8, 1978, House Select Committee on Assassinations, Box 105/5081.

19. Ibid.

20. Gavzer and Moody, "Warren Report and Its Critics."

21. Burton Turkus and Sid Feder, *Murder Inc.: The Story of the Syndicate* (New York: Da Capo Press, 2003), pp. 290–91.

22. Dean Jennings, *We Only Kill Each Other: The Life and Bad Times of Bugsy Siegel* (Englewood Cliffs, NJ: Prentice Hall, 1967), p. 17.

23. Studs Terkel, interview with the author, Chicago, Illinois, October 1975.

24. Carl Sidakis, *The Mafia Encyclopedia*, Kindle ed. (New York: Facts On File, 2005), loc. 558 of 13184.

25. T. J. English, *Havana Nocturne: How the Mob Owned Cuba, and Then Lost It to the Revolution* (Harper Collins eBooks), loc. 1710 of 7796.

26. Hinckle and Turner, *Deadly Secrets*, p. 246.

27. Peter Dale Scott, *Deep Politics and the Death of JFK*, Kindle ed. (Berkeley: University of California Press, 1993), loc. 2154 of 5628.

28. Anecdotal information discovered by the author during his research on wiretapping while assigned to the Los Angeles FBI office in 1959.

29. Confidential source.

30. Peter Dale Scott, *Deep Politics and the Death of JFK* (Berkeley: University of California Press, 1993), p. 162.

31. Hepburn and Turner, *Farewell America*, p. 271.

32. "Warren Commission Report," chap. 6, p. 342.

33. *Lee Harvey Oswald—The Patsy*, oswaldpatsy.tripod.com.

34. Seymour Ellison, interview with the author, San Anselmo, California, June 1978.

35. Ibid.

36. William W. Turner and Jonn Christian, *The Assassination of Robert F. Kennedy* (New York: Thunder's Mouth Press, 1993), pp. 194–95.

CHAPTER 5: THE NIXON NOBODY KNEW

1. Anthony Summers, *The Arrogance of Power*, Kindle ed. (New York: Penguin Books, 2001), loc. 1499 of 20387.

2. Earl Mazo, *Richard Nixon, A Political and Personal Portrait* (New York: Avon Books, 1960), p. 23.

3. William W. Turner, *Power on the Right* (San Francisco: Ramparts Press, 1971), p. 65.

4. Summers, *Arrogance of Power* (New York: Viking Books, 2000), p. 33.

5. Ibid., pp. 47–48.

6. Summers, *Arrogance of Power*, Kindle ed., loc. 1473 of 20387

7. Summers, *Arrogance of Power*, p. 32.

8. Ibid., p. 128.

9. Summers, *Arrogance of Power*, Kindle ed., loc. 4294 of 20387.

10. John F. Kennedy (speech, Democratic Dinner, Cincinnati, Ohio, October 6, 1960); transcript available online via Gerhard Peters and John T. Woolley, The American Presidency Project, http://www.presidency.ucsb.edu/ws/index.php?pid=25660 (accessed February 18, 2013).

11. Summers, *Arrogance of Power*, p. 125.

12. Ibid., p. 126.

13. Ibid., pp. 124–25.

14. Summers, *Arrogance of Power*, Kindle ed., loc. 3052 of 20387.

15. Dennis Eisenberg, Uri Dan, and Eli Landau, *Meyer Lansky: Mogul to the Mob* (New York: Paddington, 1979), p. 288.

16. Summers, *Arrogance of Power*, Kindle ed., loc. 3071 of 20387.

17. Ibid.

18. Ibid., loc. 3118 of 20387.

19. Ibid.

20. Ibid.

21. Ibid.

22. FBI report concerning Bebe Rebozo from January 9, 1959.

23. Summers, *Arrogance of Power*, Kindle ed., loc. 3142 of 20387.

24. Ibid., loc. 3143 of 20387.

25. Ibid., loc. 3110 of 20387.

26. Frank Sturgis, interview with the author, Miami, Florida, April 1974.

27. Summers, *Arrogance of Power*, Kindle ed., loc. 4289 of 20387.

28. Ibid., loc. 2455 of 20387.

29. Ibid., loc. 3119 of 20387.

30. Ibid., loc. 2647 of 20387.

31. Warren Hinckle and William W. Turner, *Deadly Secrets* (New York: Thunder's Mouth Press, 1992), p. 338.

32. Author's recollections of a conversation many years ago.

CHAPTER 6: THE ALLIANCE NOBODY KNEW

1. Rolando Salup, Minister of the Exterior, interview with the author, Havana, Cuba, 1987.

2. Frank E. Smitha, *Castro Takes Power*, Macrohistory and World Report, fsmitha .com/h2/ch24t63.html (accessed February 20, 2013)

3. Charles O. Porter, US Representative, interview, *Wall Street Journal*, January 19, 1982.

4. Anthony Summers, *The Arrogance of Power*, Kindle ed. (New York: Penguin Books, 2000), loc. 160 of 20387.

5. Anthony Summers, *The Arrogance of Power* (New York: Viking Books, 2000), p. 206.

6. William Pawley, interview with the author, Miami, Florida, November 1963.

7. "Fidel Castro's Trip to the United States," an excerpt from *Family Portrait with Fidel*, by Carlos Franqui (New York: Random House, 1984), available via J. A. Sierra, ed. and comp., historyofcuba.com, http://historyofcuba.com/history/franqui3.htm (accessed February 18, 2013).

8. Smitha, *Castro Takes Power*.

9. Georgie Anne Geyer, *Guerrilla Prince: The Untold Story of Fidel Castro*, Kindle ed. (Garret County Press Digital Edition, 2011), loc. 4918 of 9310.

10. Ibid.

11. Carlos Prío Socarrás, interview with the author, Miami, Florida, November 1974.

12. Ibid.

13. Ibid.

14. Ibid.

15. Geyer, *Guerrilla Prince*, loc. 4930 of 9310.

16. Pawley, interview.

17. Ibid.

18. Summers, *Arrogance of Power*, p. 182.

19. Hugh Thomas, *Cuba or the Pursuit of Freedom* (New York: Da Capo Press, 1998), p. 1211.

20. Ibid.

21. Summers, *Arrogance of Power*, Kindle ed., loc. 4406 of 20387.

22. Geyer, *Guerrilla Prince*, loc. 5050 of 9310.

23. Summers, *Arrogance of Power*, Kindle ed., loc. 4409 of 20387.

24. Prío, interview.

CHAPTER 7: NIXON'S RED-BAITING BOOMERANGS INTO CASTRO EPIPHANY

1. J. A. Sierra, ed. and comp., *Economic Embargo Timeline*, historyofcuba.com, http://historyofcuba.com/history/funfacts/embargo.htm (accessed February 20, 2013).

2. Frank Sturgis, interview with the author, Miami, Florida, April 1974.

3. Charles O. Porter, US Representative, interview, *Wall Street Journal*, January 19, 1982.

4. Frank E. Smitha, "Castro Takes Power," *Macrohistory and World Report*, fsmitha .com/h2/ch24t63.html (accessed February 20, 2013).

5. Ibid.

6. Herbert L. Matthews, *Castro, A Political Biography* (London: Pelican Books, 1970), p. 102.

7. Smitha, "Castro Takes Power."

8. William Pawley, interview with the author, Miami, Florida, November 1963.

9. Anthony Summers, *The Arrogance of Power*, Kindle ed. (New York: Penguin Books, 2001), loc. 3095 of 20387.

CHAPTER 8:   SETTING UP THE BAY OF PIGS AND OTHER DISASTERS

1. William Pawley, interview with the author, Miami, Florida, November 1963.

2. Hugh Thomas, *Cuba or the Pursuit of Freedom* (New York: Da Capo Press, 1998), p. 1258.

3. Warren Hinckle and William W. Turner, *Deadly Secrets* (New York: Thunder's Mouth Press, 1992), p. 42.

4. "Report on the Covert Activities of the Central Intelligence Agency," Central Intelligence Agency, p. 16, http://www.foia.cia.gov/helms/pdf/Doolittle_report.pdf (accessed February 22, 2013).

5. Pawley, interview.

6. Ibid.

7. Frank Sturgis, interview with the author, Miami, Florida, April 1974.

8. British Foreign Office records of House of Lords debate, November 28, 1959, declassified on March 22, 2001.

9. Nathaniel Weyl, *Red Star Over Cuba* (New York: Devon-Adair, 1960), p. 62.

10. Sturgis, interview

11. *Wikipedia*, s.v. "Orlando Bosch," wikipedia.org, en.wikipedia.org/wiki/Orlando _Bosch.

12. Saul Landau, "The Jeb Connection—Part I: At Our Expense; The Costly Relationship between Jeb Bush and Right Wing Cuban Exiles," *Radio Progresso Weekly*, July 25, 2002, available at the Transnational Institute, tni.org//archives/archives_landau_ jeb1 (accessed February 25, 2013).

13. Hinckle and Turner, *Deadly Secrets*, p. 106.

14. Alan J. Weberman and Michael Canfield, *Coup d'Etat in America* (San Francisco: Quick American Archives, 1992), p. 126.

15. Ibid., p. 335.

16. Sturgis, interview.

17. Unknown author, Marines' Hymn, official hymn of the US Marine Corps.

18. Pawley, interview.

19. Ibid.

20. Banana Republic, "The United Fruit Company," www.mayapariaso.com/united _fruit_company.php (accessed February 20, 2013).

21. Pawley, interview.

22. Ibid.

23. "Report on the Covert Activities of the Central Intelligence Agency," p. 8.

24. Sturgis, interview.

25. Joel David Kaplan, interview with the author, Glendora, California, September 1967.

26. Ibid.

27. Ibid.

28. Ibid.

29. Eliot Asinof, Warren Hinckle, and William W. Turner, *The Ten-Second Jailbreak*

(New York: Holt, Rinehart & Winston, 1973). The full story of the Kaplan escape is told in this book.

 30. Kaplan, interview.

CHAPTER 9: MAJOR MORGAN'S TRIPLE PLAY

 1. Gerry Patrick Hemming, interview with the author, Miami, Florida, November 1973.

 2. Fabian Escalante, *The Secret War: CIA Covert Operations against Cuba 1959–62* (Melbourne, Australia: Ocean Press, 1995), p. 19.

 3. David Grann, "The Yankee Comandante," *New Yorker*, May 28, 2012, www.new yorker.com/reporting/2012/05/28/120528fa_fact-grann?currentPage-all (accessed February 26, 2013).

 4. Frank Sturgis, interview with the author, Miami, Florida, April 1974.

 5. Grann, "Yankee Comandante."

 6. Escalante, *Secret War*, pp. 18–19.

 7. Ibid., p. 20.

 8. Ibid.

 9. See chapter 1.

 10. Escalante, *Secret War*, p. 22.

 11. Ibid., p. 19.

 12. See chapter 8.

 13. Grann, "Yankee Comandante."

 14. Escalante, *Secret War*, p. 21.

 15. Ibid., pp. 21–22.

 16. Ibid., p. 22.

 17. Hemming, interview.

 18. Fabian Escalante, interview with the author, Rio de Janeiro, Brazil, August 1991.

 19. Ibid.

 20. Grann, "Yankee Comandante."

 21. Hugh Thomas, *Cuba or the Pursuit of Freedom* (New York: Da Capo Press, 1998), p. 1238.

 22. Hemming, interview.

 23. Grann, "Yankee Comandante."

 24. Arturo Espaillat, *Trujillo: The Last Caesar* (Chicago: Henry Regnery, 1963), p. 160.

 25. Thomas, *Cuba or the Pursuit of Freedom*, p. 1238.

 26. Ibid.

 27. Espaillat, *Trujillo*, p. 160.

28. Grann, "Yankee Comandante."

29. Ibid.

30. Ibid.

31. Hemming, interview.

32. Grann, "Yankee Comandante."

33. FBI legal attaché to the Havana Embassy, interview with the author, Carmel Valley, California, 2004.

34. Hemming, interview.

35. Ibid.

36. Escalante, interview.

37. Ibid.

38. Grann, "Yankee Comandante."

39. Ibid.

40. Hemming, interview.

41. Che Guevara, *Radical Writings on Guerilla Warfare, Politics and Revolution* (New York: Filiquarian Publishing, 2006), p. 188.

42. Escalante, *Secret War*, p. 29.

43. Grann, "Yankee Comandante."

44. Ibid.

45. Hemming, interview.

46. Grann, "Yankee Comandante."

47. Boris Kitt, "George Clooney to Direct Cuban Military Drama 'The Yankee Comandante," *Hollywood Reporter*, http://www.hollywoodreporter.com/news/george -clooney-direct-cuba-yankee-comandante-334374 (accessed February 26, 2013).

CHAPTER 10: THE BEAST OF THE CARIBBEAN

1. Robert D. Crassweller, *Trujillo, the Life and Times of a Caribbean Dictator* (New York: MacMillan, 1966), p. 288.

2. Warren Hinckle and William W. Turner, *Deadly Secrets* (New York: Thunder's Mouth Press, 1992), p. 322.

3. Arturo Espaillat, *Trujillo, the Last Caesar* (Chicago: Henry Regnery, 1963), p. 154.

4. Crassweller, *Trujillo*, p. 194.

5. *Wikipedia*, s.v. "Rómulo Betancourt," wikipedia.org/wiki/rómulo_betancourt.

6. Crassweller, *Trujillo*, p. 202.

7. Bernard Diederich, *Trujillo, the Death of a Goat* (New York: Little, Brown, 1978), p. 133.

8. William Pawley, interview with the author, Miami, Florida, November 1963.

9. Ibid.

10. Joel David Kaplan, interview with the author, Glendora, California, September 1967.

11. Ibid.

12. William W. Turner, *Rearview Mirror: Looking Back at the FBI, the CIA and Other Tails* (Granite Bay, CA: Penmarin Books, 2001), p. 266.

13. Kaplan, interview.

14. Diederich, *Trujillo*, p. 159.

15. Hinckle and Turner, *Deadly Secrets*, p. 112.

16. "Kennedy's Fears of Foreign Assassinations," *New York Times*, July 23, 1975.

17. Bo Burlingham, "The Other Tricky Dick," *Esquire*, November 1975.

18. Hinckle and Turner, *Deadly Secrets*, p. 113.

CHAPTER 11: LA BATALLA DE GIRÓN

1. William Pawley, interview with the author, Miami, Florida, November 1963.

2. Leonard Mosley, *Dulles* (New York: Dial Press, 1978), p. 304.

3. E. Howard Hunt, *Give Us This Day* (New York: Arlington House, 1973), p. 38.

4. Ibid., p. 75.

5. Pawley, interview.

6. Ibid.

7. Ibid.

8. Ibid.

9. Warren Hinckle and William W. Turner, *Deadly Secrets* (New York: Thunder's Mouth Press, 1992), pp. 198–99.

10. Ibid., pp. 74–75.

11. Jay Mallin, *Covering Castro* (New York: Transaction Publishers, 1994), p. 175.

12. J. A. Sierra, "Invasion at Bay of Pigs: The Plan," historyofcuba.com/history/baypigs/pigs3.htm (accessed February 22, 2013).

13. Frank Sturgis, interview with the author, Miami, Florida, April 1974.

14. Sierra, "Invasion at Bay of Pigs"

15. Pawley, interview.

16. Richard M. Bissell, *Reflections of a Cold War Warrior: From Yalta to the Bay of Pigs* (New Haven, CT: Yale University Press, 1996), p. 210.

17. Nestor T. Carbonell, *And the Russians Stayed: The Sovietization of Cuba* (New York: William Morro, 1989), p. 127.

18. Sierra, "Invasion at the Bay of Pigs."

19. Ibid.

20. Chester Bowles, "Chester Bowles Papers," pt. 6, ser. 1, "Correspondence, 1961–

1963," box 300, folder 536, "Dean Rusk 1961," State Department Correspondence, http://hdl.handle.net/10079/fa/mssa.ms.0628 (accessed February 22, 2013).

21. Arthur Schlesinger Jr., *A Thousand Days* (New York: Mariner Books, 2002), p. 320.

22. Peter Kornbluh, *Bay of Pigs Declassified: The Secret CIA Report on the Invasion of Cuba* (New York: New Press, 1998), p. 224.

23. Ibid., p. 246.

24. Hinckle and Turner, *Deadly Secrets*, p. 86.

25. Sturgis, interview.

26. Hunt, *Give Us This Day*, p. 185.

27. Lyman Kirkpatrick, interview with the author, Rhode Island, April 1974.

28. Sierra, "Invasion at Bay of Pigs."

29. Hugh Thomas, *Cuba or the Pursuit of Freedom* (New York: Da Capo Press, 1998), p. 1358.

30. Sturgis, interview.

31. Thomas, *Cuba or the Pursuit of Freedom*, pp. 1361–62.

32. Kirkpatrick, interview.

33. Sierra, "Invasion at Bay of Pigs."

34. Ibid.

35. L. Fletcher Prouty, *The Secret Team: The CIA and Its Allies in Control of the United States and the World* (New York: Skyhorse Publishing, 2008), p. 325.

36. Ibid., p. 330.

37. Hinckle and Turner, *Deadly Secrets*, p. 102.

38. Bissell, *Reflections of a Cold War Warrior*, p. 250.

39. Schlesinger, *Thousand Days*, p. 885.

40. Sierra, "Invasion at Bay of Pigs."

41. Enrique "Harry" Ruiz-Williams, interview with the author, Fort Lauderdale, Florida, November 1973.

42. Claudia Furiati, *ZR Rifle: The Plot to Kill Kennedy and Castro* (Melbourne, Australia: Ocean Press, 1994), p. 16.

43. Anthony Summers, *The Arrogance of Power*, Kindle ed. (New York: Penguin Books, 2001), loc. 4449 of 20387.

CHAPTER 12: KENNEDY GETS HIS IRISH UP

1. Memo to Secretary of State Dean Rusk, cited in Warren Hinckle and William W. Turner, *Deadly Secrets* (New York: Thunder's Mouth Press, 1992), p. 289.

2. James Stevenson, interview with the author, Sonoma, California, August 1963.

3. Hinckle and Turner, *Deadly Secrets*, p. 104.

4. Ibid., p. 105.

5. Ibid., p. 108.

6. Jorge I. Dominguez, "The @#$%& Missile Crisis (Or, What Was 'Cuban' about US Decisions during the Cuban Missile Crisis," *Diplomatic History: The Journal of the Society for Historians of Foreign Relations* 24, no. 2 (Spring 2000): 305–15.

7. Ibid.

8. After World War II, the Huks, former resistance fighters against the Japanese in the Philippines, turned against the government to counter supposed maltreatment. They initiated guerilla warfare against the government that lasted until 1954.

9. James G. Blight and Peter Kornbluh, eds., *Politics of Illusion: The Bay of Pigs Invasion Reexamined* (Boulder, CO: Lynne Rienner, 1999), p. 125.

10. David Atlee Phillips, *The Night Watch* (New York: Atheneum Books, 1977), p. 91.

11. Claudia Furati, *ZR Rifle, The Plot to Kill Kennedy and Castro* (Melbourne, Australia: Ocean Press, 1994), p. 42.

12. Domínguez, "@#$%& Missile Crisis," pp. 305–15.

13. BBC News, "Castro: Profile of the Great Survivor," February 19, 2008, retrieved June 3, 2008. news.bbc.co.uk/2/hi/Americas/244974.stm (accessed February 22, 2013)

14. Lamar Waldron and Thom Hartmann, *Ultimate Sacrifice: John and Robert Kennedy, the Plan for a Coup in Cuba, and the Murder of JFK* (New York: Carroll & Graf, 2005), p. 409.

15. Fabian Escalante, interview with the author, Rio de Janeiro, Brazil, August 1991.

16. Hinckle and Turner, *Deadly Secrets*, pp. 216–17.

17. Ibid.

18. J. A. Sierra, ed. and comp., *Rolando Cubela Secades, AKA AMLASH*, historyofcuba.com, historyofcuba.com./history/Havana/Cubela.htm (accessed February 22, 2013).

19. "CIA Inspector General's Report on Plots to Assassinate Castro," p. 84, http://dagmar.lunarpages.com/~parasc2/mx/articles/castroreport.htm (accessed October 15, 2012).

20. Ibid.

21. Ibid., p. 99.

22. Francis Xavier Casey, interview with the author, Miami, Florida, December 1978.

23. Hinckle and Turner, *Deadly Secrets*, p. 289.

24. Ibid., p. 136.

25. Furiati, *ZR Rifle*, p. 47.

26. Ibid.

27. Ibid., p. 49.

28. Ibid.

29. Noam Chomsky and Peter Mitchell, *Understanding Power: The Indispensable Chomsky* (New York: New Press, 2002).

CHAPTER 13: THE HITS THAT MISSED

1. Gerry Patrick Hemming, interview with the author, Miami, Florida, November 1973.

2. Warren Hinckle and William W. Turner, *Deadly Secrets* (New York: Thunder's Mouth Press, 1992), pp. 410–11.

3. Ibid., p. 410.

4. Hemming, interview.

5. Arturo Espaillat, *Trujillo: The Last Caesar* (Chicago: Henry Regnery, 1963), p. 116.

6. Frank Sturgis, interview with the author, Miami, Florida, April 1974.

7. Gaeton Fonzi, *The Last Investigation* (New York: Thunder's Mouth Press, 1993), pp. 83–107.

8. Sturgis, interview.

9. Hinckle and Turner, *Deadly Secrets*, p. 51.

10. Ibid.

11. Anthony Summer, *The Arrogance of Power*, Kindle ed. (New York: Penguin Books, 2000), loc. 12572 of 20387.

12. Ibid., loc. 4631 of 20387.

13. Ibid.

14. Claudia Furiati, *ZR Rifle: The Plot to Kill Kennedy and Castro* (Melbourne, Australia: Ocean Press, 1994), p. 23.

15. Ibid., p. 24.

16. Ibid., p. 24.

17. Ibid.

18. Ibid., p. 25.

19. Ibid.

20. Ibid., p. 26.

21. E. Howard Hunt, *Give Us This Day* (New York: Arlington House, 1973), p. 173.

22. Hinckle and Turner, *Deadly Secrets*, p. 81.

23. Fabian Escalante, interview with the author, Rio de Janeiro, Brazil, August 1991.

24. Summers, *Arrogance of Power*, Kindle ed., loc. 4504 of 20387.

25. Hugh Thomas, *Cuba or the Pursuit of Freedom* (New York: Da Capo Press, 1998), p. 1296.

26. "The Tragedy of Mario Kohly," *Washington Observer Newsletter*, no. 26, October 1, 1966.

27. Ibid.

28. Letter from Richard Nixon to Judge Edward Weinfeld, dated March 9, 1965, on letterhead of Nixon, Mudge, Rose, Guthrie & Alexander law firm; a photocopy of this letter is in the author's possession.

29. Hinckle and Turner, *Deadly Secrets*, p. 114.

30. Ibid.

31. Luis Balbuena, interview by Gordon Hone, Senate Subcommittee on Administrative Practice and Procedure, Miami, Florida, April 24, 1968.

32. Ibid.

33. Hinckle and Turner, *Deadly Secrets*, p. 115.

34. Ibid.

35. Georgie Anne Geyer, *Guerrilla Prince: The Untold Story of Fidel Castro*, Kindle ed. (Garrett County Press Digital Edition, 2011), loc. 5482 of 9310.

36. David Wise and Thomas B. Ross, *The Espionage Establishment* (New York: Random House, 1970), p. 91.

37. Hemming, interview.

38. Caretaker of McLaney residence, interview with the author, Miami, Florida, June 1974.

CHAPTER 14: DECISIONS, DECISIONS: INVASION NO. 2

1. Enrique "Harry" Ruiz-Williams, interview with the author, Fort Lauderdale, Florida, November 1973.

2. William W. Turner, *Rearview Mirror: Looking Back at the FBI, the CIA and Other Tails* (Granite Bay, CA: Penmarin Books, 2001), p. 210.

3. Warren Hinckle and William W. Turner, *Deadly Secrets* (New York: Thunder's Mouth Press, 1992), p. 165.

4. Arturo Rodriguez, interview with the author, Rio de Janeiro, Brazil, September 1991.

5. Ibid.

6. Ruiz-Williams, interview.

7. Ibid.

8. Turner, *Rearview Mirror*, p. 212.

9. Ibid.

10. Hinckle and Turner, *Deadly Secrets*, p. 286.

11. William Pawley, interview with the author, Miami, Florida, November 1963.

12. Hinckle and Turner, *Deadly Secrets*, p. 147.

13. Ibid., p. 148.

14. Ibid., p. 146.

15. *New York Times*, August 27 and 30, 1962.

16. Frank Sturgis, interview with the author, Miami, Florida, April 1974.

17. Ibid.

18. Hinckle and Turner, *Deadly Secrets*, p. 225.

19. "Explosives Cache Property Lent to Cuban, Owner's Wife Says," *Times-Picayune*, New Orleans, August 1, 1963.

20. Mike McLaney, interview with the author, Miami, Florida, December 1974.

21. Ibid.

22. City of Miami Inter Office Memo, Det. Sgt. C. H. Sapp, Intelligence Unit., September 6, 1963.

23. Ibid.

24. Ibid.

25. Ibid.

CHAPTER 15: THE *FLYING TIGER* AND THE PHONY RESCUE

1. David E. Kaiser, *The Road to Dallas*, Kindle ed. (Cambridge, MA: Belknap Press, 2008), loc. 2117 of 6644.

2. Gerry Patrick Hemming, interview with the author, Miami, November 1973.

3. William Pawley, interview with the author, Miami, Florida, November 1963.

4. Kaiser, *Road to Dallas*, Kindle ed., loc. 2085 of 6644.

5. Lamar Waldron, *Watergate: The Hidden History, Nixon, the Mafia and the CIA* (New York: Counterpoint, 2012), p. 218.

6. Kaiser, *Road to Dallas*, Kindle ed., loc. 2095 of 6644.

7. Waldron, *Watergate*, p. 217.

8. Kaiser, *Road to Dallas*, Kindle ed., loc. 2091 of 6644.

9. Waldron, *Watergate*, p. 218.

10. Kaiser, *Road to Dallas*, Kindle ed., loc. 2099 of 6644.

11. Waldron, *Watergate*, p. 219.

12. Pawley, interview

13. Waldron, *Watergate*, p. 219.

14. Loran "Skip" Hall, interview with the author, Los Angeles, California, June 1968.

15. Ibid.

16. Ibid.

17. Pawley, interview.

18. Rolando Salup, interview with the author, Havana, Cuba, 1987.

CHAPTER 16: THE NAVY THAT NOBODY KNEW

1. Pepe, a crewman on *Rex* (a CIA raider ship), interview with the author, October 1973. Unless otherwise indicated, this interview is the source for all the information in this

chapter. The *Rex* was registered to a company and intended for geological research. In fact, it was used for infiltrations and aggressions, according to Gerry Patrick Hemming, in an interview with the author, Miami, November 1973.

2. Hemming, interview.

3. Warren Hinckle and William W. Turner, *Deadly Secrets* (New York: Thunder's Mouth Press, 1992), p. 153.

4. Hemming, interview.

5. Hinckle and Turner, *Deadly Secrets*, p. 158.

6. Ibid., p. 161.

7. Ibid., p. 175.

CHAPTER 17: THE CIA'S UNRULY STEPCHILD

1. David Kaiser, *The Road to Dallas*, Kindle ed. (Cambridge, MA: Belknap Press, 2008), loc. 22 of 6644.

2. Lamar Waldron, *Watergate: The Hidden History*, Kindle ed. (Berkeley, CA: Counterpoint Press, 2012), loc. 5519 of 21882.

3. Shane O'Sullivan, *Who Killed Bobby? The Unsolved Murder of Robert F. Kennedy* (New York: Union Square Press, 2008), p. 436.

4. Frank Sturgis, interview with the author, Miami, Florida, April 1974.

5. "CIA Inspector General's Report on Plots to Assassinate Castro," p. 88, http://dagmar.lunarpages.com/~parasc2/mx/articles/castroreport.htm (accessed October 15, 2012).

6. Ibid., p. 93.

7. William W. Turner, "The Garrison Commission on the Assassination of President Kennedy," *Ramparts*, January 1968.

8. Ibid.

9. Warren Hinckle and William W. Turner, *Deadly Secrets* (New York: Thunder's Mouth Press, 1992), p. 263.

10. Ibid., p. 264.

11. "Orlando Bosch Avila and MIRR," doc. 0059, Cuban Information Archives, cuban-exile.com/doc_051-075/doc0059.html (accessed February 25, 2013).

12. Kaiser, *Road to Dallas*, Kindle ed., loc. 1966 of 6644.

13. Hinckle and Turner, *Deadly Secrets*, p. 175.

14. Ibid., p. 176.

15. Gerry Patrick Hemming, interview with the author, Miami, Florida, April 1974.

16. Ibid.

17. Peter Dale Scott, *Deep Politics and the Death of JFK*, Kindle ed. (Berkeley: University of California Press, 1993), loc. 3394 of 5628.

18. Kaiser, *Road to Dallas*, Kindle ed., loc. 2824 of 6644.

19. "Warren Commission Report," National Archives, p. 413, www.archives.gov/research/jfk/warren-commission-report/chapter-7.html#cuba (accessed February 25, 2013).

20. Kaiser, *Road to Dallas*, Kindle ed., loc. 22 of 6644.

21. Loran "Skip" Hall, interview with the author, Los Angeles, California, June 1968.

22. Turner, "Garrison Commission on the Assassination of President Kennedy."

23. Hinckle and Turner, *Deadly Secrets*, p. 255.

24. Ibid., pp. 271–72.

25. Ibid.

26. Ibid.

27. William Attwood, *The Reds and the Blacks* (New York: Harper & Row, 1967), pp. 143–44.

28. Ibid.

29. Ibid.

CHAPTER 18: NIXON'S VENDETTA

1. Lamar Waldron, *Watergate: The Hidden History*, Kindle ed. (Berkeley, CA: Counterpoint Press, 2012), loc. 3583 of 21882.

2. Warren Hinckle and William W. Turner, *Deadly Secrets* (New York: Thunder's Mouth Press, 1992*)*, pp. 346–51. Unless indicated otherwise, information for this chapter comes from this source.

3. Jack Anderson, "Merry-Go-Round," *San Francisco Chronicle*, January 20, 1977.

4. Ibid.

5. Ibid.

6. Gerry Patrick Hemming, interview with the author, Miami, Florida, November 1973.

7. Ibid.

CHAPTER 19: THE COUP THAT NOBODY KNEW

1. Lamar Waldron, telephone interview with the author, San Rafael, California, August 2012.

2. "Cuba: Almeida Is More Alive Today Than Ever!" www.greenleft.org.au/node/42451 (accessed February 25, 2013).

3. "Cuban Revolutionary Almeida Dies," BBC, news.bbc.co.uk/2/hi/Americas/8252210.stm (accessed February 25, 2013).

4. Enrique "Harry" Ruiz-Williams, interview with the author, Ft. Lauderdale, Florida, November 1973.

5. Lamar Waldron, *Watergate: The Hidden History*, Kindle ed. (Berkeley, CA: Counterpoint Press, 2012), loc. 4643 of 21882.

6. Ibid., loc. 4661 of 21882.

7. Ibid., loc. 4671 of 21882.

8. Ibid., loc. 4680 of 21882.

9. Ibid., loc. 5606 of 21882.

10. Waldron, interview.

11. Waldron, *Watergate*, Kindle ed., loc. 4841 of 21882.

12. Ruiz-Williams, interview.

13. Waldron, *Watergate*, Kindle ed., loc. 4842 of 21882.

14. Ibid., loc. 5376 of 21882.

15. Ibid., loc. 355 of 21882.

16. Ibid., loc. 4955 of 21882.

17. Ibid., loc. 5207 of 21882.

18. "Almeida Lives Today More Than Ever: Reflections of Fidel," *Monthly Review*, monthlyreview.org/castro/2009/09/13/almeida-lives-today-more-than-ever.htm (accessed February 25, 2013).

19. Waldron, interview.

EPILOGUE

1. Gerry Patrick Hemming, interview with the author, Miami, Florida, November 1973.

2. David Wise and Thomas B. Ross, *The Espionage Establishment* (New York: Random House, 1970), p. 91.

3. T. J. English, *Havana Nocturne: How the Mob Owned Cuba, and Then Lost It to the Revolution*, Kindle ed. (HarperCollins eBooks), loc. 5162 of 7796.

4. William W. Turner, "The Garrison Commission on the Assassination of President Kennedy," *Ramparts*, January 1968.

5. Warren Hinckle and William W. Turner, *Deadly Secrets* (New York: Thunder's Mouth Press, 1992), p. 46.

BIBLIOGRAPHY

My own published works have been invaluable resources for details on this new volume:

William Turner, "The Garrison Commission on the Assassination of President Kennedy," *Ramparts* Magazine, January 1968.

William W. Turner. *Hoover's FBI.* New York: Thunder's Mouth Press, 1993.

William Turner. *Power on the Right.* San Francisco: Ramparts Press, 1971.

William W. Turner. *Rearview Mirror: Looking Back at the FBI, the CIA and Other Tails* (Granite Bay, CA: Penmarin Books, 2001).

William W. Turner, Eliot Asinof, and Warren Hinckle. *The Ten-Second Jailbreak* (New York: Holt, Rinehart & Winston, 1973).

William W. Turner and Jonn Christian. *The Assassination of Robert F. Kennedy* (New York: Thunder's Mouth Press, 1993).

William W. Turner and Warren Hinckle. *Deadly Secrets: The CIA-Mafia War against Castro and the Assassination of JFK* (1981; repr., New York: Thunder's Mouth Press, 1992).

———. "How the CIA and the Mafia Tried to Kill Castro," *Boulevard*, October 1981.

The following published works proved invaluable:

Anderson, Jack. "Merry-Go-Round," *San Francisco Chronicle*, January 20, 1977.

Anslinger, Harry J., and Will Oursler. *The Murderers: The Shocking Story of Narcotics Gangs* New York: Farrar, Straus, and Cudahy, 1961.

Attwood, William. *The Reds and the Blacks.* New York: Harper & Row, 1967.

Ayers, Bradley. *The War That Never Was* (New York: Bobbs-Merrill, 1976).

BBC News. "Castro: Profile of the great survivor." February 19, 2008, retrieved June 3, 2008. http://news.bbc.co.uk/2/hi/Americas/244974.stm.

Bissell, Richard M., Jr., with Jonathan E. Lewis and Frances T. Pudlo. *Reflections of a Cold War Warrior: From Yalta to the Bay of Pigs.* New Haven and London: Yale University Press, 1996.

Blight, James G., and Peter Kornbluh, eds. *Politics of Illusion: The Bay of Pigs. Invasion Reexamined.* Boulder, CO: Lynne Rienner, 1999.

Burlingham, Bo. "The Other Tricky Dick," *Esquire*, November 1975.

Carbonell, Nestor T. *And the Russians Stayed: The Sovietization of Cuba*. New York: William Morrow, 1989.

Chomsky, Noam, and Peter Mitchell. *Understanding Power: The Indispensable Chomsky*. New York: New Press, 2002.

"CIA Inspector General's Report on Plots to Assassinate Castro." http://dagmar.lunarpages .com/~parasc2/mx/articles/castroreport.htm.

Crassweller, Robert D. *Trujillo: The Life and Times of a Caribbean Dictator*. New York: Macmillan, 1966.

Diederich, Bernard. *Trujillo: Death of the Goat*. New York: Little, Brown, 1978.

Domínguez, Jorge I. "The @#$%& Missile Crisis (Or, What Was 'Cuban' about US Decisions during the Cuban Missile Crisis)." *Diplomatic History: The Journal of the Society for Historians of Foreign Relations* 24, no. 2 (Spring 2000).

Eisenberg, Dennis, Uri Dan, and Eli Landau. *Meyer Lansky: Mogul to the Mob*. New York: Paddington Press, 1979.

English, T. J. *Havana Nocturne: How the Mob Owned Cuba, and Then Lost It to the Revolution*. HarperCollins ebooks.

Escalante, Fabian. *The Secret War: CIA Covert Operations against Cuba 1959–62*. Melbourne, Australia: Ocean Press, 1995.

Espaillat, Arturo. *Trujillo: The Last Caesar*. Chicago: Henry Regnery, 1963.

Fonzi, Gaeton. *The Last Investigation*. New York: Thunder Mouth Press, 1993.

Furiati, Claudia. *ZR Rifle: The Plot to Kill Kennedy and Castro*. Melbourne, Australia: Ocean Press, 1994.

Geyer, Georgie Anne. *Guerilla Prince: The Untold Story of Fidel Castro*. Garrett Country Press Digital Edition, 2011. Kindle edition.

Grann, David. "The Yankee Comandante," *New Yorker*, May 28, 2012.

Guevara, Che. *Radical Writings on Guerilla Warfare, Politics and Revolution*. New York: Filiquarian Publishing, 2006.

Hepburn, James and William Turner. *Farewell America*. Liechtenstein: Frontiers Publishing, 1968.

Hunt, E. Howard. *Give Us This Day*. New York: Arlington House, 1973.

Jennings, Dean. *We Only Kill Each Other: The True Story of the Life and Bad Times of Bugsy Siegel*. Englewood Cliffs, New Jersey: Prentice Hall, 1967.

Kaiser, David. *The Road to Dallas: The Assassination of John F. Kennedy*. Cambridge, MA: Belknap Press, 2008. Kindle edition.

Kellner, Douglas. *Ernesto "Che" Guevara: World Leaders Past and Present*. London: Chelsea House, 1988.

Kempton, Murray. *America Comes of Middle Age: Columns 1950–1962*. New York: Penguin Books, 1972.

Mallin, Jay. *Covering Castro*. New York: Transaction, 1994.

Matthews, Herbert. *Castro: A Political Biography*. London, Pelican Books, 1970.

Mazo, Earl. *Richard Nixon: A Political and Personal Portrait*. New York: Harper, 1959.

Messick, Hank. *Lansky*. New York: Berkeley, 1971.

Mosley, Leonard. *Dulles: A Biography*. New York: Doubleday, 1978.

O'Meilia, Tim. "Cuban Dictator's Wife Gave Quietly," *Palm Beach Post*, October 5, 2006.

O'Sullivan, Shane. *Who Killed Bobby? The Unsolved Murder of Robert F. Kennedy*. New York: Union Square Press, 2008.

Phillips, David Atlee. *The Night Watch*. New York: Atheneum Books, 1977.

Prouty, L. Fletcher. *The Secret Team: The CIA and Its Allies in Control of the United States and the World*. New York: Skyhorse Publishing, 2008.

Schlesinger, Arthur. *A Thousand Days: John F. Kennedy in the White House*. New York: Mariner Books, 2002.

Scott, Peter Dale. *Deep Politics and the Death of JFK*. Berkeley: University of California Press, 1993. Kindle edition and print edition.

Sidakis, Carl. *The Mafia Encyclopedia*. New York: Facts On File Inc., 2005. Kindle edition.

Sierra, J. A., ed. and comp. "Economic Embargo Timeline." *History of Cuba*, http://historyofcuba.com/history/funfacts/embargo.htm.

———. "Fidel Castro's Trip to the United States." In *Family Portrait with Fidel*. By Carlos Franqui. New York: Random House, 1984. Available at *History of Cuba*, http://historyofcuba.com/history/franqui3.htm.

———. "Invasion at Bay of Pigs: The Plan." *History of Cuba*, http://historyofcuba.com/history/baypigs/pigs3.htm.

———. "Rolando Cubela Secades, AKA AMLASH." *History of Cuba*, http://historyof cuba.com./history/Havana/Cubela.htm.

Smitha, Frank E. "Castro Takes Power." *Macrohistory and World Report*, http://fsmitha .com/h2/ch24t63.html.

Summers, Anthony. *The Arrogance of Power*. New York: Viking Books, 2000.

———. *The Arrogance of Power*. New York: Penguin Books, 2000. Kindle edition.

Thomas, Hugh. *Cuba or the Pursuit of Freedom*. New York: DaCapo Press, 1971.

"The Tragedy of Mario Kohly." *Washington Observer Newsletter*, no. 26, October 1, 1966.

Turkus, Burton, and Sid Feder. *Murder Inc: The Story of the Syndicate*. New York: Da Capo Press, 2003.

Waldron, Lamar. *Watergate: The Hidden History, Nixon, the Mafia and the CIA*. New York: Counterpoint, 2012. Kindle edition.

Waldron, Lamar, and Thom Hartmann. *Ultimate Sacrifice: John and Robert Kennedy, the Plan for a Coup in Cuba, and the Murder of JFK*. New York: Carroll & Graf Publishers, 2005.

"Warren Commission Report." National Archives. 1964. http://www.archives.gov/research/jfk/warren_commission_report/appendix_16.html.

Weberman, Alan J., and Michael Canfield. *Coup d'Etat in America: The CIA and the Assassination of John F. Kennedy*. San Francisco: Quick American Archives, 1992.

Weyl, Nathaniel. *Red Star over Cuba*. New York: Devon-Adair, 1960.

Wise, David, and Thomas B. Ross. *The Espionage Establishment*. New York: Random House, 1970.

INDEX